LOVE, ROB

VICTORIA

SECRETS OF THE CITY

VICTORIA

SECRETS OF THE CITY

Kevin Barefoot
and the editors of

ARSENAL PULP PRESS

VANCOUVER

ARSENAL PULP PRESS
103-1014 Homer Street
Vancouver, B.C.
Canada V6B 2W9
www.arsenalpulp.com

The publisher gratefully acknowledges the support of the Government of
Canada through the Book Publishing Industry Development Program for its
publishing activities.

Book design by Lisa Eng-Lodge
Production Assistant Judy Yeung
Photographs, unless otherwise indicated, by Lawrence McLagan
Cover photo by Ross Crockford
Printed and bound in Canada

Efforts have been made to locate copyright holders of source material
wherever possible. The publisher welcomes hearing from any copyright
holders of material used in this book who have not been contacted.

Monday Magazine is a trademark of Island Publishers, Ltd.,
used under license.

CANADIAN CATALOGUING IN PUBLICATION DATA:
Barefoot, Kevin, 1971-
  Victoria: secrets of the city

  Includes index.
  ISBN 1-55152-085-0

1. Victoria (B.C.)—Guidebooks. I. Title.
FC3846.18.B37 2000   917.11'28044   C00-910921-8
F1089.5.V6B37 2000

c o n t e n t s

a c k n o w l e d g m e n t s

No poject of this kind is possible without accomplices. The authors would like to thank Brian Lam and Michael Turnpenny for agreeing to it, and all the people who shared secrets or helped put this book together, including: John Adams, Robert Ballantyne, Steve Barber, Darren Barefoot, Gordon Barefoot, John Bate, Cheryl Beaumont, Robert C. Belyk, Melaney Black, Shawn Blore, Travis Bolander, Stephanie Croft, Geoff D'Auria, Cleve Dheensaw, Susan Duhamel, Larry Eastick, Lisa Eng-Lodge, Gordon Faller, Bob Fehr, Beth Fenske, Daniel Francis, Russ Francis, Holland Gidney, Rob and Josie Grant, Diana Glennie, Jacqueline Gullion, Michael Halleran, Rania Hatz, Lynn Heenan, Roberta Hower and Judy Neil (for putting up with Kevin's extended visits), Basil Huxham, Meryl Huxham, Paul Jeffrey, Grant Keddie, Richard Kim, Blaine Kyllo, David Lai, Ken Lane, Cathy Leahy, Laura Lemay, Brett Lowther, James MacKinnon, Lawrence McLagan, Mandelbrot, James Martin, Kirsten Meincke, Robert Moyes, The Oyster Club, T.W. Paterson, Dave Preston, Lyn Quan, Terry Reksten, Martin Segger, Alisa Smith, Drew Snider, Andrew Struthers, Louise Taylor, Rob Wipond, Stewart M. Wood, everyone at *Geist*, the patient staff at the Greater Victoria Public Library and the British Columbia and City of Victoria Archives, and all the writers (including those at the *Times Colonist*) who first dug up the many stories contained herein.

Got a secret that we missed? Let us know, and we'll try to include it in the next edition of the book. Write to Arsenal Pulp Press (address on page 4) or e-mail: secretsofvictoria@hotmail.com

introduction

Cities are mysteries, even to the people who live within them.

To those visiting it for the first time, Victoria is the sweet little Garden City, the home of Butchart Gardens and flower baskets, Tudor façades and Emily Carr, tea at the Empress and cricket in Beacon Hill Park. To those who know it a bit better, it's a white-collar town of heli-jetting bureaucrats, Governor General's Award-winning poets, thoughtful bookstores (i.e., the ones that put this volume front and centre), young couples, kindly seniors ("the newly wed and nearly dead"), and leafy neighbourhoods full of antique houses where nothing ever happens.

But to those who actually live here, Victoria is something else. It's Mile Zero, the end of the Trans-Canada Highway, the burg where up-Island loggers and pulp-mill workers go on weekend sprees, where hobos and skate punks set up camp, where actors and musicians make their last stand, performing in tents or busking on the harbour causeway all summer and drowning their poverty in brewpub ales when the winter rains fall. It's a lush, rarified habitat of storm and forest, where Coast Salish Natives feasted on deer and shellfish and roasted camas bulbs, where the salmon still spawn, the whales migrate and cougars prowl the streets. It's a frontier town, the last point of civilization for old Hudson's Bay Company explorers and Klondike gold seekers headed north, now a remote outpost on the Left Coast where mystics seek transcendence and bikers grow weed — a place of fetish dungeons, demolition auto racing, radical tree-huggers, prison theatre, witchcraft, and all-night raves.

Predictably, this turbulent, exotic side of the city doesn't get much official recognition. While Olde Victoria is splashed across glossy brochures and White-Collar Victoria is fêted by the Chamber of Commerce, Wild Victoria is often suppressed by regulators and moralists of every stripe, banished to warehouses and the backwoods, beer-hall conversations and dismissive editorials in the daily paper. And yet it's this third Victoria, quietly proud and brilliantly eccentric, which really embodies the spirit of the city, and keeps it from collapsing in a heap of red brick and defaulted mortgages. Sadly, sometimes Victoria is a secret even to itself.

So it's appropriate that the editors of *Monday Magazine* would help with the writing of this book. For the last 25 years, *Monday* has entertained and infuriated readers with stories about the things Victoria's poobahs don't want publicized – the quirky societies, the brilliant artists, the outrageous scandals – the myths and characters that, in a bigger city, might end up in a sprawling social novel by Emile Zola or Tom Wolfe. But since no one else seems to be writing that novel around here (Victoria is also known as "the graveyard of ambition," after all), we've collected some of those tales ourselves in the volume you now hold.

Once a secret has been revealed, some say, it's not really a secret any more. Maybe that's true, but we figure it's a price worth paying. Victoria isn't just tea parties and bean-counters – it's stranger and more dangerous and more beautiful than that, and perhaps by giving up a few of its secrets, newcomers will understand both the maddening frustration and deep affection that longtime residents already feel for the place. Like the queen after which the city is named, Victoria can be fussy and imperious, but she commands incredible loyalty. To know her, for better or worse, is to love her.

– Ross Crockford and Kevin Barefoot

To our moms.

As one of Canada's leading tourist destinations, Victoria has its share of must-sees. Sure it's easy to find Miniature World, but what about cheater storeys, secret domes, and the city's cheapest accommodations? Read on.

Tea at the San Juan de Fuca?

In the summer of 1905, Victorians were asked to name the new prestige hotel owned by Canadian Pacific. By the end of September, the company decided on the Empress, but not before rejecting these suggestions:

Alexandra
Bulwer
Camosun
Carnarvon
Douglas Arms
Dufferin
Lotbinière
Lytton
Royal Oak
San Juan de Fuca
Van Horne

Flame is Fleeting

Once one of Victoria's most well-known features, the candle flame-shaped neon light on top of the Rockland Water Tower has been snuffed for over 10 years. Located in Rockland Heights on private property just off Terrace Avenue, the 128-foot water tower was built in 1909 by contractor Henry Kaiser, and on the city's centenary in 1962 it was topped with a 22-foot-tall neon flame donated by three local sign companies. American residents across the strait in Port Angeles could spot the flame, and for years pilots and mariners used it as a referent for navigation. The tower has a capacity of 93,000 gallons but is rarely used today, save for dry summer months and fire-fighting emergencies.

The Swallowed Anchor

Probably the most unusual monument to Esquimalt's maritime heritage can be found at 464 Head Street, just across from the West Bay Marina. That's the address of "The Swallowed Anchor," a two-storey house decorated with nautical bric-a-brac, including salvaged ship's lights, a steering wheel from an old whaling boat, and all sorts of fibreglass-and-styrofoam creatures, including dolphins, piranhas, a mermaid, and a pirate flying the skull and crossbones from a crow's nest on the roof. The house dates back to 1912, but the decorations are the work of "Barnacle" John Keziere, an old salt who worked on and around the sea all his life, and bought the place in 1967. "They say when a man retires from the sea he's 'swallowed the anchor'," he once said, explaining the title of his unique home. "Some work the land, have a garden and some chickens. This is how I swallowed the anchor." Alas, Keziere joined his mates in Davy Jones' locker not long ago, so the fate of the house floats in limbo. His family says they'll maintain the place, but Keziere's whimsical decorations probably won't qualify for heritage protection, even if the house itself does. Enjoy them while you can.

In the Doghouse

One of the narrowest houses in city (if not the country) was built in 1994 at 244 Cadillac Avenue, off Carey Road near the Town and Country Shopping Centre. The two-bedroom house measures 10 feet wide and 62 feet long and sits upon a lot only 25 feet wide. After his application failed to have the required setbacks reduced, Joe Loiacono went ahead anyway and built a 1,200-square-foot house that met all code requirements – to the chagrin of neighbours unhappy with his "overgrown doghouse." But it sure beats apartment living.

Secret Modernist Influence

Samuel Maclure and Francis Rattenbury tend to get all the press, but Victoria's other seminal architect, John Di Castri, designed most of the interesting modernist structures in the city. These include the former Canadian Institute for the Blind at 1609 Blanshard Street (until recently the home of *Monday Magazine*), the View Street and Centennial Square parkades, Prince Robert House Stores (home to Ballantyne's Florist), the Crystal Pool, McCall Brothers Funeral Chapel, and the lobby of the Royal B.C. Museum. Di Castri, who studied with Frank Lloyd Wright disciple Bruce Goff at the University of Oklahoma,

secret tunnels

They capture our imagination, but with a couple of exceptions, the stories of secret tunnels running under Victoria are entirely apocryphal. Here are the better ones:

Chinatown Tunnels

There have long been rumours about secret tunnels under Chinatown. These stories usually involve the smuggling of opium or alcohol up from the harbour during Prohibition, and were given a boost in the 1950s when a city crew discovered a large chamber five feet under Store Street near Market Square. It turns out this was only a cistern used by firemen to store water. According to UVic geographer and Chinatown expert David Lai, the storied "tunnels" of the district are just an extension of the city's storm drain system.

Wharf Street Arches

In the parking lot below Wharf Street opposite Bastion Square is a brick retaining wall that was once the footings for the Hudson's Bay Company warehouse, the city's first large commercial building, built in 1858. An arch in the wall that has since been bricked over once ran under the sidewalk and allowed access to the building's stores. Further along Wharf at Ship Point are more concrete arches set in the retaining wall, but there were never tunnels behind these – they were added in 1984 to support the crumbling wall.

Sidewalk Prisms

Those thick glass blocks embedded in downtown sidewalks suggest a network of underground tunnels, but unfortunately they're just used to light basement areas. They date from the early 1900s and create a dramatic effect when lit from underneath at night. The best examples are around the Pemberton Building on Broad Street between Fort and Broughton.

consistently creates more adventurous designs than his peers, building principally for the occupants of his buildings. For example, the CNIB building was created in 1950 before handicapped-access coding, so he used a curved front bay to lead people to the entrance. In the same year, he designed the McCall Brothers Funeral Chapel building so that daylight would enter through angled window slots and light the altar without revealing its source. Di Castri flipped the bird to the city's all too common Historical Romanticism, and Victoria's the better for it.

The Empress Hotel Tunnel

One of the two remaining tunnels in the city runs from the sub-basement of the Empress Hotel under Douglas Street to the former location of the Canadian Pacific Railway Steam Laundry and Power Plant at the corner of Douglas and Humbolt (now the Budget and Tilden rental car lot). The hotel used to truck dirty linens from its sub-basement along the tunnel to the laundry across the street, and although the plant closed in the 1960s, the tunnel remains. One end can be seen behind the concrete slab of the rental car lot, and the other behind a padlocked red door in the Empress Parkade's lower level (see photos below and on pg. 17). If you look closely, you'll see a bow in the door. The story goes that after BC Hydro completed work in the parking area, they left behind a locker room complete with showers, sinks, and urinals at the entrance to the tunnel. They later discovered a tent and sleeping bag, indicating that someone had taken up residence. Workers placed the red door over the opening to the tunnel and padlocked it, and the bow in the door is evidence of the inhabitant's attempt to bash his way out with a tire iron. It's assumed the resident escaped out the other end of the tunnel.

(see photos below and on pg. 17)

WELL WORTH KNOWING

In addition to being a great example of iron fronting from various decades, the Rithet Building (*1117-1125 Wharf St.*) is home to a secret water source. When the province bought and restored the building in 1978, workers discovered that its joists were being supported by an old cast iron pump over a bricked-in wellhead. This was the original water well for Fort Victoria, and the pipe running from the pump leads under Wharf Street and likely carried fresh water to ships. You'll now find the well in the lobby, complete with the mechanical pump.

DESIGNING WOMAN

E. Marjorie Hill, Canada's first registered female architect, did most of her pioneering work right here in the Garden City. After graduating from the University of Toronto in 1920 (the chairman of the architecture department refused to attend the convocation because Hill was a woman), she moved to Alberta, and then to Victoria in 1936. She couldn't get architect's work at first, so she earned her daily bread as a master weaver. But after World War II, commissions to design houses for returning vets started coming her way. Hill designed the first purpose-built seniors' housing in Canada

(*Glenwarren Lodge, at 1230 Balmoral Dr.*) and several prominent homes (*1905 Mayfair Dr., 2368 Queenswood Dr.*), but perhaps the best example of her work is the apartment building at 1170 Fort Street (photo below). Built in the 1950s, its clean lines, overhanging eaves and prominent windows prove that Hill was right in step with international modernist thinking, back when most Victorians were still doing mock Tudor. Hill died in 1985. Her life is currently being researched by McGill architecture prof Annemarie Adams, who points out that women in her profession haven't advanced much since Hill's time: even today, only 11 percent of registered architects in Canada are women.

Cable Vault

Telus's main exchange at 826 Yates Street has an L-shaped tunnel two stories below the building that runs from Yates to Johnson and then down another 300 feet to the intersection of Blanshard and Johnson. The vault is a repository for hundreds of phone lines.

Provincial Legislature Tunnel

Victoria's other remaining tunnel sits only 10 feet below the lawns of the Parliament Buildings behind the CNIB shop and runs under Government Street to the Ministry of Finance in the Douglas Building. In addition to allowing staff to get to and from the Parliament Buildings, the tunnel is a conduit for steam pipes, power and communications cables, and leads directly to the Douglas Building cafeteria, the largest government eatery in the city. The tunnel dates from the early 1950s when the Douglas Building and steam plant were built. The Parliament Buildings' entrance is outside room 027, but it's not publicly accessible.

exploring Chinatown

Victoria's Chinatown, while not nearly as large as Vancouver's, is the oldest surviving such district in Canada and was the first to be visited by a British monarch when Queen Elizabeth II and the Duke of Edinburgh walked through in March 1983. Here are a few little-known facts:

Tulip Dome

The Hook Sin Tong Building *(658-664 Herald St.)*, built in 1911, is an excellent example of Chinatown architecture with a recessed balcony and parapet bearing the building's name. The secret lies above the third-floor assembly room in the form of an enormous stained-glass dome that extends six feet above the roof and consists of some 5,000 pieces of stained glass in a tulip motif. Unfortunately, it is not publicly accessible.

GARDEN PARTIES

Built by Francis Rattenbury and Percy James for the Canadian Pacific Railway on the site of the former city garbage dump, the Crystal Gardens amusement centre opened on June 26, 1925. So important was the event that May Day celebrations were postponed a month so the two events could be combined into a carnival, pageant, and swim meet. At the time of construction, Crystal Gardens was not only Canada's largest swimming pool, but the largest salt-water swimming pool in the British Commonwealth. The centre also had an art gallery, twin dance floors, and a banquet room, and for years Victorians visited the gardens for Palm Court teas and dances. On August 4, 1925, Johnny "the Human Hydroplane" Weismuller, famed for his role in *Tarzan the Ape Man*, broke the 100-yard world record in the pool with a time of 51.4 seconds. The glamour of the Crystal Gardens waned in the 1950s when the roof started leaking, and where there weren't leaks, condensation collected on the framework and showered down on patrons (the bandshell became the most attractive location in the gardens). The salt water started corroding pipes and heating apparatus such that in 1955, the pool switched to fresh water. In the early 1960s, the CPR let its lease expire and the City of Victoria was forced to take over. The building continued to be plagued with mechanical difficulties, and a chlorine leak in 1967 involving a group of school children brought the issue to a head. The city decided it would be cheaper to build a new pool in Central Park (Crystal Pool) than to renovate Crystal Gardens. After years of neglect over the subsequent decades, the building was reborn in 1980 as a tropical garden and aviary. In the early 1990s, the longstanding tea service on the terrace was eliminated to make room for a tropical butterfly exhibit.

Hidden Floors

A common feature of Chinatown buildings is a "cheater storey," an extra floor created within a floor. These date from the days of less-sophisticated methods of taxation, when assessments were based on the height of a building, not total square footage. Thus an owner could create an extra storey and keep all the income it generated. A good example sits above the shops in the On Hing Company Store *(1710-1714 Government St.)*.

Great Escapes

All the suspect behaviour behind closed doors in Chinatown often meant that many participants had to disappear quickly. Back alleys that could be closed off by wooden doors or iron gates were ideal for this purpose. Someone could enter the alley, close the gate, and then exit from any number of adjoining doors or passageways. Residents also created hidden passages so that during police raids of gambling clubs, participants could enter an adjoining room through a closet, or escape into the alley through a washroom.

out of the past

J a m e s o n   M o t o r s

The elaborate tile work on the wall at 754 Broughton Street was once part of three fountains that comprised the front of the Jameson Motors car dealership located there from 1922 to 1966. At the corner of the wall is a masonry bollard that once supported an elaborate chain surrounding the fountain. The tile work dates from 1928 and is the design of W.J. Semeyn, who also did the Tweedsmuir Mansions apartments near Beacon Hill Park at the corner of Heywood and Park. Another sidewall fountain has been relocated to the courtyard behind the Law Chambers Building on Bastion Square: it can be accessed through the back door of the gardening store Dig This *(45 Bastion Square)*.

Secret Deco Monument

In his book *Exploring Victoria's Architecture*, Victoria architecture expert Martin Segger calls the B.C. Electric Bay Street Substation *(637 Bay St., 381-9800)* "one of the finest examples of Art Deco in the Northwest." Completed in 1928 using reinforced concrete construction and Deco Egyptoid motifs (check out the crest on the Douglas Street end), it has huge windows, too. Let's hope the current resident, the Westcoast College of Massage Therapy, appreciates it.

QUEENS SEEN

Although the statue of Queen Victoria is intended to greet passengers arriving at the Canadian Pacific Railway Marine Terminal (now the Royal London Wax Museum), Irish sculptor Albert Bruce was unhappy with its position, "sited [so] that anyone looking at it must stand right under it, go out on the roadway and be run over by a motor car, or fall backwards in the water of the harbour." Critics of the bust of Queen Elizabeth in Beacon Hill Park were more proactive. Installed in July 1959 to commemorate her visit, it accompanied a plaque that still stands at the parking lot between the petting zoo and the road up Beacon Hill. The bust, however, was stolen and returned once, damaged twice, and then decapitated and thrown in the Inner Harbour. Divers discovered it and returned it to the park. It now sits at Queen's Lake across the road from the cricket pitch.

Willows Exhibition Building

One of the finest structures on the west coast once stood at the Willows Fairgrounds located in Oak Bay, roughly bounded by Henderson, Fair, Eastdowne, and Neil. The Willows Exhibition Building was built in 65 days after an 1890 bylaw ensured Victoria's taxpayers covered over half of the $45,000 cost. Agricultural products were displayed on the main floor, while two galleries occupied the windowed upper storey. Two days after Christmas in 1907, the building burned to the ground. It was rebuilt, but without the same majesty; alas the remaining buildings were also destroyed by fire in 1944.

Photo: Courtesy BC Archives A-0802

The Gardens at Limekiln

Although most locals are tired of hearing it, Butchart Gardens, the 52-hectare garden on Tod Inlet developed by Robert and Jeanette Butchart back in 1904, is the province's premiere tourist attraction. Robert was a cement manufacturer from Owen Sound who bought the area for its limestone deposit, and once he'd quarried most of it, 'Jennie' developed a garden in the pit using soil from nearby farmland. With the help of landscape designer W.J. Westby, she created the Sunken Garden (see photo below), which has since become a symbol for Victoria, rivalled only by the Empress Hotel. As the gardens grew, the Butcharts had Samuel Maclure work on their house at the site and eventually paved their estate's road using concrete from the quarry, changing its name from "Limekiln" to "Benvenuto" ("Welcome" in Italian). In 1920, they started the Benvenuto Seed Company (which has offered a mail-order catalogue ever since). As the gardens became more elaborate, maintenance costs soared and by 1939, the company was running an annual deficit of $20,000. The provincial government was offered the gardens for $1, but declined, so the Butcharts started charging admission in 1941: 25 cents for adults and 10 cents for children. The gardens were lit for the first time in 1954, allowing for nocturnal visits. Nowadays, this landmark attracts nearly one million visitors annually.

Cheap Sleeps

The Gorge Strip

The Gorge was once *the* place to stay and play in Victoria, and although the motels are fraying at the edges, with names like the Oxford Castle, the Capri, and the Robin Hood, a certain cachet remains. Head out along Gorge Road East and take your pick. But be careful during the winter months when rates drop and many of the hotels become glorified rooming houses.

Hostels

Backpacker's Hostel
1608 Quadra St., 386-4471

Cat's Meow Mini Hostel
1316 Grant St., 595-8878

Hostelling International
516 Yates St., 385-4511

Ocean Island Backpackers Inn
791 Pandora Ave., 1-888-888-4180

Selkirk Guest House
934 Selkirk Ave., 1-800-974-6638

University of Victoria Housing
Parking Lot 5, 721-8395

Not-So-Cheap Sleeps

Beaconsfield

Built in 1905 from a design by Samuel Maclure, this English-style manor was a wedding present from industrialist R.P. Rithet to his daughter Gertrude, and features 11-foot-high beamed ceilings and mahogany floors. But the house has had a varied history; at one point during the 1980s it operated as a run-down rooming house. Now the place is cleaned up and many of the rooms have double Jacuzzis overlooking the fireplace.

998 Humbolt St., 384-4044

Haterleigh

This is the former home of Victoria architect Thomas Hooper, whose works include the Centennial Methodist Church, St. Michael's University School, and the Carnegie Library building, and the bed and breakfast that's in the house today is run by a couple who left the corporate world of Edmonton. It's worth a visit just to see the curved stained glass in the dining room.

243 Kingston St., 384-9995

Joan Brown's Guest House

This former home of E.G. Prior dates from 1883 and occupies an acre of land near Government House. Highlights include high ceilings, more stained glass, forest scenes plastered on the walls of the dining room, and Joan Brown, one of the friendliest innkeepers in the city.

729 Pemberton Rd., 592-5929

Alley Oops

During the early decades of this century, Fan Tan Alley, the narrow passage in the middle of the block between Fisgard and Pandora and now home to a number of retail shops, was the centre of Chinatown gambling and the home to as many as 10 Fan Tan clubs. (Fan Tan is a game in which players bet on the number of buttons left over after a cup is turned over and groups of four buttons are discarded. "Fan" means to turn over and "Tan" to spread out.) Although the police didn't want to stop gambling, they wanted to control it, so they raided the clubs, arresting participants on a regular basis. Production of opium in factories in the alley was encouraged by the provincial and federal governments as they made good money regulating this lucrative industry — an opium license in the 1890s cost $250 a year. This came to an end in July 1908, when the federal government passed an act prohibiting the importation, manufacture or sale of opium in Canada.

Other notable alleys are Trounce and Waddington (see photo). In the mid-1860s, Thomas Trounce owned the block between Government and Broad Streets. When Trounce's neighbour fenced off his lot and eliminated access to the stores on his property, Trounce cut a lane through his block which has since become known as Trounce Alley. Alfred Waddington, the inveterate crusader who used the fortune he made from the gold rush to buy three lots between Yates and Johnson Streets, cut a passageway through existing stores that allowed access to more shops. The alley is now paved with wooden bricks modeled after the original ones. One former editor of *Monday Magazine* was once told that under certain atmospheric conditions, pressure can build up under the bricks, forcing them to shoot up in the air.

Originally lit to celebrate Queen Victoria's Diamond Jubilee, Francis Rattenbury's Legislative Building, the heart of British Columbia's political scene, is illuminated by some 3,330 electric lights at night. It also contains several little-known facts. The ceiling of the Hansard lunchroom contains a piece of metal that is part of a folding staircase once used by one-time Premier W.A.C. Bennett to make quick escapes from his office a floor above. There are also tunnels under the lawn: once many years ago when the NDP was in opposition, its members hid in the tunnels to deceive the Socreds into thinking they didn't need all their members to vote on a crucial bill. (The strategy failed: the socialist horde charged out of the basement when the division bells rang, signalling the time to vote, but their numbers still weren't enough to defeat the Socreds.) But the best secret concerns the portraits of former speakers of the house lining the hallway outside the legislative chambers. Look closely at the portrait of David Higgins, speaker from 1890 to 1898: if he looks a little pallid, that's because no one thought to photograph him before he died in 1917. The photographers dressed up Higgins' body and snapped his photo afterward.

Photo: Ross Crockford

Offbeat Museums

The Royal British Columbia Museum is one of Canada's finest; its displays and exhibits attract thousands annually. But here are a couple of museums in Victoria you may not be aware of.

Ashton Garrison Museum

Located in an industrial area in Saanich, this museum houses the largest collection of women's wartime memorabilia in Canada. Among the swords, bayonets, and guns in the museum are items such as regulation hair tongs and medals for bravery. Most of the materials were donated by the families of veterans of the Canadian Women's Army Corps.

724 Vanalman Ave., 477-1117

Victoria Police Museum

Located in a corner of the main police station, the tiny Victoria Police Museum is a collection of materials from the oldest force west of the Great Lakes (dating from 1858). Among the batons, handcuffs, and medals, are charge books that date back to the the turn of the century and a display of Victoria parking meters from the last six decades. The museum also includes a souvenir section where you can purchase hats, T-shirts, and toy police cars.

850 Caledonia St., 995-7654

A DARK LEGACY

One wouldn't think a leper colony would have existed in this neck of the woods, but one did. D'Arcy Island is a tiny wooded chunk of rock located east of Island View Beach. From 1891 to 1924, it was a leper colony, with 49 interns, almost all of Chinese origin. They weren't allowed to leave or have visitors, and survived on supplies shipped over every three months, including rice, salt pork, flour, tea, tobacco, salt, fresh blankets, and coffins. Interns were forced to look after each other — the stronger ones cooking, gardening, caring for the dying, and eventually, burying the dead. There are 20 to 30 graves on the island. In 1924 the last patient was relocated to a proper medical facility on Bentinck Island, located between Rocky Point and Race Rocks. The facility at Bentinck operated for years after a cure for leprosy was found in the 1940s; the facility closed in 1958.

Sidewalk Scrabble

Cul-de-sacs, one-ways, streets that change names three times in as many blocks — it's always been difficult for newcomers to find their way around Victoria. Apparently this was even more so at the end of the 19th century, when it was popular for hooligans to steal street name and house number signs from buildings and utility poles. So in 1907, the city decided to solve the problem by writing the street names in ceramic tiles, and embedding them in concrete sidewalks.

You can still see the earthenware tiles (made by a long-defunct company in Zanesville, Ohio) at many street corners in James Bay and Fairfield. But they won't last forever. Damage, theft and vandalism are still commonplace, and the city's running low on its stock of the antique tiles, which ceramics experts say will cost up to $20 apiece to replace. In particular, the public works department says it's suffering a shortage of common letters, like A and E, and an abundance of odd ones, like Q and X. Can we buy a vowel?

Photo: Stewart M. Wood

Pioneer Bricks

If you walk up the 900-block of Government Street and then take a left into Bastion Square, you'll probably notice a double row of bricks set in the sidewalk, some of them engraved with names. This is the product of a 10-year project undertaken by a local archives society, which collected $14 per brick to record the names of people who lived in Victoria before 1914. The 2,535 bricks form the outline of the original Fort Victoria.

hotel histories

Palm Room, Empress Hotel

The Empress Hotel

If you're standing out in front of the main lobby of the Empress Hotel, look up above at the turret to the left. Two of its skinny windows are part of a room with no door. An architectural feature (or oversight), the room exists today as it did when it was completed in December 1929. A roofer who once peered in the window reported seeing a blanket and pillow in the centre of the room, perhaps waiting for some future hotel guest.

During its 92-year history, the Empress has hosted an incredible variety of celebrities. Some of the more famous include Jack Benny, Tallulah Bankhead, Prince Edward VII, Douglas Fairbanks, Rita Hayworth, Katherine Hepburn, Pat O'Brien, Ginger Rogers, and Shirley Temple. In 1944, a young Peter Lawford (later a member of Frankie and Dino's "Rat Pack") got thrown out of the hotel for making untoward advances upon a chambermaid. During Princess Margaret's stay in 1958, she upset Empress staff by visiting the hotel's roof to watch the Russian satellite Sputnik pass over the city. The staff could only watch with concern as the Princess, Lieutenant-Governor Frank Ross and his wife, and several members of the royal entourage climbed the steep ladder-style stairs to a rooftop platform and viewed the historic event. During his stay in 1931, King Prajadhipok of Siam booked an entire floor to house his 56-member entourage, who brought over 500 pieces of luggage. And during Bob Hope's visit in the 1950s, he chipped golf balls on the hotel's lawn; his stage buddy Bing Crosby was reportedly so comfortable at the Empress that he went without his toupee.

Laurel Point Inn

Laurel Point, the headland at the entrance to the Inner Harbour, is now the site of a luxury hotel, but it's served many other purposes in the past. When people arrived in the harbour 160 years ago, at Laurel Point they would've seen at least four life-size human figures made of wood, representing great orators and warriors of the Songhees natives. These figures – one wearing a European-style top hat – watched over several burial sheds on the thin rocky point. (Many isolated points of land and islands in the harbour were used as native burial sites.) Early in the 20th century, much of the land around the point was filled in, and it became the home to the British-American Paint Company (BAPCO), one of the biggest companies in Canada. In 1978, another division of the company reclaimed the land and built the hotel that stands there today, which is currently owned by the heirs of Paul Arsens, the entrepreneur who built the popular copper-topped Paul's Motor Inn and restaurant on Douglas Street.

Gatsby Mansion

For many years, this stately pile at 309 Belleville Street was the home of the wealthy Pendray family, which owned a soap works and the paint factory that used to stand across the street at Laurel Point. The Pendrays were famous for their industry, but they were also known for suffering an unusual series of mishaps. The patriarch W.J. Pendray was killed in 1913, when a fire-sprinker pipe broke at the paint works, and he fell 40 feet onto his head. His son Ernest was killed in 1909, when he was thrown from his wagon right in front of the mansion, and the second son Herbert accidentally shot himself in the chest in 1893 with a .22 pistol. Only the third son, Carl, escaped unscathed: he became general manager of the paint factory, sold the soap works to the giant Lever Brothers in 1913 after his father's death, and went on to become the mayor of Victoria from 1925 to 1928.

Oak Bay Hotels

Today's travellers visit Victoria to see the Empress Hotel, but once they padded their way to the grand hotels of Oak Bay. Named for the snow-capped peak across the water in Washington State, the five-storey Mount Baker Hotel opened in 1893, and played host to such guests as the Duke and Duchess of York (later known as King George V and Queen Mary). It was developed as part of a plan to build docking facilities in Oak Bay so steamers could save an hour's sailing time by using it as their embarkation point. Unfortunately the plans went nowhere, and the hotel burned to the ground in 1902. In 1905, it was replaced by the Oak Bay Hotel, later renamed the Old Charming Inn. This hotel was reportedly built in only 19 days, and was a favourite haunt of Rudyard Kipling, who wrote this bit of doggerel about his stay there: "A gilded mirror and a polished bar; myriads of glasses strewn ajar. A kind-faced man all dressed in white; that's my recollection of last night. The streets were narrow and far too long; sidewalks slippery, policemen strong. The slamming door; the sea-going hack; that's my recollection of getting back. A rickety staircase, and hard to climb. But I rested often, I'd lots of time. An awkward keyhole and a misplaced chair informed my wife that I was there." The Inn was demolished in 1962 to make way for the Rudyard Kipling apartments. The remaining hotel from this era is the Tudor-style Oak Bay Beach Hotel, home to the Snug, the favourite pub of many Victorians. It was added in the 1950s when cocktail lounges were legalized, and is named after the small room attached to old English pubs to allow the vicar or constable to drink in privacy. The pub has unobstructed views of Mount Baker and is one of the better places to while away an afternoon in Victoria.

Secret Vistas

Yates Street Parkade
There aren't many publicly accessible places where you can get above the bustle of the city. One of the best is also the least glamorous: the city parkade at 575 Yates Street. Take the easy-access elevator from the street up to the eighth floor, and you'll get a fine view of the harbour, the Johnson Street bridge, and the mossy red brick of the Old Town district to the north.

Chateau Victoria
Vista 18, the bar and restaurant at the top of the Chateau Victoria Hotel (749 Burdett Ave.), has the best bird's-eye view of town and beyond, from majestic (and volcanic) Mount Baker to the east, and the Sooke Hills to the west.

Moss Rocks
The best view of Fairfield is from Moss Rock Park on Master's Road off Fairfield Road (there's a sign if you're coming from downtown). Climb up to the benches where you get an excellent view of Government House, the Gonzales Observatory, Trial Island (see photo), the Parliament Buildings, and some suburban backyards.

Highrock Park

Just northwest of Lampson and Old Esquimalt Road, the streets go steeply upwards. Park your car, take one of the unmarked paths and climb even higher, and in a few minutes you'll reach a mossy peak with great views of Esquimalt Harbour, Portage Inlet, and the surrounding hills.

JUST THE WAX, MA'AM

With its imposing Romanesque pillars and stark white façade, the Royal London Wax Museum adjacent to the Inner Habrour is tough to miss, but architecture alone is not what makes this old CPR steamship terminal such a hit; it's the characters inside. Like God's cocktail party, you'll find celebrities, world leaders, and historical figures, mixing and mingling in groups they never dreamed of.

The figures themselves, which have fibreglass bodies, and faces and hands made from beeswax, are constructed in England. But the choice of who gets into Victoria's museum is made locally. It's not as simple as just deciding who you want or not ("Bump the Queen Mum"); orders sent to England must also include a description of the context and setting, and include the required facial expression and limb position ("Annoyed with Ginger Spice's stage antics, Posh scowls and boots her in the ass."). The average price tag for each wax figure is $10,000, depending how popular they are: U.S. Presidents go cheap; Canadian Prime Ministers are pricy. By the way, no matter how hot it gets, that wax ain't gonna melt ... at least, not anymore it won't. But back in 1970, a lighting mistake apparently put a hot spot on Joe Stalin's noggin, and the subsequent runoff was enough to bump him from the display for good. Guess he was hot to Trotsky.

Sooke Harbour House

The Sooke Harbour House, the exclusive inn/restaurant west of Victoria, is a favourite of celebrities who are trying to keep a low profile. Here are some of the big names who've stayed there:

Gillian Anderson
Cindy Crawford
Robert DeNiro
French president Valéry Giscard d'Estaing
David Duchovny (he also proposed to his wife
Téa Leoni there)
Jodie Foster
Richard Gere
Jane Goodall
Angela Lansbury
Hal Linden
Bonnie Raitt
Wesley Snipes
Patrick Stewart
Sharon Stone

downtown's mystery properties

The Janion Building

Probably the most prominent undeveloped site in the city is this derelict masterpiece at 1612 Store Street, across the street from the Swans Hotel. The building started out in 1891 as the Janion Hotel (named after a prominent local merchant), a luxurious 48-bedroom inn for passengers on the E&N railway, which passed right beside it. But the hotel was a bust (despite ads in papers of the day announcing that "only white cooks" worked in its kitchens!), so the railway took it over in 1895 and turned it into offices. In 1933 the Janion was turned into a warehouse, which it remained until 1981, when it was boarded up. Currently the old hotel is owned by a kindly (and presumably wealthy) widow, who's still waiting for a buyer willing to restore it to its former glory. She also owns the boarded-up series of old buildings across Johnson at 1314 Wharf Street, which include the defunct store known as Northern Junk.

Photo: Ross Crockford

your membership fees are $95 per month.) Obviously, you can't get in if you're poor, but at least you won't be barred because of your gender: women got the right to become voting members in 1994.

VANISHING NEON

While most people are keen to preserve Tudor shop façades or Samuel Maclure mansions, others worry about the commercial symbols of the city's modernist past: its neon signs. These date from the development boom after World War II, and before the advent of cheaper and easier to maintain plastic signs. A good example is the Turner's Confectionary sign at the corner of Birch and Richmond, which dates from 1946. Unfortunately, city heritage rules don't extend to buildings constructed after World War II, much less to the signs on the buildings, so it's up to aficionados to preserve them.

Those fans include Todd and Cindy Ryan (see photo above), who back in 1993, loved a 1940s-era sign so much, they named their café after it. Sally was once a clothing store on the corner of Douglas and Cormorant Streets, and after it closed, the Ryans bought one of its neon signs. It continues to light Cormorant Street.

Nelson's Music

This imposing Georgian-revival edifice at 1600 Quadra Street was built in 1912, and served as the First Baptist Church from 1925 until 1973, when it was purchased by the London Boxing Club. After a few years as Victoria's house of pugilism (now you have to go to Stan Peterec's kickboxing studio, around the corner on Fisgard Street), the building was occupied by Nelson's Music until 1991, when it was acquired by Lloyd Cartwright, the guy who owns the incredible collector's store that's currently on the ground floor, packed with old magazines, books, and vinyl records. (Raves have been held in this building, too.) A few years ago, the manic local music promoter Deborah J. Cameron went in on a deal with Cartwright to buy the joint for $725,000 and turn it into an arts centre, but the scheme collapsed and the old church has been stuck in development purgatory ever since.

Songhees Rocks

At the southwest corner of Tyee and Esquimalt Road sits a giant chunk of rocky land that looks ready-made for more monolithic condo towers, just like the ones nearby on the Songhees waterfront. The B.C. government, the owner, will let you have the whole parcel for $13 million – as long as you're willing to clean up the contaminated soil left from the property's years as a public dump.

Rock Bay

North of Herald Street, the cafés and tony live-work studio apartments give way to gravel pits, warehouses, and a dilapidated old BC Hydro plant. This is the turf known as Rock Bay, which a consortium of architects and developers would like to turn into Victoria's "next downtown." (Rock Bay is the name of a hidden barge-filled cove fronted by the LaFarge cement works; there used to be a bridge across it, which is how Bridge Street got its name.) Plans have even been drawn up for what the new neighbourhood could look like, but it probably needs one big project to get the ball rolling. Can you say "sports arena"?

Looking for a new home? How'd you like to win Craigdarroch Castle? While that may sound like a BC Lottery Corportation come-on, back in 1908, raffling off Rockland's most famous pile (at 1050 Joan Crescent) was just a canny way of selling real estate.

Following the deaths of Robert and Joan Dunsmuir, the castle was sold to Griffith Hughes, a former owner of the *Victoria Daily Times*. Rather than keep the castle in the style to which it had become accustomed, Hughes proceeded to subdivide the surrounding land into 144 ready-to-build lots. In order to attract buyers for the new Joan Crescent, Hughes then put the castle up for raffle: buy a lot, get a shot at the castle. Names were drawn and Craigdarroch was subsequently won by lumber baron Solomon Cameron. Alas, however, Cameron's days as lord of the manor were numbered. Shortly thereafter he lost ownership to the mortgagee, who paid a mere $35,000 to take the castle off his hands. As for what happened next ... well, you'll just have to take the tour.

And when you take that tour, ask about the door in the pantry. Rumour has it there's a hidden servant's passage about 2½ feet wide that leads to the dining room. So if you were rich enough to buy the castle, you could ensure the help was neither seen nor heard.

COLLECTOR'S ITEMS

It's tough to call the Royal British Columbia Museum a secret — it has attracted some 27 million visitors since the current exhibit building opened back in 1968. Although it's difficult to judge the value of the museum's collection since many of its items are irreplaceable, it has been estimated to be worth at least $50 million. Here are some of the more interesting artifacts:

- The 1968 Rolls Royce owned by the late Beatle John Lennon is one of the largest items in the collection. Currently stored with a local specialty car dealer, it was a gift to the museum from B.C. entrepreneur Jimmy Pattison. Renowned for the psychedelic paintings on its exterior, it is often loaned to other museums around the world.

- The hat worn by explorer Simon Fraser over 200 years ago when he navigated the river that now bears his name. It is one of the most precious items in the museum's large clothing collection, which also includes a bonnet owned by Queen Victoria.

That's Some Waterpipe, Dude

Photo: Courtesy Sooke Regional Museum

• Specimens of 179,000 vascular plants from across the province dating back to the turn of the century are stored in the museum's herbarium. Many are so rare and unusual that they're loaned around the world for study. For example, 394 specimens of B.C. orchids are with the New York State Museum in Albany, and some 155 specimens of marine worms are at the state university in Moscow, Russia.

• The 1912 Model-T Ford in the history gallery is in running condition. With right-hand drive (B.C. had British road rules until 1921), its most interesting feature is the acetylene gas headlamps. It cost $690 new.

• 8,000 stuffed shrews.

One of the city's most interesting megaprojects from bygone days is the old Sooke waterpipe. In the early days, Victorians first got their water from a spring near Wharf Street, and then out of a pipe from Elk and Beaver lakes. But when the city boomed in the aftermath of the Klondike gold rush, local politicians decided to pipe in more water from Sooke Lake.

Four hundred men laboured in 1914 and 1915 to build the pipe, which was hauled into place by a specially-built narrow gauge steam train; as each of its 36,000 four-foot sections were positioned, the track beneath was dismantled, leaving behind a continuous concrete tube above the ground that was 27 miles long. But landslides wiped out several sections of the pipe during the brutal winter of 1915-16, and soon the town fathers thought it wiser to build another pipe underground. Today, it's broken and green with moss, but for a pleasant meander through the old growth along the edge of Sooke Hills Park, the top of the original pipe can't be beat.

The Barn on Blanshard

Few structures in Victoria are more loved – and hated – than Memorial Arena. Constructed in 1946, this "concrete bread loaf" (as one sportswriter called it) has been home to countless hockey and lacrosse games, wrestling matches, skating parties, public ceremonies, political conventions, teen dances, raves, and extravagant concerts, all despite acoustics no better than an aircraft hangar. Housing 5,021 seats (give or take a few, as some people have), Memorial Arena was and still is the place for Victoria's biggest indoor events.

As you can imagine, it's also had its share of strangeness. According to several news stories, in the early days the rink engineers used to colour the ice white with milk, mixing 300 gallons of moo juice from a nearby dairy with briny water and then spraying the mixture onto the surface. One night in 1950, the big scoreboard clock fell from the roof and smashed onto the ice; fortunately, no one was nearby at the time. And in 1957, workers discovered a bag of safecracker's

MUNICIPAL HALL DE CORBU

There's no question that Victoria City Hall on Douglas Street is a piece of work; the clock alone cost $5,000 back in the 1890s. But Saanich wins the contest for the most boss seat of government. John Armour's design of the Saanich Municipal Hall (770 Vernon Ave.) was inspired by the work of architectural titan Charles-Edouard Le Corbusier and features fountains, ponds, and manicured lawns overlooking the Swan Lake nature sanctuary. Inside is lots of exposed concrete and terrazzo floors, and the most pleasant place in Victoria to get a building permit.

tools that had been left behind after thieves tried to nab the gate receipts from a big lacrosse match; incredibly, after the workers had thrown the bag around and used some of the tools in it, police discovered that it also contained a jar with enough nitroglycerine to blast the arena to smithereens. Several schemes have since threatened to demolish the venerable old building. The most famous of them was a recent plan by David Pasant (see photo above), a California car dealer, to raze the arena and replace it with a 12,500-seat "multiplex" that would play home to the Spiders, his International Hockey League franchise. But after giving Pasant over two years' worth of deadline extensions to come up with the development money, in 1999 Victoria's city hall finally put the

kibosh on the deal, and so the old Memorial still stands.

Some of the stars (and star horses) who've performed at Memorial Arena:

Louis Armstrong
The Beach Boys
Chuck Berry
Johnny Cash
Bill Cosby
Dire Straits
Duke Ellington
Gracie Fields
Harry James
Spike Jones
Montovani and his Orchestra
Roy Orbison
The Red Army Choir
Kenny Rogers
The Royal Lipizzaner Stallions
The Seattle Cossacks Motorcycle Team
Supertramp
Tina Turner

Transportation

Being on an island, Victoria has come up with some sophisticated (and some not-so sophisticated) modes of transportation. Here are their stories, from big blue bridges to facelifted ferries.

The Blue Bridge

At the foot of Johnson Street is one of Victoria's most obvious secrets, a bascule-type drawbridge raised and lowered by counterweights. Built in 1924 for the sum of $918,000, it was based on a design by Joseph Strauss, who went on to design the Golden Gate Bridge in San Francisco. The two concrete bascules (one for the railway section and one for the roadway), which weigh 780 tons, are actually hollow. The original bridge deck was made of wood, so in wet weather, it absorbed water; extra concrete would be added to the

bascules so the span (since replaced by an open steel grid) could be lifted. In 1979, the bridge was given major repairs and painted a colour called Juan de Fuca blue. Why that particular shade? Because the oxides of its pigment are the same colour as the paint, so little fading occurs.

Getting a Lift

Need to get your schooner in the upper harbour but find that pesky Johnson Street Bridge is in the way? Call 385-5717 or radio VAH20 on VHF channel 12 (156.6 mHz) to arrange a bridge-lifting just for you. But don't bother during rush hour; it's closed. On late evenings and weekends, it'll cost you $75. Call an hour in advance.

Chop Shop

The BC Ferry Corporation has never been afraid of re-purposing its stock. During the 1960s, suspended platform decks were installed in the car decks of nine ships. Then in 1970, the corporation dealt with rapid traffic growth by "stretching" seven ships in the fleet. Although it took an engineering study and evidence of successful execution elsewhere to convince insurers and Canada Steamship inspectors it could be done, the corporation sliced the ferries in two and inserted 84-foot mid-sections in each one, adding capacity for an additional 42 cars. Finally, in the 1980s, it sliced the vessels linearly, using 129 hydraulic jacks to split each boat apart so an additional car deck and support beams could be built in the middle.

Photo: Courtesy of Maritime Museum

Ferry Wake Surfing

Surfers on Gabriola Island never have to watch tide tables or weather charts for a big swell. If the PacifiCat ferry is running, there's a break going off. Although the Strait of Georgia doesn't normally have surf, the provincial government's $200-million wave generators, better known as the "Fast Cat ferries" running between Nanaimo and Horseshoe Bay, produce a consistent curl for those who live in its wake. The waves break in both directions, and under certain tides, can be taller than five feet. Not quite the Pipeline, but it'll do.

The History of Gettin' Around

You can catch a glimpse of Victoria's transportation past at these two museums:

British Columbia Aviation Museum

Every Thursday, veterans of the aviation industry gather in the restoration hangar behind this museum and reassemble classic airplanes. Their work, displayed in the main hangar, includes a 1910 Gibson once flown at Lansdowne Airport near Camosun College, and a Tradewind like the one that jetted Minister of Highways "Flying" Phil Gagliardi around the province. The Eastman Sea Rover on display was reassembled from a wing strut discovered in the Yukon and sent to the Smithsonian Museum for identification. Other highlights include a display of historic plane engines and a Memorial Room with a collection of wartime flying memorabilia.
1910 Norseman Rd., Sidney, 655-3300

Maritime Museum of BC

Located in a former Victoria courthouse, this museum's highlights include a replica of the *HMS Temeraire* constructed entirely of beef and chicken bones by French naval prisoners captured during the Napoleonic wars, and a heritage courtroom renovated by Francis Rattenbury — on the right hand side of the room, draw the red velvet curtain aside to see his original sketches of the moulding. Also check out one of Victoria's most ornate elevators (see left). *28 Bastion Square, 385-4222*

10 Most Dangerous Intersections

These are the corners in Victoria you're most likely to bugger up your car. They may also be the busiest, so might as well avoid 'em altogether (see Driving Secrets). The stats are totals for the last five years.

Douglas at Finlayson
Number of accidents: 86

Hillside at Quadra
Number of accidents: 78

Bay at Quadra
Number of accidents: 73

Hillside at Shelbourne
Number of accidents: 70

Blanshard at Hillside
Number of accidents: 69

Bay at Cook
Number of accidents: 67

Douglas at Hillside
Number of accidents: 67

Cook at Johnson
Number of accidents: 66

Bay at Blanshard
Number of accidents: 65

Blanshard at Finlayson
Number of accidents: 57

Note: the stop sign at Douglas and Tolmie has become particularly nasty (19 accidents in 1998), so look both ways coming out of the Mayfair Shopping Centre, eh.

Hard Landing

Photo: Courtesy of BC Archives #G-5364

In 1913, two of the best-known stunt pilots (or "barnstormers") around were Alys McKey and John Bryant, a wife-and-husband flying team from California. In August that year they travelled to Victoria to exhibit their skills at a festival of waterfront events, and set a few flying records.

They'd already set one on their tour: on July 31 at Vancouver's Lulu Island, McKey became the first woman to fly a plane in Canada. She flew again in Victoria on August 5, but had to land prematurely because the notorious ocean winds kept thumping her plane. The following day her husband attached a float to the plane's undercarriage and attempted the same flight. He managed to pilot the plane over downtown – becoming the first person to fly over a Canadian city – and landed in the Inner Harbour, to the cheers of thousands.

A few hours later, Bryant took off from the harbour, and circled back over downtown. He'd only been in the air a few minutes when the aircraft went into a steep dive over City Hall – and, to the crowd's horror, crashed onto the roof of a building on Pandora Street, a few doors up from what is now the Swans Hotel. Bryant was killed instantly. Tragically, he'd set another record: he was the first person to die in a plane crash in Canada.

Alys McKey saw everything from a building nearby. Although she later did important work for U.S. aviation plants during both world wars, she was so heartbroken by her husband's death that she never flew again.

Air Traffic

First-time tourists who've paid big coin to stay at a hotel on the Inner Harbour are often unpleasantly surprised to discover they're sleeping smack dab in the middle of a busy airport. Around 40 seaplanes take off and land at the harbour every day between sunrise and sunset, making a terrible racket every time they rev their engines.

Watching those Otters and Beavers nose-dive over the city for a landing, you're bound to wonder whether any of them have ever crashed. Transport Canada says "only three or four" have crash-landed in the harbour over the past decade (including the Air BC plane in the 1989 photo above), but none has collided with boats or buildings – pretty lucky, considering that the Inner Harbour's landing strip is only 50 metres from the Songhees condo towers.

If you want to try landing your own plane, call the harbour master (380-8177) at least 48 hours before you arrive, and find out how to file your flight plan. Then make your arrangements with Hyack Air (384-2499), the only company that'll let you park at their dock; rates start at $75 to tie up a single-engine aircraft for a few hours.

When the pace of Victoria's city living gets to be too much, spend an afternoon at the Victoria International Airport watching everyone leave and pretend you're one of them. One of the best spots is on the bank by the Legion on Mills Road. If you want to get closer to the runways, try the picnic tables west of the main terminal.

"THE FOUNTAIN'S ALL BACKED UP..."

A hundred years ago the corner of Hillside and Douglas, now one of Victoria's busiest intersections, was one of the city's top residential areas. Joseph Heywood, who owned a house on Douglas at this time, felt impelled to provide a drinking fountain for the horses of wagoneers heading into the city. He built a water trough and drinking fountain in 1887, and for decades afterwards, the intersection of Hillside and Douglas was referred to as "the fountain." The drinking fountain now stands at the Johnson Street entrance of Market Square (see photo above).

ICE AND SNOW SUPPLIES

Every time the snow flies, rumours surface that all our snow-clearing equipment went to Calgary years ago. Not so. The city still has:

2 front-mounted snow plows on tandem trucks

6 underbody plows

6 sanding/salting units

1 front-end loader

4 backhoes

1 bobcat with snow blade for sidewalk clearing

Approximately 500 tons of salt

Victorians can easily recall the blizzard of 1996 (photo above), but during January and February 1916, the city experienced its other "Snowfall of the Century." In early February of that year, the snow lay four feet deep (photo below), and drifted to heights of 10 to 15 feet. Streetcars were given rotary brushes and put to work clearing the streets. They started in the suburbs of Mt. Tolmie and the Uplands, but were soon confined to the downtown loop (often rescuing cars that had already been stuck). Eventually the 103rd Battalion, camped at Willows Beach and waiting to go overseas, was deployed. The soldiers created a big wooden snowplow which 900 men took turns dragging downtown to clear Fort Street. Later, they took to shoveling Government Street from the Parliament Buildings northward.

Photo: Courtesy of BC Archives #E-0847

the unbearable rightness of bicycling

Non-motorized transport is a big deal in Victoria. Thanks to the city's fair weather and compact dimensions, up to 10 percent of all trips around town are made by bicycle – a stat that's led keen local politicians to brand Victoria the "cycling capital of Canada." Whether the title is warranted or not (*Bicycling* magazine thinks Montreal is best), there's no doubt that Victorians are seriously into pedal power.

Advocates

More and more public facilities are built for Victoria cyclists every year, and a good part of the credit goes to the Greater Victoria Cycling Coalition, a small (719 members at last count) but influential lobby group. Aside from needling politicians, the GVCC also organizes social rides and seminars on cyclists' legal rights and traffic planning issues. To join, call 480-5155 or check out their comprehensive website at www.gvcc.bc.ca, which includes schedules of events and ready-to-print maps of trails around town.

The Right Path

Without a doubt, the most important trail for getting around is the Galloping Goose, an old train right-of-way that starts just west of the Johnson Street Bridge and winds 70 kilometres past swimming lakes (Thetis, Matheson), suburban communities, esteemed colleges (Royal Roads University and the Pearson College of the Pacific) and farmland, all the way out to Sooke, and only rarely crossing the paths of those nasty automobiles; another fork of the Goose heads north, enabling you to get most of the way to the Swartz Bay ferry terminal. If you're interested in recreational riding, many districts have their own networks of trails; to locate them, check out the Victoria Cycling Map, available at many city bike shops.

Go Play on the Freeway

Some people think keeping your balance is all you have to learn to ride a bicycle. Dead wrong. There's also the tricky

GAS LIGHT

When it opened on June 19, 1931, the Causeway Garage (now the home of Tourism Victoria, located across from the Empress Hotel in the Inner Harbour) had a Spanish tile roof on the main building and pump islands, and acted as both a vehicle repair shop and storage area. Designed by Townley and Matheson, who also did Vancouver's City Hall, the Sperry navigational beacon on the top of the garage's 80-foot tower beamed 10,000,000-candle-power light across the harbour, for a distance of almost 60 miles (96 kilometres). At night, eight huge floodlights illuminated its Imperial Oil sign. The lights were permanently turned off just before World War II, taking Victoria out of the spotlight and into the shadows.

Bicycle Stores

Get off your duff and into one of the following so you too can cycle the Victoria way:

Bicycleitis
1623 Bay St., 370-2282

Chain, Chain, Chain
1410 Broad St. (in the alley),
385-1739

Fairfield Bicycle Shop
1275 Oscar St., 381-2453

Fort Street Cycle
1025 Fort St., 384-6665

Oak Bay Bicycle
1968 Oak Bay Ave., 598-4111

Russ Hay's
650 Hillside Ave., 384-4722
2480 Beacon Ave., Sidney,
656-1512,

West Shore
#1-1610 Island Hwy., 391-1980

matter of learning how to ride in traffic, and that's where Can-Bike instructor Ray Hall comes in. Several times a year Hall teaches a course on survival skills which aren't even obvious to veteran riders: instead of hewing to the curb, for example, he tells cyclists to "take the lane" and ride confidently out on the roadway, where drivers can see them. "If you want to be given the same respect as a car, you've got to act like one," Hall says. To find out more about his course, call 380-0172.

Legalities

According to B.C.'s Motor Vehicle Act, a cyclist has "the same rights and duties" as a driver. That means cyclists are just as entitled to use the road – and just as subject to its rules and regs. In 1997, Victoria police issued 1,165 tickets to cyclists, slapping them with $86 fines for traffic violations (riding on sidewalks, etc.) and $29 penalties for failing to wear helmets. Sometimes it's worth fighting such tickets in court, though. One helmet-hating Victoria cyclist and devotee of "simple living" has made a point of disputing all nine helmet tickets he's received since 1996, and, so far, eight of them have been thrown out because the cops didn't bother showing up at the trials.

Free Bikes!

Even if you can't afford a used Raleigh, you can still pedal around Victoria thanks to the noble citizens behind the Blue Bikes, the baby-blue two-wheelers occasionally seen leaning up against lamp-posts around town. Like Amsterdam's famous white bicycles, these blue numbers are free to anyone, on the understanding that you'll leave the bike out for someone else to use when you're done – thereby preserving the environment and the social contract at the same time. If you'd like to donate a bike, or find a blue one in need of repair, call 381-BLUE.

Get Moving

If you've got goods to deliver or an apartment's worth of furniture to get across town, you can do it without burning nasty fossil fuel. Instead, recruit the athletic folks at Bike CartAge – "powered by digestion, not combustion" – who can move just about anything on their sturdy trailers. For more info, call 480-7285.

(For mountain biking, see Sports, Leisure and the Outdoors.)

A Streetcar Named Disaster

On the afternoon of May 26, 1896, a streetcar headed to Macaulay Point in Esquimalt to watch a mock military battle celebrating Queen Victoria's birthday was loaded with 142 passengers. (It was licensed to carry only 60.) The car started to cross the Point Ellice Bridge (now called the Bay Street Bridge, though the name has never officially changed) when the bridge cracked and dropped a foot. The car ran on for another 15 feet before the entire span collapsed and fell into the 260-foot-deep waters of the Gorge and struck bottom. As the car rose again, observers reported, air pressure expelled passengers out broken windows. Onlookers in boats pulled survivors from the wreckage and lined them up on the shore. In total, 55 people died and 27 were seriously injured. Among those who perished, 12 were children. It remains the worst streetcar disaster in North American history.

Streetcar Sell-Off

With the conversion of the streetcar to bus lines in the mid-1940s, in July 1947 the BC Electric Company began advertising the former cars for sale – $100 for the smaller "Birneys," $150 for the wooden cars. The streetcars were re-purposed as chicken houses, outhouses, hamburger stands, and a few even became a home in Luxton. One streetcar in Langford became the Night Owl diner (destination: Esquimalt) and Birney 401 became the "Jolly Trolly," a children's mini-theatre and play area, on Tattersall Drive in Saanich. This contrasts the ignoble means of disposal over in Vancouver, where streetcars that finished their careers were pushed off the tracks and set alight.

TAKE THE TRAIN

Okay, so you don't own a car, but you want to take a trip up-Island. You could take a bus – but who wants to be trapped for hours next to some kid blasting Megadeth on his Walkman? Plan ahead, and ride the rails. You'll travel with a more international class of passenger, and save money at the same time. While a bus to Courtenay costs $70 return from Victoria, the same trip on VIA Rail's dayliner will only set you back $53.50 (less for children, students, and seniors) if you book at least seven days in advance. The train travels just as fast, and instead of looking at the strip-mall junk along Highway 1, you'll pass through lovely farmland, over spectacular trestle bridges, and right past cheerful Islanders drinking beer and playing in their back yards with their Rottweilers. For more info, call 1-800-561-8630.

PARKING TICKETS

A few years ago a bumper sticker appeared on cars around the Garden City, expressing the frustration of suburban drivers with our cozy, olde-Brit downtown: "Victoria – Parking Ticket Capital of the World." That moniker's an exaggeration (hey, what about Manhattan?), but it's true that the City of Victoria issues an awful lot of parking fines. Around 250,000 tickets were handed out in 1999 alone, bringing in $2.7 million for the municipal coffers. Keep a close watch on the time, even if you're not at one of the city's 1,900 meters; the commissionaires are famous for nailing cars that stay even a few minutes over the one- or two-hour limit on side streets. (And don't rub off the chalk they mark on your tires to keep track: there's a $100 fine for that, too.)

DRIVING MISS PAT

Cab drivers always pray for big fares, but few can top the one paid in January of 1996 by Pat Fry, a 68-year-old lady who hopped in a taxi in Pasadena, California — and got out 10 days and 4,800 kilometres later in Victoria. The meter ended up reading $7,600 US (the driver knocked the tab down to $4,000), but Pat came out ahead on the deal. Aside from getting a tour of lovely Victoria, she was interviewed by news media outlets from the *Times* of London to the *National Enquirer*, appeared on talk shows with Jay Leno and Conan O'Brien, and eventually had a made-for-TV movie made of her story, *Cab to Canada*, for which she and the driver reportedly both pocketed six-figure paycheques.

On May 20, 1901, Captain John Voss and local journalist Norman Luxton left Oak Bay on one of the most fantastic voyages to ever begin in Victoria. Earlier in the year, Luxton proposed to Voss that they attempt to circumnavigate the globe in the smallest vessel on record (while raising a $5,000 prize and writing a book about the journey). Voss agreed, and procured a dugout canoe on the east coast of Vancouver Island and named the boat the *Tilikum* (a Chinook word meaning "people" or "friends"). He fitted the 38-foot boat with necessary refinements to weather the voyage: a deck and a five-by-eight-foot cabin, a rudder, tiller, 300 pounds of lead attached to the keel, and three masts. His friend's wife constructed the sails on her sewing machine.

Although Luxton lasted less than a half a year as first mate (he got off in Fiji), Voss sailed on to Australia and New Zealand, across the Indian Ocean and north to Europe, arriving in London over three years later. Although he managed to cross three of the world's oceans and arrive in England with his boat unharmed (he burned through 11 other mates, one of whom was swept overboard), he didn't cross all the meridians necessary to claim the feat of sailing around the world.

His account of the odyssey was published in 1913 as *The Venturesome Voyages of Captain Voss*. His sailing tips contained in the appendix include practical instructions such as "How to manage a small vessel in a typhoon" and "The proper time to heave to when running before a strong wind and sea," and are still cited by sailors today. Luxton's bitter account of one-sixth of the journey was published by his daughter in 1971 as *Luxton's Pacific Crossing*.

After displaying the *Tilikum* at the Navy and Marine Exhibition at Earl's Court in 1905, Voss sold the boat, which lingered on the Thames until the Victoria Publicity Bureau arranged to have it shipped back to the city in 1929. It sat at Crystal Gardens and in Thunderbird Park before finally finding a home at the Maritime Museum, where it is on exhibit today.

driving secrets

Despite what you might think, Victoria does have its traffic trouble spots. Here are a few pointers to get you driving-savvy:

To the Gorge from downtown

Avoid the mess at Douglas at Hillside. It was workable as a roundabout back in the 1950s, but with 14 accidents last year? Forget it. Instead take Government to Bay, the first right on Rock Bay and a left on Gorge and you'll be at Craigflower Manor in minutes.

Avoid the horses in James Bay

Forget Belleville, Government, Menzies or Dallas. To navigate through James Bay, stick to the lesser-hoofed side streets: Cook or Quadra to Southgate, then take a left on Douglas, a right at Toronto, and straight on through Simcoe and the "five corners" to Oswego and the heart of James Bay. No horses, just jaywalkers.

Navigating the maze that is Fernwood

More and more people are using Cook Street to get around Blanshard, but the single lane stretch between Pandora and Bay often clogs at rush hour, and Fernwood Road is a 30-km zone. The solution? Chambers Street parallels Cook just one block east and offers easy north-south access; for an east-west connection between Fernwood and Richmond, take Cook Street to Balmoral, then Begbie to Shelbourne.

CAR SHARE CO-OP

Cars are like dogs: you've got to keep them clean and well-fed, and find a place for them to stay at night. That adds up to a lot of trouble, and expense. You can always live without a dog. But can you live without a car? Fortunately, you don't have to make that terrible choice, thanks to the Victoria Car Share Co-op, which enables you to own as much or as little car as you need. After paying an entry fee of $400 (refundable when you leave the co-op) you can rent a Tercel, minivan, or pickup truck from one of the co-op's three locations for $2 per hour and 35 cents for every kilometre you drive. To book a car, ring the 24-hour reservation line; it's best to call a day or two in advance if you want a vehicle for a few hours, farther ahead if you want a full day or more. (If no car's available, they also have a discount rate with a local taxi company.) It's more convenient than you might think, and cheaper than owning — especially when you consider that you don't have to pay extra for maintenance or insurance. For more info, call 995-0265 or see www.vvv.com/~carshare.

MERMAID OF ACTIVE PASS

Splash alert! On the evening of June 12, 1967, travellers on four BC Ferries

reported seeing a long-haired blonde woman sitting on a rock at Helen Point on the northwest corner of Mayne Island at Active Pass. George Harrison of Sioux City, Iowa managed to get a picture from the deck of the *Queen of Saanich*, and a Cobble Hill man took an aerial photo. Observers described a long-haired blonde with the lower body of a fish or porpoise who appeared to be eating a salmon.

A nameless observer with a pair of 10-power binoculars said, "The salmon had a big bite out of it," and that "she seemed to enjoy the wake of the ferry washing over her." Despite the fact that newspapers put her on the front page, she hasn't reappeared in the 30 years since.

A CLOSE CALL

If you take the *Coho* ferry from the Inner Harbour to Port Angeles and experience a particularly thorough search by U.S. customs officers upon arriving, blame it on Ahmed Ressam. The accused Algerian terrorist was caught coming off the *Coho* on December 14, 1999 with bomb-making materials and four timing devices in the spare-tire compartment of his rental car, creating pre-millennial panic across the U.S. and leading to the cancellation of big New Year's Eve celebrations in downtown Seattle.

Sling shot past the campus crawl

Stay on Fort Street until it turns into Cadboro Bay Road, which then takes you directly to Sinclair on the back side of UVic. There are no school zones and little traffic, and it puts you on the right side to find parking. Another option: Johnson Street turns into Shelbourne which takes you to McKenzie – a quick right and you're only a few blocks from campus. The advantage of this one is its double lanes and lack of speed zones.

Europe in Victoria

Want to show the kids the old country but can't afford it? Pack them in the station wagon and head into Rockland. Take Richardson to Lotbinere and follow the one-way along the rock wall past Government House. For 15 seconds, the narrow, winding road will make you think you're in the Apennines. (For a particularly authentic European experience, drive the wrong way on Lotbinere – kidding!)

One of Victoria's most colourful characters of the last century was Bill Nye. No, not the wacky PBS scientist for kids, but the Bill Nye whose real name was Thomas Chaplin, who arrived in Victoria in the early 1890s and worked as a longshoreman for many years. In addition to wearing gold earrings, sleeping on a mattress of newspapers in his cabin on Humbolt Street, and having a photographic memory, he salvaged bottles by paddling around the Inner Harbour in a barrel using a shingle in each hand to propel him.

Photo: Courtesy of BC Archives #D0371

MOTORCYCLE CITY

If life is a highway, it's best travelled on two wheels — a sentiment that seems to be shared by many in Victoria. Given our nearly year-round sun, low levels of rain, and the cheaper ferry price, travelling by motorcycle may be the most logical choice of Island transportation. Certainly that's the view of *Canadian Biker*, our national motorcycling monthly, which is based in the Garden City and regularly hosts such events as the Ride for Sight and the Christmas Toy Run, both of which get well over 1,000 riders annually. Publisher Len "Layback" Creed started the mag with lottery winnings over 20 years ago, and he's been riding tall in the saddle ever since. (You can find him at 735 Market St., 384-0333.) Need servicing? For Japanese bikes, the best choice is Victoria Suzuki; their friendly and knowledgeable staff will truck your dead machine in, and then stick to their estimate like glue *(858 Esquimalt Rd., 386-8364)*. For Harleys, the only choice is Steve Drane Harley-Davidson, the Island's

centre for all things "hog"; if you can believe it, their Nanaimo store also features a sushi bar *(735 Cloverdale Ave., 475-1345)*. Don't own but still want to ride? Renting is always an option. For big-ass Harleys, check out the up-island Coastline Motorcycle Tours and Rentals *(250/338-0344)*; for zippy Japanese street bikes, try Cycle Victoria Rentals *(811 Wharf St., 995-1661)*. While the choices for Island riding are many and marvellous — Highway 1 to Campbell River, the 14 to Port Renfrew (watch the curves; they're literally deadly), the 4 to Tofino, and the gracefully curving 19 (the old Island Highway) — the best rides in the city include the scenic James Bay-Uplands route along the waterfront; the scream along Old West Saanich Road to East Sooke Park; McKenzie from UVic to Highway 1; the Malahat (watch for the Lake Cowichan speed traps); and the Pat Bay Highway straightaway, where you can easily crack 180 kph off the ferry before worrying about curves.

It's synchronized swimming with a big twist. Imagine 20-foot, diesel-powered ballerinas, pirouetting to the strains of "The Blue Danube," and you've got the most unique ballet performance in town — the dance of the harbour ferries, gracing the waters in front of the Empress Hotel every Sunday morning at 9:45, mid-June to mid-September.

The ballet is choreographed by Victoria Harbour Ferries owner Paul Miller, the former Port Hardy boatwright who designed the sturdy little 12-passenger vessels. (He also built the similar Aquabuses that ply Vancouver's False Creek.) But they're not just frivolous boats for tourists: many people who live in James Bay and Vic West walk or bus downtown in the morning and use the ferries for a relaxing afternoon commute home. A one-way trip is $3, although you can also get a frequent traveller's discount card.

The ferries run to various points on the harbour from March to October. In the summer, Miller's company also runs tours up the Gorge waterway (leaving every half-hour from the Empress docks), and does weekday look-sees of Esquimalt Harbour (leaving hourly from the museum at the HMCS Naden naval base), the home of Canada's Pacific Fleet. Call 708-0201 for more information.

The secrets of Beacon Hill Park and other green spaces to park yourself. Plus defunct sports teams, the "Human Polar Bear," and the best places to get public nookie.

Those Pioneering Patricks

Photo: Courtesy BC Archives D-07 15

Victoria is a pioneer hockey town. Patrick Arena, which opened on Christmas Day 1911, was built by Lester and Frank Patrick, and stood at the corner of Epworth and Fort, across from Oak Bay Secondary. Not only was it the largest wooden structure ever built on the island, it was also Canada's first artificial ice surface and head office of the Western Hockey League for many years. In the building's first game, the New Westminster Royals skunked the Victoria Senators 8-3. The arena burned down early one morning in November 1929. But during the league's early years, the Patricks invented the following contributions to our national pastime: numbers on jerseys (1911-12), forward passing in the centre zone (1913), post-season playoffs (1918), and line changes on the fly (1925). In addition to coaching his hometown Cougars to a win in the finals in 1925, Lester Patrick (the namesake of the National Hockey League's Patrick Division) coached the New York Rangers to three Stanley Cups. His sons Muzz and Lynn also won the cup with the Rangers.

Cougars Win the Stanley Cup!

Believe it or not, in 1925, the Victoria Cougars beat the storied Montreal Canadiens to win the Stanley Cup. They were coached by the great Lester Patrick, who left the following year to lead the newly formed New York Rangers. Pro hockey left Victoria at the end of the next season when the Cougars moved east to Detroit. They played as the Detroit Cougars for the 1926-27 season, and changed their name to the Red Wings the following year.

Beacon Hill Larks

Except for the botanical gardens he proposed as a centrepiece, Beacon Hill Park remains true to the plan that won Scottish landscape architect John Blair the prize to develop it in 1888. Here are a few things you might not know about it.

Bear Pit

For 26 years in the early 1900s, a corner of Beacon Hill Park (now occupied by the petting zoo) was home to Ursus Kermodei, a rare white bear captured in 1924 on Princess Royal Island off the mouth of the Skeena River. She was named after Francis Kermode, a former director of the BC Museum of Natural History (who, along with Dr. William T. Hornady, discovered her species). Kermode bears are some of the world's rarest and exist in the wild only on the islands and mainland of Canada's northwestern coast. For years Victorians delighted in the bear's antics and debated over the adequacy of housing her in a small cage with only a cement floor, a concrete water tank, and a dead tree. Ursus died in 1950 and was stuffed and put on display at the Provincial Museum, but when the light started to fade her fur, she was moved into storage, where she remains today.

Missing Statue

In August 1998, the statue of Scottish poet Robbie Burns and Highland Mary Campbell went missing from its location on a seven-foot high pedestal in the middle of the Beacon Hill Park putting green. Installed in November 1900 by the William Wallace Society, the first Scottish society in Victoria, the statue has long been a treasure for the highlanders of Victoria. It was discovered days later in a driveway on Island Road, after a mysterious anonymous phone call to Victoria police insisted that the reward money be split between the Cancer Society and the Robbie Burns Society in Scotland. The statue has since been returned to the putting green.

Mayor's Grove

Near the Quadra Street entrance is the Mayor's Grove, a collection of trees dedicated to local and visiting dignitaries, between 1927 and 1985. Among the

Green Miles

Private and public golf courses.

PRIVATE

Gorge Vale
1005 Craigflower Rd., 386-3401
18 holes, 6,452 yards, par 72

Royal Colwood
629 Goldstream Ave., 478-9591
18 holes, 6,543 yards, par 70

Uplands
3300 Cadboro Bay Rd., 592-1818
18 holes, 6,310 yards, par 70

Victoria
1100 Beach Dr., 598-4322
18 holes, 6,015 yards, par 70

PUBLIC

Ardmore
930 Ardmore Dr., Sidney, 656-4621
9 holes, 2,603 yards, par 34

Cedar Hill
1400 Derby Rd., 595-3103
18 holes, 4,975 yards, par 67

Cordova Bay
5333 Cordova Bay Rd., 658-4444
18 holes, 6,668 yards, par 72

Glen Meadows
1050 McTavish Rd., Sidney, 656-3921
18 holes, 6,859 yards, par 72

Henderson

2291 Cedar Hill X Rd., 370-7200

9 holes, 679 yards, par 27

John Phillips

2197 Otter Point Rd., Sooke,
642-6344

9 holes, 2,242 yards, par 32

Juan de Fuca

1767 Island Hwy., 474-8621

9 holes, 1,123 yards, par 27

Metchosin

4100 Metchosin Rd., 478-3266

9 holes, 2,830 yards, par 34

Mount Douglas

4225 Blenkinsop Rd., 477-8314

9 holes, 1,537 yards, par 30

Olympic View

643 Latoria Rd., 474-3671

18 holes, 6,530 yards, par 72

Prospect Lake

4633 Prospect Lake Rd., 479-2688

9 holes, 1,985 yards, par 32

Royal Oak

540 Marsett Pl., 658-1433

9 holes, 1,933 yards, par 32

Sayward

5300 Cordova Bay Rd., 658-3996

9 holes, 816 yards, par 27

Sunshine Hills

7081 Central Saanich Rd.,
Saanichton, 652-5215

18 holes, 1,130 yards, par 54

honoured are Sir Winston Churchill (who planted a hawthorn), Lord Baden-Powell (oak), and Miss Helen Mackenzie, chatelaine to Lieutenant-Governor Randolph Bruce (Douglas fir). But good luck finding the tree to match the dignitary. Although they're numbered, the trees can be difficult to find, especially in the spring when the grass is long and the markers are all but hidden.

Burial Cairns

Just down the wide grassy slope from Signal Hill that faces Dallas Road, you'll find several clusters of large rocks. Although they look like primitive fire pits, they're actually what's left of several dozen native burial cairns that used to be spread across the hilltop. The point of land across from Signal Hill once was a defense post, which Coast Salish peoples used for refuge from raiding parties of rival tribes; the natives buried their dead on the hill, and covered over each body with earth and a pile of stones. (Most of the people buried on the slope were probably victims of smallpox rather than warfare, however.) After the white colonists moved in, they broke up many of the rocks and used them for road construction, or moved them around so they could cut the grass; four of the 300-year-old cairns have since been reconstructed. They're now protected by law, and occasionally used by local pagans for their nocturnal rituals.

Hot Plants

It's illegal, but that doesn't stop some people from taking souvenirs of Beacon Hill's greenery home with them. Every year over 200 plants are stolen from the park, mainly geraniums and begonias, although the occasional rose bush has gone missing as well. Park staff say the thieves usually strike right after the first planting of the flower beds in June, and then again in September when the winter annuals go in. No one's ever been caught, though, because the thieves do their dirty work in the middle of the night.

53

Blue Camas

If the apocalypse (earthquake, global computer virus, BC Ferries strike) suddenly descends and all the Thrifty supermarkets are closed, don't panic. You can always eat the bulbs of the Blue Camas, a type of lily that flowers on the dry grasslands of Beacon Hill Park every spring. The Coast Salish peoples visited these grasslands for centuries to harvest the sweet bulbs and roast them in pit ovens. But if you're ever tempted to do the same, collect them only when the Blue Camas is in bloom: the bulbs look identical to that of the white-flowering Death Camas, which was often responsible for killing the grazing sheep of Victoria's pioneers.

Mile Zero

Over 30 tour buses per day stop at this spot at the corner of Douglas and Dallas Road marking one end of the 7,821-kilometre (4,849-mile) Trans-Canada Highway, the longest national highway in the world. Plans are afoot to turn our "Mile Zero" into a swanky monument with pavilions and a phone booth linked to the other end, in St. John's, Newfoundland – which, oddly enough, is also called Mile Zero. Perhaps that's a tribute to vagabond Canadian optimism: east or west, we always like to think we're at the start of a journey, rather than at its conclusion.

Fonyo Beach

Just across from Mile Zero is the beach where, on May 29, 1985, Steve Fonyo dipped his artificial leg in the Pacific, completing his cross-Canada run for cancer research. Fonyo raised over $13 million and was awarded the Order of Canada, but fame took its toll on him: in 1996 he pleaded guilty to 16 charges for criminal offences he'd committed in Edmonton, including assault, fraud, theft, perjury, driving while disqualified, and possession of an unregistered 9mm handgun. Fonyo now lives quietly in Vancouver, where he's studying aircraft engine maintenance.

Pool Parties

Public swimming pools in Victoria.

Commonwealth
4636 Elk Lake Dr., 727-7108
50 metres; 26°C, dive tank, 1-metre board, 3-metre board, 3, 5, 7.5, and 10-metre towers, wave pool, tot pool, whirlpool, sauna, waterslide

Crystal (see above)
2275 Quadra St., 361-0732
50 metres; 28°C, 1-metre board, 3-metre board, tot pool, whirlpool, waterslide, underwater viewing room (beware of mooning teenagers)

Esquimalt
527 Fraser St., 386-6128
25 metres; 31°C, 1-metre board, tot pool, weight room

"The Human Polar Bear"

Photo: Courtesy BC Archives H-0291

Gordon Head

4100 Lambrick Way, 477-1871
25 metres; 30°C, 1-metre board,
whirlpool, sauna, climbing wall

Juan de Fuca

1767 Island Hwy., 474-8677
25 metres; 30°C, 1-metre board,
tot pool, whirlpool, sauna

Oak Bay

1975 Bee St., 595-7946
25 metres; 28°C, rope swing,
drop slide, spiral slide, tot pool,
midnight swim $2

Panorama

1885 Forest Pk., 656-7271
25 metres; 28°C, 1-metre board,
climbing wall, tot pool, sauna

University, McKinnon

McGill and Ring Rd., 721-8484
25 metres; 28°C, steep drop-in prices

University, Gordon Head

3964 Gordon Head Rd., 472-4000
25 metres (outdoor)

YMCA

880 Courtney St., 386-7511
25 metres; 28°C, tot pool, whirlpool

Most Victorians know Marilyn Bell, the teenaged heroine who became the first woman and the first Canadian to swim across the Strait of Juan de Fuca. For some reason, though, no one ever talks about Bert Thomas (pictured at left), the guy who did the Strait before anyone else. In 1954, Marilyn Bell swam across Lake Ontario, a first-time feat that won so much international attention that the *Victoria Dailey Times* decided to offer $1,000 to anyone who'd be first to swim the 18-mile (33 km) stretch between Port Angeles and Victoria. Over the following months, 53 people braved the Strait to try for the prize money, but the first to make it was Bert Thomas, 29, a 275-pound ex-logger and former navy frogman from Tacoma, Washington. After 11 hours and 17 minutes plowing through frigid currents, Thomas staggered ashore in Esquimalt on the morning of July 8, 1955 – whereupon he reportedly kissed his wife and asked for a cigarette. Thomas was showered with honours: the city named him the third "freeman" in Victoria's history, entitling him to vote in civic elections without holding property. Along with $1,000 from the *Times*, the town of Port Angeles chipped in $1,800 and Victoria residents gave Thomas another $1,400 just to thank him. (A year later, though, when Marilyn Bell swam the Strait and beat Thomas's time by 38 minutes, the *Times* paid her 30 grand.) Thomas kept paddling. In 1956 he swam from Seattle to Tacoma, and in 1958 he tried to become the first to swim across the English Channel and back again, but he only made it halfway on the return trip. He became a commercial diver, and then managed a boathouse; he died in Tacoma in June of 1972. So why do Victorians remember Marilyn Bell instead? Maybe it's because hundreds of people stroll past her monument on Dallas Road every day, while Bert Thomas's stands in Esquimalt's quiet Saxe Point Park.

Dallas Road Rocks!

Don't tell the souvenir shops, but Victoria has its very own pet rock. Dallasite can be found well beyond city limits, but the best place to check it out is along the beaches that line Dallas Road, which the rock is named after. You'll need a good eye for detail, however; the stone is volcanic in origin, and typically has thin bits of brown or green lava set in quartz.

Smash-Up Derby

Since 1954, Langford's Western Speedway has been the region's home of full-throttle auto racing, and the training ground for many great drivers, including Billy Foster (brother of music producer David Foster), who won many big races at the track in the early sixties, and in 1965 became the first Canadian to qualify for the Indianapolis 500. (Sadly, Foster died in a practice-lap crash at Riverside, California in 1967.) Stock cars, drag racers, wing-tipped sprint cars, and classic "old-timers" are just some of the types of vehicles that take to the 4/10ths-of-a-mile oval every weekend; there's also an annual "Denomination Derby," a race for local preachers.

Without question, though, Western Speedway's biggest draw is "hit-to-pass" demolition racing, a sport unique to the Pacific Northwest. While regular demolition derby cars chug around an enclosed pit, in hit-to-pass they're racing flat-out at highway speeds, guaranteeing plenty of rollovers, engine fires, and pulverized metal – it's like a Mad Max movie come to life. For a schedule of events, call 474-2151.

Secret Parking Spaces

Here are some peaceful plots where you can park yourself for some downtime.

Art Gallery of Greater Victoria

Sit in the mossy garden at the AGGV (1040 Moss St.) and listen to chestnuts falling on the copper roof of the Shinto shrine, which dates from the Meiji era (1868-1912).

Royal Theatre

If you're downtown and looking for a quiet place to have lunch, visit the Lawrie Wallace Garden adjacent to the parking lot between the Royal Theatre and CFAX Radio's headquarters on Broughton Street. Barely 10 feet wide, this parking space rescues you from the frenzy of downtown, and comes with wooden benches and shady trees.

Saxe Point

At the end of Fraser Street in off Esquimalt Road, Saxe Point Park offers cultivated gardens, forested paths, and an incredible vista of the Olympic Mountains across the Strait of Juan de Fuca. But bring a sweater, as winds on the point can blow the cobwebs out.

The Sound of Cricket

Given the city's old-empire roots, it's pretty easy to find a cricket match somewhere in town:

Metchosin

The ground is at the end of Happy Valley Road, behind the Metchosin council chambers. The tree in the middle of the pitch is in play — hit it on the fly it's a six, a roller it's four. Changerooms and washrooms are in the adjacent municipal hall.

Beacon Hill

Located at the corner of Park and Heywood. Fans can watch matches from their cars in the parking lot around the field, a tradition in Victoria since the turn of the century.

Windsor

Surrounded by the Tudor buildings of Oak Bay, the pitch is located in Windsor Park *(Windsor Rd. and Newport Ave.)*, and has an excellent clubhouse with a barbeque on the viewing deck.

St. Michael's

This pristine pitch is located on the campus of St. Michael's University School *(3400 Richmond Rd.)*.

Blood on the Wicket

Cricket in Victoria hasn't always been the genteel pursuit of tea-slurping men in white. The pitch at Beacon Hill bore witness, in 1858, to a "misunderstanding" between players John Collins and William Morris serious enough to be settled with pistols at 10 paces. Three shots were exchanged before Collins was bowled out for his final innings and sent to the Great Wicketkeeper in the sky. Morris fled the country. While news of this bloody duel must have shocked the good citizens of early Victoria, at least they knew where to fix blame for such lawlessness: both men were Americans.

Fight Club

The earliest prize fight on Vancouver Island was held on February 23, 1866, when Constable Joe Eden (6 ft, 175 lbs) took on George Baker (5 ft 10 in, 154 lbs) at an outdoor ring in William Head because prize fighting was prohibited in the city. The fight employed London Prize Ring rules (otherwise known as bare knuckles) and lasted an incredible 128 rounds. In the 46th, Eden injured his left hand and was unable to use it for the rest of the fight. By the 63rd, both men were exhausted but Baker managed to last until the 120th, when it was clear the fight was over: a few more right-handed blows by Eden "knocked Baker out of time." Spendthrift fight fans avoided the box office by assembling in the oak tree above the ring. Organizers tried to prevent this by coating the tree with oil.

on the beach

Nestled as we are down at the tip of Vancouver Island, more than a few travellers arrive ready to hit the beach, expecting to see more of a seashore than really exists. For big sand and tides that go waaaaay out, take an up-Island drive to Rathtrevor or Long Beach; here in town it's more rocks and logs than tanning oil and thongs. Don't chuck the sunscreen, though. While few, there are some choice beaches no more than a bus ride away from downtown.

Cadboro Bay

Up towards UVic is charming Cadboro Bay, quite possibly Victoria's most picturesque cove. Filled with families and kids (usually playing on the whimsical creations of Gyro Park) during the day, Cadboro Bay often empties come early evening, making it the ideal place to dig your feet in the sand and watch the moon rise. Keep your eyes peeled for Cadborosaurus.

Gonzales

Hippies new and old will find a home down at Gonzales, where big-as-a-car driftwood and sandy tucks into the surrounding rockface provide the privacy to peel. A favourite among Fairfield locals, it may be a bit of a trick to find someone who'll point the way.

Island View

If you're looking to spread out a bit or set up a volleyball net, try this stretch in Saanich, 15 minutes north of town on the Pat Bay Highway. Island View also features a First Nations reserve (watch where you park), a marginally clothing-optional section (depending on the year), and the occasional rave.

Skater Rinks

In these skate-park havens you can skateboard without having to battle security guards, bylaws officers, or the rough patches in the road.

Saanich
Lambrick Park Sports Centre
4115 Torquay Dr.
Concrete, free, street course

Sidney
Eighth St. and Pat Bay Hwy., Sidney
Concrete, free

Sooke
Journey Middle School
6522 Throup Rd.
Concrete, free, snakerun

Vic West
Next to Victoria West
Lawn Bowling Club
407 Alston St.
Concrete, free, street course

ROLLERBLADE COASTERS

In-line skates may at first seem like a perfect way to see Victoria, but don't be fooled: the two most obvious places to skate — downtown and Dallas Road — are also two likely places for 'blade-busting. Rollerblades, like skateboards, are banned in the downtown core and infractions can net you a fine and possible equipment seizure. And while you won't be ticketed for zipping along Dallas Road's paved pathways, you won't make any friends either; 'blades are generally unwelcome in that place of pedestrian-and-puppy perambulation.

The same is true for Esquimalt's Inner Harbour seawalk, where you'll encounter more scowls than smiles while rolling along. So what's left?

Try the streets. Forced away from the obvious, you'll discover more of Victoria's peculiar charm while quietly scooting through its neighbourhoods. James Bay is best seen rolling; from there to Fairfield through Beacon Hill Park is a favourite route, where slow roads give way to smooth paths with plenty of crosswalks. If you're looking for the best place to learn, grab your pads and head to UVic, where quality concrete with plenty of surrounding greenery make it the smoothest place to 'blade in town. Past noble totems on the fringes of the Mystic Vale forest over to the sunny patio at Felicita's Pub, you can't beat the campus for a fine afternoon of skating.

West of Sooke

For truly spectacular beaches, hop on Highway 14 east towards Port Renfrew and explore the out-of-town wonders that await. China Beach is close to Jordan River, which offers the best winter surfing this side of Long Beach (photo above). Mystic Beach sports an amazing waterfall plus a beachfront campsite, just a two-kilometre walk in. French Beach has 1,600 metres of sand plus great views of migrating whales in spring and fall. The secret sea gardens and tidal pools of Botanical Beach near Port Renfrew are not to be missed, but remember: look, don't touch.

Willows

The teen scene thrives down at this sandy but small piece of waterfront in Oak Bay, where buff bodybuilders beef up their bronze before a gaggle of giggling goils. On sunny days, Willows' shallow waters let the ocean get at least warmish, although even on the nicest days no one really makes a habit of swimming hereabouts.

Starting at the Inner Harbour and heading out along the coast in either direction, you'll soon find a place to jump in the ocean in a kayak. There are loads of options for gear, but a great start is Ocean River Sports *(1437 Store St., 381-4233)* where you'll find everything you need, including rentals, sales, and lessons. Before you head out, pick up Mary Ann Snowden's *Island Paddling: a Paddler's Guide to the Gulf Islands and Barkley Sound* for advice on the best spots. For beginners, the Gorge waterway is calm and leads from the Inner Harbour up to Portage Inlet, but be careful when the tide is going out: the reversing falls under the Tillicum bridge can build up a head of a metre and are tough to navigate. Launching from Willows Beach in Oak Bay, paddlers can easily get out to the Chatham and Discovery Islands. The Sooke Basin provides some easy paddling to offshore islands; launch from Anderson Cove in East Sooke Park. The shoreline on the southwest side of the park provides some challenging paddling to Whiffin Spit. Other good launch spots along the west coast are at Albert Head Lagoon, Weir's Beach or Pedder Bay. Out near Sidney, launch from Island View Beach, Saanichton Bay or Sidney to reach James, D'Arcy, Sidney, Mandarte, Rum, and Reay Islands. From Swartz Bay, trip out to Portland or Moresby Islands. For lessons, workshops, and more paddling destinations, contact the Victoria Canoe and Kayak Club *(355 Gorge Rd. West, 361-4238)*.

CALLING ALL TURKEY HEADS

If the membership fees at larger yacht clubs are putting you in the poorhouse, try the Turkey Head Sailing Association. For $75 you'll get a full membership, allowing you to join one of their weekly sailing events. With the emphasis on fun, these include games such as the Bassackwards race or Sookesure, allowing any member the chance to experience sailing. The association is based out of the Oak Bay Marina, and named after Turkey Head, the point of land the marina sits on. See www.thsa.bc.ca or call the Oak Bay Marina (598-3369) for more information.

Putting at Windmills

Miniature golf courses in Victoria.

All Fun
2207 Millstream Rd., 474-7225

Beacon Hill
Simcoe Street entrance, across from
the petting zoo
Free and open 24 hours

Blenkinsop
4239 Blenkinsop Rd., 477-4104

Bushwhackers
3766 Sooke Rd., 474-4544

Colwood
1772 Island Hwy., 474-7432

Elk Lake
5411 Hamsterly Rd., 658-4737

Mattick's Farm
5325 Cordova Bay Rd., 658-4053

Come Sail Away

Named for a survey vessel that sounded the Swiftsure Bank in the 1890s, the Swiftsure Classic sailing race started in 1930, with three boats in a race out around the lightship marking the bank. Held every May, it now consists of over 400 entries and three distinct races: from Clover Point to Swiftsure Bank and back (136.8 nautical miles), to Neah Bay and back (100.6 nm), and to Clallam Bay and back (76.2 nm), plus the Sooke Harbour Classic for non-competitor boats. Weather always plays the most important role in the races, and although some years the seas are so calm that competitors give up and power back to shore, other years the weather wreaks havoc. The 1976 race stands as the most tumultuous in Swiftsure's 50-year history: gale force winds and seas up to 25 feet caused over a dozen boats to break away from the race, and Seattle yachtsman Wilbur Willard drowned after a wave swamped the cockpit of his boat, *Native Dancer*. The best spots for viewing are along Dallas Road and the Ogden Point breakwater. Arguably, the best part of the weekend is the pre-race pancake breakfast put on by the Fairfield Community Association.

Survival Suit

Back in 1983, three University of Victoria professors got together to design a lifejacket with enough thermal protection to keep shipwrecked boaters alive. The result of their efforts, the Mustang UVic Thermofloat lifejacket, has since sold over 100,000 units and become the industry standard. Martin Collis, John Hayward, and John Eckerson each spent over 100 hours immersed in frigid water analyzing how the body loses heat, and discovered that the groin, sides of the chest, and the head and neck are most in need of protection. So they developed a type of mini-wetsuit resembling a conventional lifejacket, but with a Velcro-secured flap in the back that can be pulled between the legs to insulate the groin, and a thermal hood in the collar. This allows boaters more mobility than a conventional survival suit, and the protection they need if something ever goes wrong.

old glories, done dynasties

In addition to the Stanley Cup-winning Cougars, Victoria has had quite a colourful history of successful sports teams.

Maple Leaf Baseball Club

One of Victoria's first sports teams, the Maple Leaf Baseball Club started back in 1898 and had the distinction of having a black player on the roster, Victoria-born Jimmy Banswell: an anomaly, as black players were banned from the major leagues until the 1950s. He caught barehanded and was reportedly good enough to have played in the big leagues if not for his colour.

Victoria Dominos / Blue Ribbons

During the first half of this century, Victoria sported a basketball dynasty to rival the Chicago Bulls of the 1990s. The Victoria Dominos and their forerunners, the Victoria Blue Ribbons, won five national titles in the Canadian Amateur Senior Basketball Association; two as the Blue Ribbons in 1933 and 1935, and three as the Dominos in 1939, 1942, and 1946. The rules were different back then: players could only take one step with each dribble, and there was no palming the ball or touching the rim. The Dominos even beat the famed Harlem Globetrotters in 1939 in a game played at Victoria High, with the help of a 16-year-old rookie named Norm Baker who scored 33 points. Team members Doug Peden and Chuck Chapman also helped the Canadian Olympic team win the silver medal at Berlin in 1936 – they were thumped by the United States in a game played outside on a clay court in the pouring rain.

LUCK OF THE IRISH

Victoria hasn't won a Stanley Cup since 1925, but it continues to clean up in Canada's "other" national sport. Victoria's Foundation Lacrosse Club first won the Mann Cup, the national prize in senior lacrosse, for the Garden City back in 1919, and since the Victoria Shamrocks team was created in 1950, it's won six more – most recently in 1999, when the 'Rocks were led by home-town superstar twins Paul and Gary Gait, arguably the greatest-ever players of the sport. The 'Rocks play from May to August; for a game schedule, call Memorial Arena at 361-0506.

GOING SKY HIGH

If you've got a thing for jumping out of planes, there's only one choice in town: Sidney's Ultimate High Parachute Centre (9564 Hurricane Rd., 656-6111), which will teach you, train you, and drop you all in the same day. Their one-day skydiving course won't break your bank – or your back – but they will guarantee that plunging from 3,000 feet will give you a whole new perspective of the Island.

AND THEY DIDN'T LIVE HAPPILY EVER AFTER

In 1962, Alfred J. Petersen started a five-acre theme park on leased land in Beaver Lake Park, which he called Wooded Wonderland. The entrance consisted of sculptures of giant books and the park itself contained over 60 life-sized storybook characters located in the middle of the forest; a gigantic Humpty Dumpty greeted visitors at the entrance, visible from the highway. The inclusion of the park in the Greater Victoria Regional Parks System in 1967 spelled the end of this fairy tale of private enterprise on public property. In 1968, Petersen's lease expired and was not renewed.

WAR ZONE

When the Spencer's Department Store burned down in October 1910, the entire lot bounded by Fort, Government, Broad and Trounce Alley became a pile of rubble. Within three weeks David Spencer had purchased the adjacent Driard Hotel and converted it into a department store, but the lot behind remained vacant for part of World War I. Returned soldiers used the detritus to recreate the trenches of the Western Front, and charged 25 cents for tours.

The Jokers Foul Bay Lacrosse Club was awarded the 1942 Minto Cup 43 years after winning the season. The Jokers club, which was managed by George H. "Joker" Patton, won the B.C. Junior Lacrosse Championship that year, but because of World War II, the playoffs were cancelled and no national championship was awarded. At a dinner at the Union Club in 1985, former members of the Jokers decided to challenge Etobicoke, winners of the Ontario Lacrosse League, to a match to decide who could rightfully claim the 1942 Minto Cup. Unfortunately, they couldn't find enough Ontario players to field a team, so at a dinner at Victoria's Holyrood House later that year, Peter Avender, president of the B.C. Lacrosse Association, presented the Jokers with the cup.

A Taste of SALTS

Ever wonder about the fancy boat often at the dock in front of the Empress Hotel? It's the *Robertson II*, a fishing schooner from Nova Scotia that Dr. Philip Ney brought to Victoria in 1972 when he started the Sail and Life Training Society. This Christian non-profit organization focuses on youth training, taking crews of 30 out for 10-day trips during the summer, and shorter trips during the spring and fall. In 1986, the society created The *Pacific Swift*, a topsail schooner built in an exhibit at Expo, and launched in October of that year. Between 1988 and 1995 it was used for offshore training programs, the longest being 22 months. The society is now building a replica of the *Robertson II*, named the *Pacific Grace*. Anyone can visit the shipyard (*#2-203 Harbour Rd.*, *383-6811*) to see the work that's going on.

tender in the grass

With breath-taking scenery, ocean breezes, the sensuous pull of surrounding tides, Victoria is – dare we say it? – a sexy town. Sometimes the amorously adventurous feel the need to take their intimacy outdoors for a heavy breather or two. And why not? Oscar Wilde once said they best way to get rid of a temptation is to yield to it. But before you get tender in the grass, remember: flora and fauna can play havoc with even the most well-planned sexual encounter. Plants can be prickly, and ants, geese, and shocked tourists can bite. Not to mention the invasive nature of beach sand. So if you're planning to make love al fresco, bring a blanket. And although being seen or caught is part of the attraction for some people, it helps to be discreet. You and your partner may *feel* sexy, but you might not *look* sexy. Some places to try:

Golf Courses

A playground for the sexually mischievous, Victoria's courses offer lush green fairways perfectly suited to a private moonlit encounter.

Beacon Hill Park

The park and cove beaches under the crumbling cliffs of Dallas Road are well known places to fool around. Here, like the hungry traveler at the buffet on a BC Ferry, the willing participant can choose from a "wide selection of hot and cold entrées."

Horsedrawn Carriages

You both stare up at the stars, smell the pungent fragrance of summer flowers, and listen to the charming clop-clop sound of your horse; take a night tour of Beacon Hill Park, and the peacocks won't be the only ones screeching.

Mount Tolmie

This hill in Gordon Head remains a perennial favourite. Choose your backdrop from any number of panoramic views before turning your attention to the matters at hand.

(Thanks to Brett Lowther, who originally wrote this piece for *Monday*.)

Athletes of Note

Maybe it's the mild climate, or maybe it's the healthy lifestyle, but the Garden City is home to an incredible number of notable athletes.

Athlete: Norm Baker
Sport: Basketball
Achievement: Four titles with Victoria Dominos, only non-U.S. player selected for the "stars of the world" team in 1950.

Athlete: Dawn Coe-Jones
Sport: Golf
Achievement: Most career money won by a Canadian on the LPGA tour.

Athlete: Billy Foster
Sport: Auto Racing
Achievement: First Canadian to race in the Indianapolis 500, in 1965 (dropped out in the 90th lap due to a broken water line).

Athlete: Silken Laumann
Sport: Rowing
Achievement: Two world single sculls championships, bronze in the 1984 Olympics, bronze in 1992, and silver in 1996. Perhaps best-known for her remarkable Olympic comeback following a terrible rowing accident in 1991.

Athlete: Ed Murray
Sport: Football
Achievement: Spent 18 seasons

in the NFL and became the seventh-leading scorer in NFL history. He won a Super Bowl ring with the Dallas Cowboys in 1994.

Athlete: Steve Nash
Sport: Basketball
Achievement: Highest Canadian pick in the history of the NBA draft, when the Phoenix Suns picked him 15th overall in 1995.

Athlete: Muzz Patrick
Sports: Hockey, Basketball, Boxing
Achievement: Stanley Cup with New York Rangers, national championship with Blue Ribbons/Dominos, Canadian amateur heavyweight title.

Athlete: Lynn Patrick
Sports: Basketball, Hockey
Achievement: National basketball title with Victoria Blue Ribbons, Stanley Cup with New York Rangers (1939-40).

Athlete: Doug Peden
Sports: Basketball, Cycling, Tennis, Track, Baseball, Rugby, Hockey
Achievement: Olympic silver medal in basketball; won seven international cycling races; played on the national junior tennis team; was a junior city track champ; hit over .300 in Class A Eastern League baseball; the only Canadian to score against New Zealand's All Blacks during their 1936 tour; was invited to sign for the New York Rangers' farm team.

Run for Your Life

Victoria is a runner's town. Attendance in the annual Garden City 10K increases every year – when it started in 1990, it had 2,262 entries, but last year it drew over 7,600 runners. And there are loads of running groups in the city: Team Westcoast, the Peninsula Plodders, the Island Road Racers, to name a few. Check in at Frontrunners (382-8181) or the Running Room (383-4224) for guidance on one that's right for you. One group that deserves special mention is the Hash House Harriers. Started by a group of British expatriates in Malaysia in 1938, the Harriers are an international running organization with hundreds of local chapters or "hashes." Their runs are modeled after British public-school paper chases; the name Hash House refers to the food at their original social centre in Kuala Lumpur, the Royal Selangor Club. Their events involve a runner laying out a trail using blotches of flour on various landmarks, and the pack following it to a checkpoint where they usually down a beer, and then resume the trail until it ends at a pub for the "after-hash" party. Some runs are "live" hashes, where one runner is picked to be the hare that is chased by the pack. Dress for the runs can involve anything from kimonos to underwear to Easter Bunny costumes. The hotline for those interested in hashing is 995-8733.

Mountain Biking

The South Island Mountain Bike Society (477-2455) has all the information about where to ride (www.coastnet.com/~simbs). The most popular trails are at Hartland near the landfill and Millstream out beyond Western Speedway, but other trails are at Burnt Bridge near Shawnigan Lake, Mt. Tzouhalem near Duncan, and Bamberton. Trail work happens the third Sunday of every month from 9 am to 12:30 pm, and SIMBS provides lunch.

wild, wild life

Victorians have unusual relationships with some of the other species that call this place home.

Birds of Prey

Some unique predators reside in our town (and we're not talking about divorce lawyers). Peregrine falcons, once famous because their numbers were decimated by DDT, sometimes rest on aerial wires outside the Chateau Victoria Hotel and on the steeples of St. Andrew's Cathedral. Greater Victoria also hosts the second-highest density of Cooper's hawks in North America, squeezing themselves into the city at a ratio of one for every three square kilometres. A good place to spot them is around the public library on Broughton Street, where the hawks hunt house sparrows attracted by seed laid out by well-intentioned citizens.

Bullfrogs

They've been common back east for millennia, but bullfrogs didn't exist on Vancouver Island until the 1930s, when Depression-era residents imported them to build frog farms and get rich selling the legs to French restaurants. But Victoria didn't really *have* any French restaurants at the time, so the would-be farmers let the bullfrogs loose, and now the croakers have taken over most of the lakes on the Saanich peninsula. This wouldn't be a problem, except that the big frogs (weighing up to one pound each) eat everything that moves, including snakes, rodents, fish, small birds – and the tiny Pacific tree frogs that are native to the island.

Cougars

Whenever a police report goes out over the radio that a cougar has been sighted, a shiver of excitement goes through town. The big cats are frequently spotted out in the 'burbs, but sometimes they come right into the heart of the city; in 1992, for instance, a cougar was caught and tranquilized in the parkade of the Empress Hotel. That's a better fate than many cougars have faced. Until 1958, they were considered no-good varmints (there was a bounty of $40 on their heads), and though there are only around 800 left on Vancouver Island, around

Athlete: Derek Porter
Sport: Rowing
Achievement: Olympic gold in 1992 and silver in 1996, and single sculls world championship in 1993.

Athlete: Gareth Rees
Sport: Rugby
Achievement: Played in a world-record fourth World Cup in 1999.

Athletes: Peter Reid and Lori Bowden
Sport: Triathlon
Achievement: This husband-and-wife team won the men's and women's Ironman titles in Hawaii in 1999, and the men's and women's Canadian triathlon championships in 2000.

Athlete: Alison Sydor
Sport: Mountain Biking
Achievement: Seven world championships and a silver medal at the 1996 Olympics.

Athlete: Luraina Undershute
Sport: Kickboxing
Achievement: Ranked number one in the world in 1999.

Athlete: Simon Whitfield
Sport: Triathlon
Achievement: Gold medal (the sport's first) at the 2000 Summer Olympics.

60 or 70 cougars are killed every year by hunters and conservation officers, especially if the cougar's attacked a farm animal or a pet. Domestic dogs, though hardly endangered, rarely suffer the same fate for the same crime.

Garry Oaks

Legend has it that Walt Disney got the idea for the scary forest scene in *Sleeping Beauty* from these jagged trees, but that's not what makes the Garry oak important. The only type of oak indigenous to western Canada, it grows best in grassy meadows alongside dozens of unique species, including food plants (Chocolate Lily, Nodding Onion) once harvested by Coast Salish natives. Garry oak meadows are also endangered: though they exist in Canada only on southeast Vancouver Island and a few Gulf Islands, they're steadily being wiped out by "development" (e.g., Langford's controversial Costco outlet). If you want to see a Garry oak meadow as it should be, check out the grounds of Government House, or Mill Hill Regional Park.

Gypsy Moths

Every couple of years, Victoria gets into an uproar about government plans to douse the city with insecticide to wipe out a local infestation of the European Gypsy moth. A voracious little insect (accidentally released on this continent by a Massachusetts scientist in 1869), the moth's caterpillars can strip dozens of different tree species of their leaves in just 24 hours, posing a serious threat to Vancouver Island's forest-products industry. As critics point out, though, we humans are to blame for the moth's success: it thrives in areas like Victoria where there are few caterpillar predators (shrews, toads) and the trees have been weakened by urbanization.

Salmon

Every October and November, when the creeks swell with the autumn rains, Victorians migrate to Goldstream Provincial Park to witness the spectacular return of up to 60,000 salmon to the Goldstream River. Nearly all of the

---

BANKING THE LAND

Southern Vancouver Island and the Gulf Islands are beautiful, environmentally unique places — which is why a lot of people worry that when its secret gets out, development will explode, replacing the lovely forests with mega-malls and instant "communities." To contain that growth, the push is on to create a sea-to-sea "greenbelt" around the city, led primarily by the Land Conservancy of British Columbia. In just three years, the conservancy has raised more than $4.2 million to acquire and protect more than 32,000 hectares (around 78,000 acres) of land across the province, including Sooke's salmon-spawning Ayum Creek, and Matthews Point, one of the most spectacular sites in Active Pass and on the ferry route to Vancouver; in July of 2000 the conservancy announced plans to buy another 1,376 hectares (3,400 acres) in the Sooke Hills for the greenbelt. If you want to help this noble and important cause (especially with fundraising!), call 479-8053.

fish are chum (one of the seven species of salmon), guided by smell back to the place they were born four years earlier; after laying and fertilizing some 3,000 eggs apiece, they die in the river, providing food for the bald eagles circling overhead and (as UVic studies have shown) vital nutrients for the surrounding forest. The Goldstream Visitors' Centre conducts helpful interpretive tours during the salmon run; for more info, call 478-9414.

Scotch Broom

A hardy bush that bursts into bright yellow flowers every fall, especially alongside rural roadways, Scotch broom is an invited guest that has long overstayed its welcome. In 1849, a homesick Scotsman, Captain Walter Colquhoun Grant, planted a few broom seeds in Sooke to remind him of the old country, and they took root. (He didn't know it, but broom isn't native to Scotland: it was brought north from the Mediterranean by the Romans, who used it in wine- and broom-making.) Now the prolific broom is choking out native wildflowers across the region, leading concerned Victorians to hold annual "broom bashes" to rip out the invasive plants.

To find out more about these and other creatures that live here, call the Victoria Natural History Society (479-2054), which organizes hikes and publishes a fine newsletter.

The Daffodil King

Every spring people around the world buy daffodils to support cancer research, thanks to Geoffrey Vantreight, a Saanichton farmer and florist. Vantreight instigated the fundraising idea in 1956 when he donated 10 boxes of the flowers to the Canadian Cancer Society to sell as *boutonnières*. The idea bloomed, and now hundreds of thousands of boxes are shipped worldwide every year, raising tens of millions of dollars. Vantreight himself died of cancer in May 2000, but his legacy lives on with his family, which has 12 farms on the Saanich peninsula—and 200 acres of daffodils.

DIVING IN

While it may be the earth-bound plant life that earned us our Garden City nickname, Victoria also sports a world of watery wonders to explore. Don't forget that dry suit, though; the ocean rarely warms up enough to make diving in a wet suit comfortable. For local land dives, the folks at Frank White's Scuba Shop (1855 Blanshard St., 385-4713) recommend either end of Dallas Road, off Clover Point or Ogden Point. High points of that stretch include kelp forests, sea pens, and a diverse cross-section of aquatic life, plus occasional visits by seals, sea lions, and whales. Low points include the fishing lines off the Ogden Point breakwater and periodic bursts of sewage from the Clover Point outflow pipe. Ogden Point also sports its own dive centre (199 Dallas Rd., 380-9119), where you can fill your tanks. Another good shore dive is in Sidney's Deep Cove (off Land's End Road), where you'll find a sunken barge to explore.

For boat dives try the Saanich Inlet, specifically at Willis and Henderson Points, and McKenzie Bight, off Gowlland Tod Provincial Park. Ten Mile Point off Cadboro Bay is another favourite, but tricky currents make it risky for all but the most advanced divers. And if you're looking for something really exciting, four miles east of Sidney — and 100 feet down — you'll find the HMCS *McKenzie*, a 366-foot, 2,900-ton escort ship that was sunk just off Gooch Island by the Artificial Reef Society of B.C. in 1995. Sometimes there are strong currents and the average visibility in the water is about 25 feet, but you'll find three marker buoys attached to the ship (bow, bridge and stern) that allow direct access from the surface.

RVYC AND A BOTTLE OF RUM

The history of the Royal Victoria Yacht Club seems inexorably tied up with booze. During prohibition in the 1920s, many club members, sympathetic to the plight of their "dry" American neighbours, took to hauling cases of Scotch across the straits. Canadian customs officers approved shipments officially destined for Mexico, in boats that would be hard-pressed to make Port Angeles. One of the largest bootlegging outfits was Rithet Consolidated on Wharf Street, which became known as "Rum Row." The outfit was managed by RVYC Commodore Harry Barnes, whose 42-foot yawl *Minena* was so well-known to American authorities that it would be subject to immediate seizure if it entered American waters. This prevented Barnes from competing in many of the club's longer-distance races. During a 1925 regatta hosted by the club, Ernie Adams of Victoria broke the open outboard world record in his powerboat the *Miss Victoria II*. It was designed with the peculiar V-shaped hull favoured by rumrunners, and it was suspected that many boats competing in the regatta were entering the bay in daylight for the first time.

The Garden That Love Built

The story of the Abkhazi Garden is as beautiful as its flowers. It was started in 1946 by Peggy Pemberton Carter, who came to Victoria after spending over two years in a Japanese internment camp outside Shanghai. Soon after that she was reunited with Prince Nicholas Abkhazi, a member of the Georgian nobility she'd met in Paris in the 1920s, and who'd been a prisoner of war in Europe. They were married in Victoria, where they created their one-acre masterpiece – featuring native Garry oaks, ornamental evergreens, and alpine plants set into a dramatic piece of glaciated rock with views of the city and the ocean. Nicholas died in 1988 and Peggy died in 1994, and the property was sold to a developer who planned to build townhomes upon it. But in 1999, the Land Conservancy of BC came to the rescue and bought the garden; it's now paying off a mortgage to protect it as a heritage site. The garden, gift shop, and tea room, are all located at 1964 Fairfield Road *(598-8096)*.

Above All Else

The Garden City's got some mighty impressive foliage, but one particular plant towers over the rest. Victoria's Heritage Tree Society says that, without a doubt, the biggest tree in town is a giant sequoia that stands at the corner of Moss and Richardson. The last time it was measured, the tree stood 150 feet (45.7m) tall, and its trunk was 76 inches (193cm) across. Pretty impressive, although it's relatively small compared to its cousins in the Sierra Nevada. The sequoia was given to the province by the governor of California in 1886. Back then, several large trees were transplanted to Victoria (another giant sequoia stands in front of the legislature), but many of them were cut down after the estates they stood upon were subdivided into smaller lots. Standing at Moss and Richardson, it's not hard to see why: if the big sequoia ever toppled, it would demolish any house in its way.

Dining

Some of us pine for the days of breakfast at the Red Mango, lunch at Johnny's, and dinner at Chez Daniel. But Victoria still has some 487 other restaurants (at last count), from greasy spoons to the country's finest dining. You just need to know where they are.

Best Breakfast

The croissants at Demitasse (1320 Blanshard St., 386-4442) are filled with scrambled eggs steamed using a cappuccino nozzle (dates from the days of a much smaller kitchen) or try their sublime bowl of mixed fruit. Also try the waffles at Sally (714 Cormorant St., 381-1431), the granola-topped pancakes with real maple syrup at Banana Belt (281 Menzies St., 385-9616) or practically anything at the Blue Fox (#101-919 Fort St.,

380-1683), which the *Zagat* guide calls "the best breakfast in B.C." The Fox always seems busy, so if you want a table, arrive a few minutes before they open. We're not joking.

Best Brunch

The winner here is the original, ever-busy John's Place (723 Pandora St., 389-0711) or John's Other Place (1652C Island Hwy., 474-6417). The first is located in the former Maynard's shoe store, the second in a former Smitty's Pancake House on the Colwood strip. In the latter, check out the huge painting of Detroit's Tiger Stadium from high in left field by local artist Garth Buzzard. For a classier brunch, try Cassis Bistro (253 Cook St., 384-1932) or, of course, the Empress Hotel's buffet (721 Government St., 389-2727).

tea time

Ever the proper pseudo-English town, Victoria has numerous places to have a proper afternoon tea. These are just a few:

Adrienne's Tea Garden

5325 Cordova Bay Rd., 658-1535
Decor: Outside covered in ivy; inside paintings of birds.
Crustless Sandwiches: yes
Royal Sightings: none
Price: $10.95
Comments: Ask for the "rower's special" breakfast of French toast (not on the menu). Run by Fay Hextall, mother of Philadelphia Flyers goalie Ron Hextall.

Blethering Place

2250 Oak Bay Ave., 598-1413
Decor: Wood beams and frumpish outfits on the servers.
Crustless Sandwiches: yes
Royal Sightings: Dour Mary and George V, Elizabeth II during a happy visit to town.
Price: $14.95
Comments: Royal Family memorabilia available for sale in the shop.

Empress Hotel

721 Government St., 389-2727
Decor: High-end chintz.
Crustless Sandwiches: yes
Royal Sightings: Mary and George V (not amused)
Price: $32 ($39 June - October)
Comments: The city's number two tourist destination. Despite the price, you gotta do it.

Gatsby Mansion

309 Belleville St., 388-9191
Decor: Queen Victoria meets Queen Anne in soap magnate W.J. Pendray's former residence.
Crustless Sandwiches: yes
Royal Sightings: Only W.J. himself
Price: $16.95
Comments: Lace curtains, light rooms, good value.

BEST BOWL OF SOUP

The Vancouver Island Soup Company *(1057 Fort St., 920-7687)*, located in the newly renovated Mosaic building, has many to choose from, or try the Corn Chowder at Moss Rock Café *(143 Moss St., 995-5516)*.

BEST BOWL OF NOODLES

The hot and sour soup at J&J Wonton Noodle House *(1012 Fort St., 383-0680)* is made from shredded pork, bamboo shoots, carrots, black mushrooms, eggs, and Chinese vinegar. Joseph and John Wong make the noodles weekly in the basement on equipment they imported from Hong Kong.

**BEST AFFORDABLE
BUSINESS LUNCH**

If you want it quick and there aren't any dueling egos, try Eugene Vasiliabis' Greek snack bar, which moved to its current location *(1280 Broad St., 881-5456)* in the mid-1980s (it used to be in the walkway between Fort and Broughton) and has been filled with downtown lunch crowds devouring tiropita and gyros ever since. There is a second Eugene's at Fort St. and Foul Bay Rd. *(592-7373)*. Or if you're out near Quadra and Hillside, head for the clean, well-lighted back room at San Remo *(2709 Quadra St., 384-5255)*.

James Bay Tea Room

332 Menzies St., 382-8282
Decor: Lace window coverings, pictures of the Queen.
Crustless Sandwiches: no
Royal Sightings: Charles and Di in happier times.
Price: $10 ($7 once the trifle is gone)
Comments: Souvenir tea cozies.

Princess Mary

344 Harbour Rd., 386-3456
Decor: Brassy, woody, like the inside of a ship.
Crustless Sandwiches: yes
Royal Sightings: none
Price: $12.95
Comments: Once the apogee of upscale dining in Victoria.

Windsor House

2540 Windsor Rd., 595-3135
Decor: Four wallpapered rooms in a converted house.
Crustless Sandwiches: of course
Royal Sightings: The Royal Family owns the stairwell.
Price: $25.95 (for two)
Comments: Ask for the room with wedding photos by "Pen," a friend of the owners.

get outta town

Maybe it's because we're on an island. Or maybe it's because the outdoors are at our doorstep. But Victorians spend lots of time going to other places. And we often get hungry in the process.

B l a c k i e ' s

Most people speed by on the way to the ferry, but those who stop at Vern and Angela Schreiber's café are rewarded with old-fashioned home cooking amid one of the most eclectic collections of 1950s and 1960s collectibles in the city. Named after their dog, the café and deli *(6105 Patricia Bay Hwy., 652-5109)* is filled with ceramic fruit, magazines, and over two dozen "blue-lady" paintings by the king of kitsch, Vladimir Tretchikoff. Almost all the food is prepared on site (they even peel the apples for the pies) and the deli offers classics like saltwater taffy, rock-candy sticks, and jawbreakers the size of croquet balls. Sit by the wood stove in the winter or on the deck out back in the summer. Any entrée on the seven-item lunch menu not served in ten minutes is free.

B l e u e   M o o n / S p i t f i r e

Mary's Bleue Moon Café *(9535 Canora Rd., Sidney, 655-4450)* has been in the same location for six decades and has collected flying memorabilia (some grand model airplanes) and a loyal following. They're busy year around. The relatively new Spitfire Grill *(9681 Willingdon Rd., 655-0122)* is across the field, and offers a better view of planes spewing exhaust over the Saanich peninsula.

C a r d e n   S t r e e t   W e s t

Named for a street in Guelph, Ontario where the original restaurant resides. After running it for four years, owner Michael Mino moved out west and opened Carden Street West *(1164 Stelly's Cross Rd., 544-1475)* with Paulette Jolley and Connie O'Brien. They offer a concise menu: soup, salads, a few appetizers, and a half dozen entrées such as Malaysian Prawn Curry and Sweet Potato Kofta. Small dining room and deck with aviaries. Closed Sunday, Monday.

BEST BAGELS

The Mount Royal Bagel Factory *(#6-1115 North Park St., 380-3588)* takes its name seriously and offers only take-away out of a garage in Fernwood. It also offers the best hand-rolled, Montreal-style cinnamon bagel in Victoria. Other locations are at #2- 4649 West Saanich Road and 1827 Fairfield Road. The Tillicum Bagel Oven *(2902 Tillicum Rd., 920-3697)* also doesn't mess around. The brick wood-fired oven occupies most of the shop (enter through the back door to witness the volume of wood it requires). More fine examples of the doughnut with rigor mortis.

BEST OLD EMPIRE FOOD

Despite the recent demise of Marks and Spencer, that bastion of all things English, there are still sources for food from the old world.

Robert Shaw Specialty Pies
2865 Foul Bay Rd., 592-3314

Slater's First Class Meats
2577 Cadboro Bay Rd., 592-0823

Lilac Tree

Located on a quiet corner of the peninsula, the Lilac Tree (6006 West Saanich Rd., 652-0675) offers substantial portions of Hungarian home cooking. In Hungary, before the advent of modern signage, roadside inns known as "Chardas" were identified by lilac trees planted at the approach. (Chef Eva Domonkos claims Hungarians blend paprika like Asians blend curries; some 200 varieties of red pepper are used to make approximately 2,000 paprika blends depending on the region or village.) You'll find purple tablecloths, lilac-coloured walls, and cut flowers on every table.

Seahorses Café

Located in a former boathouse at the Brentwood Ferry dock, Seahorses (799 Verdier Ave., 544-1565) offers some of the finest dining in all of picturesque Brentwood Bay. When they roll up the boathouse door at the end of the restaurant, the dining room expands with another 70 seats outside (some under brilliant hanging baskets), and on Saturdays from July to September they offer dinner and a cruise to the fireworks at Butchart Gardens. But book early; it sells out every night. Chef Christian Collins sources local produce, seafoods, and meats to create entrées like New York steak with a red wine demi-glace.

Dock 503/Blue Peter

Some of the best dining at the end of the peninsula is in the largest full-service marina on the west coast. Walk past the laundromat at the north end of the marina to Dock 503 (2320 Harbour Rd., Sidney, 656-0828), a restaurant with white tablecloths and a hardwood floor, offering casual fine dining during the day. The menu changes twice a year and chef Simon Manvell makes the aioli in-house and creations like Fraser Valley Duck Confit and House Smoked Chicken Bucatini. At the other end of the marina is the Blue Peter Pub & Restaurant (2270 Harbour Rd., Sidney, 656-4551) where guests arriving by water can use the moorage slips out front, and play darts in the pub or have a sit-down meal in the dining room next door. Its owners also have the Harbour Road Deli up the street (17-2235 Harbour Rd., Sidney, 655-0005) that lays claim to offering the best cinnamon buns in town.

ROMANTIC ROOMS
Cassis Bistro

Named after the village near Marseilles and the favourite drink of owners Lisa and John Holl, and David Abersek. Dishes such as Pork Loin Chop Daniel pay homage to the time John spent working for Daniel Rigollet, the famed owner of Chez Daniel. The law degree (found at a yard sale) that once hung in the washroom was purchased by a nostalgic customer. Dishes include Sooke Hills Rainbow Trout and Salt Spring Island Mussel and Spring Loin Ragout. Candlelight and white tablecloths.
253 Cook St., 384-1932

Deep Cove Chalet

Housed in a building built in 1914 as the terminus of BC Electric railway line, this French restaurant offers stunning views of Deep Cove and some of the finest food on the west coast. Bring your plastic though: the one guest suite must be booked in advance and goes for $300 a night.
11190 Chalet Rd., Sidney, 656-3541

greasy spoons

Gone are the days of the Gorge Coffee Shop, and the Metropolitan on Fort Street, but there are still lots of places to plant yourself on a sticky vinyl seat and get your Swedish Gasoline in an Armorlite cup. And no, they don't serve espresso. Standard price is for a burger and fries.

Beacon Drive In

126 Douglas St., 385-7521
Decor: Pink sculpted booths with high backs and an outdoor patio. Yellow signs light up the parking lot like day. Soft-serve ice cream.
Standard Price: $4.90
Bottomless Coffee: no
Comments: The burgers are so-so, but the location (across from Beacon Hill Park) can't be beat.

Day and Night

622 Yates St., 382-5553
Decor: Life viewed through a yellow lens filter.
Standard Price: $3.75
Bottomless Coffee: yes
Comments: Texas Delight "special of the month" held over for years.

BEST VEGETARIAN

It started as a juice bar and continues to make over 80 varieties of fruit and vegetable drinks, but Re-Bar *(50 Bastion Square, 361-9223)* now offers "Modern Food" like a Yam Quesadilla and Monk's Curry. The Parsonage *(#1-1115 North Park St., 383-5999)*, opened by Elsa Tudor in July 1992, is named after an old parsonage off Wilkinson Road near her house, and is Victoria's best rendition of a '60s coffeehouse. Check out the Bavarian coffee urns but watch your step climbing into one of the wooden booths. Green Cuisine *(#5-560 Johnson St., 385-1809)* is a sprawling, cafeteria-style restaurant in the basement at Bastion Square, and has a piano, kids' play area, and cosmic murals on the wall. The pay-by-weight self-serve buffet is vegan, with all the ingredients listed on cards above each dish. Treats include Not Nanaimo Bars and the Xanadu Shake (strawberry, tofulati, soymilk). The Lotus Pond *(617 Johnson St., 380-9293)* is also vegan and serves a variety of imitation meat dishes including Lemon Mock Chicken and Veggie Mock Salmon in Peking Sauce, along with a pay-by-weight lunch buffet.

Ian's Jubilee Coffee Stop

2004 Richmond Ave., 595-8121
Decor: Brown vinyl seats with brown duct tape,
13 Golden Cup trophies lining the wall, the friendliest
cook in the city.
Standard Price: $3.95
Bottomless Coffee: no
Comments: Consistently judged best doughnut shop
in the city.

Oak Room, Paul's Motor Inn

1900 Douglas St., 382-9231
Decor: Booths are uncomfortably snug.
Standard Price: $4.45
Bottomless Coffee: Server's discretion.
Comments: When the diner was built in 1956, it
sported the largest plastic sign in the world, and the
copper-topped roof was treated with a non-oxidizing
coating so it wouldn't turn green like that big hotel on
the harbour.

Pluto's

1150 Cook St., 385-4747
Decor: Housed in a former gas station with the
old garage serving as the dining room.
Standard Price: $7.25
Bottomless Coffee: no
Comments: Purple booths. Mesquite grill.
Open stage Tuesdays.

Scott's

650 Yates St., 382-1289
Decor: Pink vinyl booths with framed posters of sailing
ships provided by the National Bank of Greece. Lots
of hanging plants and mirrors between the booths.
Standard Price: $6
Bottomless Coffee: no
Comments: Witness entropy at work on club kids
at 2:30 am.

secret dining rooms

The dining room at the Provincial Legislature serves B.C. oysters, Vancouver Island eggs, and B.C. salmon at suspiciously cheap prices. There are embossed napkins and flowers on tables, but the restaurant is accessible only when the house is in session, with some weird hours: open Monday at 9:30 am, Tuesday to Friday 8 am; closed Monday-Thursday at 8 pm, Friday 2:30 pm. Ask the commissionaires for directions and ignore the "No Public Access" signs. *Parliament Buildings, 387-3959*

Dunlop House on the Lansdowne campus and the classroom on the Interurban campus of Camosun College have students in the Hotel and Restaurant Administration program serving food like Pheasant Dunlop and Belgian Chocolate Truffle Torte. A vegetarian menu is available with 48 hours' notice. Open during the winter and spring terms. Best to make reservations Thursday or Friday. *1960 Lansdowne Rd., 370-3144; 4461 Interurban Rd., 370-3775*

George Stelly's Dining Room is a 65-seat eatery near the front entrance of Stelly's High School in Central Saanich. Student chefs, waiters, and waitresses in training serve lunch Tuesday to Thursday, 11:30 am-1 pm. Reservations are recommended. *1627 Stelly's Cross Rd., 544-0305*

MEAL WITH GRANDMA

For a panoramic view of North Saanich, call ahead to reserve one of the nine window tables at Dunsmuir Lodge *(1515 McTavish Rd., Sidney, 656-3166)* or take Gran for a spin on the maple floor at McMorran's Beach House *(5109 Cordova Bay Rd., 658-5527)*. She might even forget there's a ring in your nose.

BEST SLICE

Try either location of Pacific Rim Pizza *(523 Pandora St., 385-7746 or 704 Broughton St., 385-1167)*, or get a quarter-pizza sized slice at Ali Baba *(1011 Blanshard St., 385-6666 and 1-310 Goldstream Ave., 474-6666)*. Surly's Diner *(1296 Gladstone Ave., 386-8446)* in Fernwood serves vegan pizza, beer on tap, and a wicked creamsicle milkshake in one of the few pizza joints where you can actually hang out. If you're in Brentwood, try Pizzaz Gourmet Pizza *(#5A-7103 West Saanich Rd., 652-0055)* located in the Trafalgar Square mall.

GREASY FISH

At Barb's Fish and Chips *(310 St. Lawrence St., 384-6515)*, dine amid the boats and seagulls on the dock at Fisherman's Wharf. Get your cod, oysters, or halibut grilled, steamed or deep-fried, "any way you like it." The Old Vic *(1316 Broad St., 383-4536)* has been a chipper off and on since the building was built in 1892. Wooden booths, brass finishings, and everything covered in grease — what else could you ask for? A suburban location? Try Haultain's *(1127 Haultain St., 383-8332)* or Fairfield Fish and Chips *(1275 Fairfield Rd., 380-6880)*. You can also go to Willows Galley to get some of Victoria's best fish and chips, plus chowder and even an ice-cream cone to go, then make a picnic of it down at Willows Beach *(2559 Estevan Ave., 598-2711)*.

garden city sushi

Ebizo
604 Broughton St., 383-3234

Futaba
1420 Quadra St., 381-6141

Hime Sushi
680 Broughton St., 388-4439

Izumi
739 Pandora Ave., 995-8432

Japanese Village
734 Broughton St., 382-5165

Kazu
#100-1619 Store St., 386-9121

Koto
510 Fort St., 382-1514

Senzushi
940 Fort St., 385-4320

Tamami Sushi
509 Fisgard St., 382-3529

Yokohama
980 Blanshard St., 384-5433

Yoshi Sushi
#601-771 Vernon Ave., 475-3900

Café Brio

944 Fort St., 383-0009

Café Brio is west coast cuisine with a Tuscan influence with appetizers like duck confit and entrées like Grilled Cured Pork Chop and Braised Ling Cod. The patio can be noisy, though.

Camille's

45 Bastion Square, 381-3433

Located in the basement of the Law Chambers Building in Bastion Square, the restaurant resembles a wine cellar. And for good reason: there are over 150 offerings on the list. They go with entrées such as Pumpkin Seed-crusted local Salmon and Spinach, and Goat Cheese and Marsala Braised Carrot Terrine.

Herald Street Caffé

546 Herald St., 381-1441

Upscale but friendly, with sublime floral displays. West coast-international fusion results in dishes like Curried Kashmir Tiger Prawns. Lineups most nights.

The Marina

1327 Beach Dr., 598-8555

Try booth three for a panoramic view of the Oak Bay Marina. Entrées can vary depending on what's fresh and available, and might include Slow Roasted B.C. Spring Salmon with Red Wine Braised Shallots, Scallion Oil, and Smashed New Potatoes. Also a separate sushi bar.

Sooke Harbour House

1528 Whiffen Spit Rd., Sooke, 642-3421

International food critics stay up nights dreaming of superlatives to describe this quiet country inn, consistently rated one of the best restaurants in Canada. Bring the platinum Visa and judge for yourself.

THE ISLAND CHEFS' COLLABORATIVE

The farms around Victoria produce the most incredible variety of food in all of Canada. Blessed with a climate like northern California, here you can find locally harvested ingredients as wildly different as geoducks and sea asparagus, emu steaks and ostrich eggs, and dozens of types of heirloom apples and tomatoes (Calabash, ox-heart) that'll never turn up at Safeway. To celebrate that diversity and help the farmers who keep it growing, some of the best chefs in Victoria have banded together in a group known as the Island Chefs' Collaborative. Founded by John Hall of Cassis Bistro, its members include chefs at such fine establishments as Café Brio, the Sooke Harbour House, Camille's, Il Terrazzo, Dock 503 in Sidney, and the dining rooms at Butchart Gardens and the

Dunsmuir Lodge (pictured are Café Brio's Sean Brennan and farmer Tina Fraser). All are committed to using locally grown, organic ingredients, and they regularly meet with local farmers to plan their crops for future menus — something that's nearly impossible for big-city chefs to do. For a delicious survey of their collaborations, be sure to check out Feast of Fields, an event that happens every

September at a different farm in the Victoria area, where you can nosh all you like on fabulous local cuisine and award-winning regional wines. Tickets are around $65, but they sell out early; for more information, call the local agriculture advocacy group Farm Folk/City Folk at 743-4267.

UNEXPECTED ETHNIC

Pounders

Choose the contents of your Mongolian-style stir-fry from the buffet and get the chef to cook it up in the back. Choices include musk ox, ostrich, and escolar. *535 Yates St., 388-3181*

Korean Gardens

Although the menu is more North-Asian fusion, this is the best source for Bi Bim Bap east of Pusan. *3945C Quadra St., 744-3311*

DESIGNER FOOD TO GO

Cheryl's Gourmet Pantry

2007 Cadboro Bay Rd., 595-3212

Complete Cuisine

2020 Oak Bay Ave., 595-3151; 2014 Oak Bay Ave., 595-3115

Hotels on the Harbour

The Coast Harbourside Hotel is home to one of the city's best seafood restaurants. The Blue Crab *(146 Kingston St., 480-1999)* offers panoramic views of Songhees, and regular entrées include Digby Scallops and Jumbo Prawn Sauté, and Pacific Halibut Fillet. The blackboard specials allow the chef to wing it with whatever catch is at the dock. Across the harbour at the Ocean Pointe Resort, the Victorian Restaurant *(45 Songhees Rd., 360-5800)* has equally epic views, and fine, if pricey dining, and the Boardwalk Restaurant *(360-5889)* downstairs serves a grand Sunday brunch.

Best New York-Style Restaurant

Judging from the line most nights, it's hardly a secret, but Pagliacci's *(1011 Broad St., 386-1662)* is definitely a favourite. It was opened in 1979 by brothers David and Howie Siegel and Alan Difiori when, after seeing a movie one night, they couldn't find a decent espresso. (Or cheesecake? Or cappuccino? It depends on which story you believe.) Named after the Italian word for clown, most nights it's elbow-to-elbow. They serve huge portions of pasta with names like Ravioli Paradisio and Bicycle Thief II (owner Howie Siegel also owns the Roxy Theatre and is a huge film buff).

BEST ESPRESSO

Looking for an expedient injection of caffeine? Try the espresso at Bean Around the World *(533 Fisgard St., 386-7115)*, Torrefazione *(1234 Government St., 920-7203)*, Paradiso Di Stelle, which also has the best *gelati* in town *(10 Bastion Square, 920-7266)*, or one of the three types at 2% Jazz Espresso Bar *(2621 Douglas St., 384-5282)*.

Best Quick Italian

Tucked away in behind London Drugs you'll find Zambri's, a fabulous little gem owned by a sister and brother who spent 20 years cooking in different regions of Italy. Try the several types of fresh pasta (e.g., spinich linguine with squid, chanterelles and fresh tomatoes) on offer every day, the delightful soups, or the inspired breaded chicken sandwich. Since it's only open till 7 pm during the week (5 pm Saturdays), Zambri's really is just for lunch or a quick after-work dinner – but you'll wish it could last for hours.
#110-911 Yates St., 360-1171

FASTER FOOD

Find respite from intimidating teenagers and bus exhaust at one of the most attractive fast food restaurants in the city. The downtown McDonald's *(1200 Douglas St., 384-6111)* has a 20-foot chandelier in the lobby and mosaic art-deco tiles salvaged from the Kresge's department store that occupied the spot for years. A block down, try the seven-layer burrito at one of the province's few Taco Bell restaurants *(1300 Douglas St., 360-1377)* located in the former E.C. Kellog Druggist building. Management plays classical music on speakers outside to encourage loiterers to make a run for the border. For a burrito the size of a professional football, and Coronas on ice, try La Fiesta *(1001 Douglas St., 383-6622)*.

Photo: Mandelbrot

Chinatown Chow

After exploring the alleys of Chinatown, take a break at Don Mee *(538 Fisgard St., 383-1032)* which specializes in Chinese seafood and dim sum. Foo Hong Chop Suey *(564 Fisgard St., 386-9553)* is the cheapest Chinese food in town, and retains its original 1960s décor (check out the ceiling neon), is cash only, and take-out or eat-in (go for the loft). They have great wonton soup. Or if it's late (like 2 am) try the Fan Tan Café *(549 Fisgard St., 383-1611)*.

by David Leach

Monkey-loving painters. Haunted bookstores. Quantum Catholic art cults. James Bond at the Empress. Plus: readings, galleries, flying machines.

Emily's House

The Victoria art scene is still very much the house that Emily built – one that the eclectic Ms. Carr dubbed the "House of All Sorts." Painter, author, slumlord, zoo-keeper – Emily Carr set a standard of excellence and eccentricity that still leaves even the most boho of local artists in her shadow. She ran a rooming house and kept a vast menagerie that included a pet rat and a monkey who squirted paint into her shoes. She drew inspiration for her canvases from Vancouver Island's rain-soaked forests and the totems of the Queen Charlotte Islands (where the Haida people dubbed her *Klee Wyck*, or "laughing spirit"). She won a Governor General's literary award for her memoir about life as an artist in Victoria.

While largely ignored before her death in 1945, Carr has since become Canada's best known female artist – a canvas recently sold for over a million dollars – and something of a cottage industry for local enthusiasts and entrepreneurs. There have been Emily Carr books, films, plays, festivals, retrospectives, and all manner of memorabilia. One devotee, missing the double entendre, suggested that the Beacon Hill greenspace she loved so much be renamed "Emily Carr Park." Another admirer wrote a collection of stories from the point-of-view of Woo, her pet monkey.

To experience a slice of Emily's life, visit Carr House in James Bay (*207 Government St., 383-5843, mid-May until mid-October*), where you can wander through her family home, listen to an actor read from her journals, and admire Carr originals and works by local artists in the "people's gallery" that the painter always dreamed of opening. (The House of All Sorts, the rooming house Carr ran with an iron fist, also remains standing; it's now an apartment block on 646 Simcoe Street, often rented to young artists and authors, with the decorative eagles she painted still on the attic ceiling.)

To best appreciate Carr's bullheaded artistic spirit and her rocky relationship with her often complacent hometown, seek out the city's current roster of struggling artists and authors in Victoria's hidden galleries and book nooks.

group therapy

Emily Carr had little patience for artistic meekness or pretense – an attitude that didn't sit well, as she recounts in *The House of All Sorts*, with the dabbling *artistes* and conservative patrons of the local painting society:

In Victoria I had only come up against my own class. The art society, called "Island Arts and Crafts", were the exponents of Art on Vancouver Island, an extremely exclusive set. They liked what they liked – would tolerate no innovations. My change in thought and expression had angered them into fierce denouncement. To expose a thing deeper than its skin surface was to them an indecency. They ridiculed my striving for bigness, depth. The Club held exhibitions, affairs of tinkling teacups, tinkling conversation and little tinkling landscapes weakly executed in water colours. None except their own class went to these exhibitions.

Emily didn't have it in for *all* clubby painters, though. In 1928, she visited the Group of Seven in Ontario, and the Canadian art stars made her an honourary member. The magnificent Seven's support convinced Carr to return to her own painting, after a 12-year hiatus from the easel, and create some of her most memorable works.

Victoria has been home to several "art groups" of its own since then. It's hard to know what the cantankerous Ms. Carr would have said about them.

Group of Eleven

If a jealous rival had dropped arsenic into the appies at an early meeting of the Limners, Victoria's visual arts scene would have been set back half a century. When they first gathered in 1971 at the suggestion of elder states-brush Maxwell Bates, the Limners (who take their name from the wandering portraitists and sign-painters of the Middle Ages) weren't a band of starving young artists looking to grab headlines as a "movement" through shared styles and radical manifestoes. Rather, the 11 founding members were all established artists seeking the

Hidden Galleries

Art Gallery of Greater Victoria

It might seem odd to describe Victoria's major civic gallery as "hidden," but many locals still can't find the AGGV's Rockland hideaway. That just means you can wander the renovated Spencer Mansion in peace and quietly enjoy the gallery's fine collections of Asian and First Nations art, as well as regular exhibitions of contemporary artists. (Check out the gallery's internet insallations at www.aggv.bc.ca.) Thinking of making Victoria home – or at least look like home? The AGGV also runs an art rental program with works by local artists.
1040 Moss St., 384-4101

Open Space

Founded as an artist-run cultural centre in 1971, Open Space continues to host the city's most innovative events and exhibitions – experimental theatre, avant-skronk jazz, head-scratching conceptual installations, guerrilla film screenings, and performance art "happenings" that seem straight out of Chelsea.
510 Fort St., 383-8833

Rogue Art

Mall-walking takes a turn for the weird when you slip through Rogue Art's unremarkable door on the fourth floor of the Eaton Centre. There you'll find works in a mix of media by the most *avant* of Victoria's *garde* in the main gallery and two annexes. The Rogue's curators also organize the popular Antimatter Festival of Underground Short Film and Video — three bucks a ticket, free vodka, and mind-bending movies you'll never see in the cineplex. Tip: Take the elevator to the gallery rather than the escalator to avoid the odorous food court.
4th floor, Eaton Centre, 385-3327

Xchanges Gallery

This artist-run gallery had to relocate from downtown to a residential street in View Royal, but still runs an eclectic series of programs, from drop-in drawing classes to triple-X erotic art shows. Warning: a grumpy neighbour calls the cops whenever gallery happenings get too hopping.
420 William St., 382-0442

Community Arts Council Gallery

If any space lives up to Emily Carr's unfulfilled dream of a democratic civic gallery where the works of humble artisans can rub frames with those of their more forward-looking peers, it's the slim exhibition hall known as the CAC. (Imagine coughing up a hairball as you affectionately pronounce it the "Cack.") A mere sneeze from Victoria's busiest intersection, this city-run gallery makes an eye-pleasing escape from the bustle of downtown.
#6G-1001 Douglas St., 381-2787

camaraderie and convenience of meeting and exhibiting as a group.

Notable names signed to the guestbook for that formative meeting at the home of Herbert Siebner include: Myfanwy Pavelić, a friend of Emily Carr who has painted actress Katharine Hepburn, violinist Yehudin Menuhin, and former prime minister Pierre Trudeau, and was the first Canadian to have a work hung in the National Portrait Gallery in London; poet, professor, collagist, and witch Robin Skelton and his calligrapher wife Sylvia; sculptor Elza Mayhew, whose monolithic castings can be found on the university campus and whose senile dementia was brought on by styrene poisoning from making her moulds; Nita Forrest, owner of one of Victoria's earliest serious commercial galleries; and Karl Spreitz, photographer and documentary filmmaker. Eight members joined later, including fabric artist Carol Sabiston and ceramicist Walter Dexter, both of whom have won the prestigious Saidye Bronfman Award for Excellence, and internationally acclaimed printmaker Pat Martin Bates. While the group hasn't accepted new Limners since the mid-'80s, surviving members continue to exhibit as a group and to inspire new generations of artists with their spirit of cooperation and creativity.

Catholic Art Cult

Catholic theology, revolutionary politics, and quantum physics combine in "topologism," the odd philosophy behind the controversial local art cult, the Chapman Group. The loose collective of painters, sculptors, and poets argue that their literally warped creations (imagine curvy Picassos) address a "crisis of space" that other artists have ignored — a claim that hasn't exactly endeared them to local colleagues. While the group officially disbanded after the 1999 death of their charismatic Mexican guru, members such as nationally distinguished painter James Gordaneer still exhibit regularly at the Chapman West gallery-cum-flower shop *(#4-1010 Yates St., 382-2512).*

Watermelon Worshippers

After one too many Chapman Group boasts, the performance art duo known as the Hermaphrodite Brotherhood challenged the Chapmans to go *mano a mano* and bring their artistic attitude to court — the basketball court, that is. The Chapmans declined, but the Hermaphrodites – campus radio DJ and cow-punk accordionist David P. Smith, beat poet and pet portraitist Roy Green, plus a revolving cast of "monkey boys" – remain Victoria's reigning merry pranksters. Their irregular but always memorable shows have included worshipping watermelons, distributing adult diapers and pastrami-filled CD cases, and committing unspeakable acts upon stuffed lobsters.

Public Art Shockers

Sculpture-seeking tourists usually content themselves with taking pictures of the pigeon-pooped pate of Captain Cook in the Inner Harbour or asking locals if the golden boy atop the legislature is really Wayne Gretzky. (Damn Yankees! Can't they recognize Gordie Howe?) Full-time Victorians indulge in a more lively pursuit: complaining about public art. It's strange habit considering that, aside from a few statues and more orca murals than you can shake a harpoon at, the Garden City doesn't have very many street-level creations to either like or loathe. Still, that doesn't stop citizen critics from crapping on what there is.

Any tour of unsightly sites should begin with the barren metal tree and gurgling ponds installed in front of the medical building at Fort Street and Foul Bay Road. Four out of five dentists agree: *Bowker Accord* is butt-ugly. Apparently the aluminum arbutus makes an eco-conceptual nod to a now paved-over creek. Whatever. The branchless wonder is still put to shame by the whimsical topiary on the traffic island across Foul Bay Road, pruned every summer by the avant gardeners of the Oak Bay parks department. Flowers in the shape of a Volkswagen? Now, *that's* art!

Closer to downtown, fast-living local sculptor Jay Unwin unveiled his *Trust and Harmony* in front of the new Victoria Police Station *(850 Caledonia St.)* shortly before he died in a highway crash in 1996. It's not his best work – far better is *Truth, Duty and Valour* (or, *Three Nude Guys and a Big Rock*) at Royal Roads University. Still, a cop shop sculpture that appears to depict a crowd being crushed by a giant monolith does pack symbolic weight.

No stranger to controversy, mega-installationist and University of Victoria professor Mowry Baden has built an international reputation for winning civic commissions and public bewilderment. (After his *Wall of Death* was

previous year as a New Year's gift. Subsequent *Gems* incorporated the previous years' portraits, until her final versions squeezed 20,000 cherubs into each frame. (Maynard also took police mug-shots and bragged that she had photographed every person in Victoria.)

Her most surreal pictures were the composite self-portraits she made using multiple exposures in which repeated images of herself appear together in morbidly playful scenes — in one, Hannah leans from a picture frame to pour tea on her unsuspecting triple; in another, multiple Maynards pose beside a pedestal holding up her grandson's severed torso. And you thought *your* grandma was creepy!

Herbert Siebner

Photographer Karl Spreitz once described Herbert Siebner as the "Energizer Bunny of the local arts scene," and true to this metaphor, he keeps going and going and going … averaging a new work every day-and-a-half for the last five decades — expressionistic oil paintings, watercolours, drawings, lithographs, and striking graffito murals. (Siebner sometimes dips his brushes in vodka

unveiled under Seattle's University Bridge, one newspaper opined: "The person who was paid to make it is more confidence artist than artist.") He hit the mark again with a 1996 piece in front of the Landmark condo tower (605 Douglas St.), two rust-coloured mattresses and a sheet metal banner declaring: *Night is for Sleeping, Day is for Resting.* If you parse Baden's massive Zen koan as revealing the secret motto of bored government employees, you'll understand why they hate it so much.

Old Town 1880 by local artist Luis Merino is the colourful Cubist centrepiece of Market Square, and one of the largest and most climbed-upon public sculptures. The square's caretakers, however, hope to install a stage in the space currently occupied by the multi-hued homage to life in colonial Victoria, so they're willing to give it away to a good home. Any takers?

Few civic art controversies, though, have rivalled the uproar over the city's revitalization of Broad Street, the rough-edged downtown *rue* which bisects the Eaton Centre. As part of the public art commission, Pender Island poet Michael Kenyon composed a verse epic about the street's chequered past to be etched on sculptured pylons. Broad Street merchants objected to the poem's unsavoury references to hookers, hustlers, and rats, and the word "bazoobies." We haven't heard if Broad Street's hookers, hustlers, and rats had any complaints. And what's a "bazoobie" anyway?

The only public art that gets a thumbs-up from the general public seems to be the nude-frolicking-with-dolphins fountain on the Westsong Way promenade. Cast by John Barney Weaver, a sculptor who *has* made a Gretzky statue (though you have to go to Edmonton to admire it), the bronze babe in front of the Songhees development has proven so popular that ardent art-admirers have thrice made off with one of her accompanying nymphs. Collect 'em all!

Poet, teacher, witch, scholar, father, patron, and ghostbuster all: from the moment Robin Skelton moved from England to Victoria in 1963, he seemed to live a life destined for biography. In addition to the renowned artistic salons that ran for years in his Oak Bay manor house, Skelton published over 100 books of poetry, fiction, art criticism, and biography. He also managed to find time to found UVic's Creative Writing Department, co-found the prestigious literary magazine *The Malahat Review*, and raise three children with wife (and fellow Limner) Sylvia.

Present authors-of-note Marilyn Bowering, Susan Musgrave, Rhonda Batchelor, and Margaret Blackwood are just a few past students who consider Skelton both an inspiration and an influence. But while it may be his academic and poetic works that are most referenced, Skelton also gained fame as one of Victoria's most prominent practicing witches. As well as penning such occult how-to guides as *Spellcraft*, *The Practice of Witchcraft Today* and *Talismanic Magic*, Skelton also wrote *A Gathering of Ghosts*, a fascinating (and completely true) account of his experiences with fellow witch Jean Kozocari as Victoria's pre-eminent ghostbuster. Roundly respected as an honoured elder by local Wiccans and pagans, Skelton's passing at 71 in 1997 left a hole in both the local occult and artistic communities that is unlikely to ever be filled by a single person again.

so that his watercolours dry faster.) Born in Settin, Germany, the young artist survived three wartime bombing raids and was transferred to safety from a Russian POW camp after switching his stool sample with that of a sick soldier. After immigrating with his wife to Victoria in 1954, he quickly infused the provincial capital with the avant garde energies and cosmopolitan heritage of the European art world. An original member of the Limners, Siebner has mentored countless students and exhibited in hundreds of shows. His works hang in galleries and private collections around the world (although they remain conspicuously absent from the National Gallery in Ottawa). With Spreitz, he concocted elaborate art pranks (rarely carried out), including plans for a Rumour Centre (they'd start one for a dollar then undo it for a thousand) and a Rent-a-Shadow service (to help tourist-photographers create the illusion of sunshine on overcast days). Siebner also jazzed up local art soirées by getting buck naked and pretending he was a bull. Now in his 60s, he continues to paint with the same flair and irreverence at his home by Prospect Lake. *En plein air* and *au naturel*, of course.

Victoria lit up

Sure, the guidebooks gush and *Condé Nast Traveler* has written up Victoria as one of the top 10 cities in the world to visit. But full-time authors are a tougher lot to impress, so the reviews have been mixed from both the transient and resident scribes who've parked their pens in the Garden City. They came, they saw, they complained about the tea.

Joe Average

Anything but average, this local Joe (born Brock Tebbutt) has become one of the west coast's most celebrated artists for his giddy, rainbow-hued Pop Art paintings and his dedication to the fight against AIDS. An Oak Bay High dropout who's been HIV-positive for over 15 years, Average left Victoria to live in Montreal and Toronto before settling on doing his starving artistry in Vancouver. His bold, hopeful, colour-soaked acrylic work was used as the signature image for the 1996 International Conference on AIDS, has earned Average the Governor General's Caring Canadian Award and other commendations, and has been seen around the world on a Canada Post stamp.

Rudyard Kipling

If you stuck members of the local tourist board and the chamber of commerce in a room and force-fed them happy pills, you still wouldn't get the ecstatic gush of superlatives that British author Rudyard Kipling poured upon Victoria. He first visited the city in 1889, returned several times, and even considered immigrating to Canada when war threatened to break out between Britain and the States. In a letter to his family, he offered the following panegyric to the Garden City – ready-made PR bumpf that's been shamelessly cribbed by civic boosters ever since.

To realize Victoria you must take all that the eye admires most in Bournemouth, Torquay, the Isle of Wight, the Happy Valley at Hong Kong, the Doon, Sorrento, and Camps Bay; add reminiscences of the Thousand Islands, and arrange the whole round the Bay of Naples, with some Himalayas for the background.

Real estate agents recommend it as a little piece of England – the island on which it stands is about the size of Great Britain – but no England is set in any such seas or so fully charged with the mystery of the larger ocean beyond. The high, still twilights along the beaches are out of the old East just under the curve of the world, and even in October the sun rises warm from the first Earth, sky, and water wait outside every man's door to drag him out to play if he looks up from his work; and, though some other cities in the Dominion do not quite understand this immoral mood of Nature, men who have made their money in them go off to Victoria, and with the zeal of converts preach and preserve its beauties.

… I tried honestly to render something of the color, the gaiety, and the graciousness of the town and the island, but only found myself piling up unbelievable adjectives, and so let it go with a hundred other wonders… .

Of course, tourist brochures don't quote as liberally from the imperialist address Kipling delivered to the local Canada Club while on his government-sponsored tour of 1907:

The time is coming when you will have to choose between the desired reinforcements of your own stock and blood, and the undesired races to whom you are strangers, whose speech you do not understand, and from whose instincts and traditions you are separated by thousands of years.

Rupert Brooke

Dashing young British poet Rupert Brooke travelled across the Great White North in 1913, just two years before he died of blood poisoning during World War I. Onboard a ship to Victoria, he complained in a letter to his mother that "Canada is a most horribly individualistic place, with no one thinking of anything except the amount of money they can make, by any means, in the shortest time."

Five days later, Brooke could at least rhapsodize about the natural beauty of his surroundings in a postcard from the city:

You think B.C. means before Christ But it doesn't. I'm sitting, wildly surmising, on the edge of the Pacific, gazing at mountains which are changing colour every two minutes in the most surprising way. Nature here is half Japanese….

Raymond Chandler

Although born in Chicago, the hardboiled author of *The Big Sleep* and other private dick novels had become a naturalized British citizen during a boyhood in England. So when the U.S. jumped into World War I, the adventure-seeking Chandler was ineligible for the American forces, and decided to enlist in the Canadian forces instead. He did his basic training with the Gordon Highlanders near Victoria, which he considered drearily provincial. Three months later he was in Halifax, then on to France. He never returned to Canada, although 30 years after the war he recollected his time on the Island in a letter to a Canadian journalist: "[I have] strong pro-British feelings and also

Throw a stone in Victoria, and you'll likely nail a novelist then catch a poet and a playwright on the rebound. (That's no reason to stop throwing stones, of course.) Maybe it's the inspiring natural beauty. Maybe it's the chance to apprentice as a student or earn real coin as a prof in the University of Victoria's writing department. Maybe the lack of winter road salt keeps literary awards from rusting. Whatever the case, Victoria has always had a wealth of wordsmiths. Add to this cast of scribblers the many pen-wigglers who have visited Mile Zero over the years and sent postcards from its edge, and there's little wonder that the Garden City has been so often memorialized in prose and poetry, and doesn't lack for new and used bookstores, or readings and open mic nights where local tale-spinners and out-of-town bookies can mingle.

Readings
Mocambopo

A name-brand author (or two) reads each week after a motley crew of open mic junkies at the longest running local reading series. *Mocambo Café, 1018 Blanshard St., Fridays at 7:30 pm*

pro-Canadian, since I served in the CEF and spent months at Victoria in Gordon Highlands of Canada not long ago…. If I called Victoria dull, it was in my time dullish as an English town would be on a Sunday, everything shut up, churchy atmosphere and so on. I did not mean to call the people dull. Knew some very nice ones."

The only (semi-) local reference in his writing, though, appears in *Playback*, an unproduced screenplay (which Chandler considered "one of the best films I wrote") about a stalwart Canadian cop who thwarts devious American villains. (Wonder why Hollywood didn't run with that pitch….) One scene features the changing of the guard in front of the B.C. legislature — which the author has airlifted from Victoria to Vancouver.

Fleur Adcock

In 1980, New Zealand-born expat poet Fleur Adcock arrived in Victoria for a transcontinental reading tour with two other British writers. As she later mused in her poem "Coast to Coast," the trio of travelling authors came expecting maple syrup; instead they got bangers and mash:

"From shore to shining shore."
Or, as we now say, coast to coast:
from coast to bleeding coast and back again
in fourteen days. Three British poets,
jet-lagged already, and it's only Sunday;
and this is Victoria, B.C.
"You'll like Victoria, it's so English,"
English? We can have that at home:
we've just flown over the Rockies,
we want grain-hoppers and grizzly bears.
Lead us to your trackless forests,
your endless prairies under snow,
your lumberjacks and fur-trappers.
When shall we need snowshoes? Give us clichés!

Marilyn Bowering

To All Appearances a Lady (1989), by Victoria-raised poet and novelist Marilyn Bowering, tells a historical ghost story that sweeps across the Pacific from 19th-century China to the leper colonies and opium dens of colonial Victoria, as the secrets and lies of the Garden City's past rise from its compost:

D'Arcy Island. The island of lepers. Nobody went there, except for the lepers, of course. They were supplied by the

Sundays at the James Bay Inn
Usually three featured performers, with an open mic/poetry slam every third week. Poets have stripped to their gaunch, smeared guacamole over their cheeks, and brawled on-stage at this pubby lit night.
James Bay Inn, 270 Government St., Sundays at 8 pm

Open Voice
An irregular showcase of Can Lit canon-fodder. The late, great Al Purdy did one of his final public performances here. *Open Space, 510 Fort St., 383-8833*

Sidney Reading Series
Monthly Friday night readings and music in Sidney-by-the-sea. *Breakwater Café, Seaport Place, 656-2430*

Victoria Storyteller's Guild
Tell-me-a-story types gather on the third Monday of every month, except during the summer.
1831 Fern St., 7:15 pm, 477-4177

City of Victoria, which was responsible for imprisoning them. It was not a subject much talked of: it tended to be bad for morale. And the lepers were all Chinese, so far as he knew. Once sent to the island they ceased to exist for the rest of the world. Even passing ships avoided their shores, arcing away from the coastline where the lepers had their colony. People were superstitious about it, as well as frightened. The Indians said the island was cursed.

(Reprinted with permission from Random House Canada.)

John Gardner

Even James Bond packed his license to kill for a jaunt to Victoria. In the second chapter of John Gardner's *Broken-Claw* (1990), the superspy plays "two rounds of golf with indifferent partners at the Victoria Golf Club," then hits all the guidebook hotspots along the Inner Harbour (whose "specific cleanliness … reminded him of Switzerland"), including the Empress Hotel, the Legislature, and a tour of the Royal B.C. Museum described in such blueprint-precision that Gardner, Ian Fleming's literary successor, surely visited the city with notepad in tow. (He even mentions the daily rag, the *Times Colonist*.) Gardner introduces the local setting with one of those hilariously abrupt "… and in another part of the forest" segues as Agent 007 proves to be as finicky about the tea service as any holidaying Brit:

Eventually, the autopsy of Robert Allardyce would give the cause of death as deep trauma resulting from the spinal cord and left lung being penetrated by two .45 bullets. But, at the moment those bullets hit the unfortunate Professor, James Bond was sitting only some five miles away, in the opulent Palm Court Lounge of the Empress Hotel on Victoria's pleasant waterfront.

People who knew Bond well would have noticed that his manner, and expression, were ones of disapproval: the eyes hard and restless, his face frozen into the look of someone who has just been served bad fish. In fact Bond was irritated by the way this old, and famous, hotel served what it called an English Tea….

(Reprinted with permission from Hodder & Stoughton.)

Mark Anthony Jarman

Before swapping coasts for New Brunswick, University of Victoria grad, instructor, and frequent *Monday* contributor Mark Anthony Jarman let a few of the bruisers, boozers and losers from his

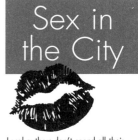

Sex in the City

Local authors don't spend all their time between the covers. Here's a few of their tips on where else to get off while in the Garden City.

Susan Musgrave

While her literary reputation has been overshadowed by her notoriety as wife to bank-robber-turned-author-turned-bank-robber Stephen Reid (see Notoriety), Susan Musgrave remains one of Canada's most adventurous poets and essayists. And one of the Island's most conspicuous writers, too, arriving at local readings in an eye-stopping "art car" that's glue-gunned with toy figurines and found objects. As she confesses in a story in the anthology *Desire in Seven Voices*, the always original Ms. Musgrave also pioneered what's since become a popular pursuit among the wild rabbits and wilder co-eds who roam the grounds of the University of Victoria: on-campus bonking.

At the age of fourteen I found my virginity. No sacred spring gushed forth to mark the spot, though years later the University of Victoria erected its Faculty of Law where my blood stained the grass.

W.D. Valgardson

University of Victoria prof W.D. Valgardson loaded his second novel *The Girl with the Botticelli Face* (1992) with Victoria references, leaving many local readers trying to fit their *clefs* into his *roman*: which café does the neurotic narrator hang out in? (Demitasse, we suspect.) Who was inspiration for the book's Botticelli-pussed object of affection? (Jury's still out.) None of the references is more knee-trembling, though, than when the novel's hero, a middle-aged English prof (Who's that?), has a quickie in his office at the University of Vice:

Hate fucking, I thought. Sex is supposed to go with love. But it didn't stop me from standing up so she could undo my buttons. At least she's not dressed like a nun, flashed through my mind. What if the secretary knocks and thinks I'm not here and lets herself in to drop off some papers? The rest of me was busy trying to get the chair out of the way so we'd have enough space to lie down. I was in such a hurry, I jerked the chair, hit a pile of books, knocked over the tower of saints, which toppled other piles like dominoes. Someone in American foreign policy was afraid of this, I thought, and nearly laughed out loud.

hard-edged, hilarious stories call Victoria home. In "Backhoe" (published in *Prism* magazine), the narrator does time in Metchosin's William Head penitentiary (i.e. "Club Fed") after stealing a van of doughnuts. Later, he reflects on a pre-prison workday on Ten Mile Point in this quintessential Van Isle vignette. Hey, Shamu, leggo my Fido!

Twelve killer whales cruised by my backhoe one sleepy afternoon, a pod blowing water like steam trains and rolling their long black fins like nightsticks in the waves, harassed the entire time by whale-watching Zodiacs and sundry small craft and even a red and white floatplane carving circles above us. A dog swam in the cove and I wondered would an Orca swallow a giant poodle.

J o n a t h a n   R a b a n

Aside from being Victoria's classiest bookstore, Munro's Books on Government Street is also ground-zero for the favourite sport of local literary observers: spot the Alice Munro character. The *New Yorker* regular and Can Lit icon lived in Victoria until 1972, while married to bookstore owner Jim Munro, and although most of her finely wrought stories are set in southwestern Ontario, several draw on Victoria and Vancouver Island for characters and colour. Even the English-by-way-of-Seattle travel writer Jonathan Raban can't resist reading between her lines, as he admits in a passage from *A Passage to Juneau* (1999):

I slightly knew Alice Munro's first husband, who owned the handsome, dark-paneled bookshop, once a bank, on Government Street in Victoria. I enjoyed spotting him, or bits of him, in the husband-figures in her fiction. At his gray-stone house on a hill overlooking Juan de Fuca Strait, I had, or so I fancied, met many of the women characters, 25 years on; gray hair swept back and tied with Indian scarves; ruefully bright talkers. They still did things on the fringes of the arts; and as I sat smoking in a wicker armchair on the porch, the black strait glittering below in the starlight, I wondered if they still looked across the border for their dangerous men – like Miles [a Munro character], showing up from Seattle on his motorbike, a human time bomb designed to blow marital life apart in tame Victoria.

(Reprinted with permission from Pantheon Books.)

the good book

In addition to a downtown location of the Chapters chain, Victoria has a number of interesting bookshops catering to every whim, cementing its reputation as a bookish town (as is Sidney, see below).

Bolen Books

Expect to get shelf-shocked wandering the vast selection of volumes at this independent bookstore. Bolen Books also organizes in-store readings and signings, and "author breakfasts" in the food court of its Hillside Mall home. *1644 Hillside Ave., 595-4232*

Dark Horse Books

Sci fi, new age. *623 Johnson St., 386-8736*

The Deanery

A religious book nook behind Christ Church Cathedral. *930 Burdett Ave., 382-2636*

Hawthorne Books

This cozy Cook Street shop makes a good stop for used book buying. *1027 Cook St., 383-3215*

Ivy's Bookshop

Since 1964, *the* place to book-browse behind Oak Bay's "tweed curtain." It's also the site of a famous poetry punch-up: after being dismissed from the university's English department, visiting poet-in-residence Robert Sward decked literary lion and UVic prof Robin Skelton at an Ivy's reading in 1969. *2184 Oak Bay Ave., 598-2713*

Munro's Books

A central location, gorgeous interior, and bibliophilic staff make this former bank the top stop for local book-hounds. During floor restorations, a spent cartridge was found from a shooting in 1948. It's also haunted by the ghost of a teller who was caught with her hand in the till, then hung herself in the basement vault. Now the only danger is from bargain-hunters jostling around the remainder shelves. *1108 Government St., 382-2464*

Linda Rogers

After a tumble in the groves of academe, the next hotspot for literary lovin' is the beachfront below Dallas Road, its reputation cemented by *Woman at Mile Zero* (1990), the cover of which features local poet Linda Rogers lounging across the shoreline rocks in a sea-soaked dress.

Last night, the sea was wild on Dallas Road. It hit the restraining wall with the angry slap of a mother when she and her child share the same strangely sexual fear of death, when he perversely dangles himself from a tenth story window or runs in front of a car. Or my hand on your cheek when we are too far apart for kissing. Or yours on mine. I saw you on the wall. We danced together in the waves and headlights. Maybe we were trying to push each other off.

DO-IT-YOURSELF PUBLISHERS

Think you've got a book in you? Several Victoria companies want to play midwife to your words. (Just don't call them "vanity" publishers.)

Trafford Publishing is one of the world's leading on-demand publishing houses — digitally storing authors' manuscripts, then printing only as many paperback copies as are ordered. They've released everything from engineering textbooks to political thrillers to slim volumes of modern verse, and won't be satisfied until every person on the planet has become a published author (www.trafford.com, 383-6864). If you're a writer of more modest means and manuscripts, Fine Words Chapbooks will help you design and produce a paperback folio-edition (plus 100 copies) of your dream book for an average fee of $650. Fine Words also organizes group readings for its local authors (721-WORD).

Poor Richard's

Come for the cats, the free coffee, and the cozy reading corners in this showcase for bricklayer's work and classy book-selling. *968 Balmoral Rd., 384-4411*

Renaissance Books

Great selection of used literary and scholarly titles. *579 Johnson St., 381-6369*

Russell Books

Vancouver Island's largest used bookstore stocks out-of-print, remaindered, and otherwise homeless tomes on two floors of towering shelves. *734 Fort St., 361-4447*

SUBText

Get a bargain at this UVic campus consignment shop. Bonus: unintentionally hilarious marginal notes penned by earnest undergrads! *Student Union Building, 721-8810*

Tell Me a Story

Crawl through for ankle-biter books. *1848 Oak Bay Ave., 598-8833*

University of Victoria Campus Bookstore

Practice the joy of texts — and find a wide selection of literary titles and faculty publications. *University of Victoria, 721-8311*

Wells Books

Sail in for nautical and antiquarian titles. *832 Fort St., 360-2929*

Booktown-by-the-Sea

Sidney was once only known as home to sleepy retirees and disgruntled youth. But Victoria's peninsular neighbour has rebranded itself as "Booktown." Check out the general selection of books and magazines at Tanners *(2436 Beacon Ave., 656-2345)*, the kids' lit at the Children's Bookshop *(2442 Beacon Ave., 656-4449)*, metaphysical manuscripts at Lotus Books *(9803 Third St., 655-6479)*, nautical volumes at Compass *(9785 Fourth St., 656-4674)*, escape reading at Time Enough For Books *(2424 Beacon Ave., 655-1964)*, used books at the Haunted Bookshop *(9807 Third St., 656-8805)*, antiquarian volumes at Beacon Books (2372 Beacon Ave., 655-4447), and whodunnits at the Mystery Bookshop (2372 Beacon Ave., 655-4447). Then score a bench by the pier for an afternoon of seaside page-turning.

Advanced Book Exchange

Can't find the title you want in the city's bookstores? Hop online and surf to Advanced Book Exchange (www.abe.com). This website plays matchmaker for buyers and sellers of rare and sought-after volumes. It's also one of Victoria's biggest dot-com successes.

mystery theatres

While a sizeable and experienced performing arts community calls Victoria home, the lack of small and mid-sized venues means that local theatre impresarios have had to reconsider what exactly a "performance space" is. Plays have sprung up in cafes, malls, tents, loading docks, living rooms, even parked cars. Here's an overview of local thespians and the odd places you'll find them acting up.

William Head on Stage

Where: a prison William Head Institution runs the only theatre in Canada where the actors are more captive than the audiences. One inmate/thespian tried to escape from the penitentiary's peninsular grounds in the stage coffin from a production of *Dracula*. Curious audiences should be that eager to get *in* to catch this unique dramatic experience.
6000 William Head Rd., 363-8585

Belfry Theatre

Where: a former church
Top-notch Canadian and international drama in the intimacy of this restored Baptist church.
1291 Gladstone Ave., 385-6815

WATER MUSIC

What's got 72 legs, floats in the Inner Harbour, and goes out with a bang every summer? Symphony Splash, of course. For over 10 years, the Victoria Symphony Orchestra has boarded a barge, risked *sturm und drang*, and performed a free evening concert of water music for an audience of 40,000 or more gathered on the lawns of the Empress Hotel and the Legislature. On the Sunday of the August long weekend, dedicated Splashers wake early to score a prime spot on Belleville Street or the lower causeway. Rent a kayak or canoe to get genuine front row seats when the orchestra closes their annual fundraising show with Tchaikovsky's *1812 Overture*.

BASSES LOADED

No less than *Time* magazine declared Victoria's own Gary Karr the "world's best bassist." That's not news to aspiring classical performers, as students lug their bulky instruments from the four corners of the globe to attend his summer Karr Kamp at the University of Victoria. Karr recently retired from an international performing career to concentrate on recording and teaching, so the only way to hear him create his sonorous sounds live is to visit the city when the world's number one player joins his happy Kampers for their annual Basses Loaded recital.

THE AMAZING SVEN AND HIS FLYING MACHINE

With few resident companies, Victoria's hardly a major centre for modern dance and ballet. But that could all change thanks to Sven Johansson, artistic director of Discovery Dance, inventor of an on-stage flying apparatus, and self-styled Leonardo of the leotard set. Despite little formal training, the Swedish-born Johansson claims he's able to "channel" choreography out of thin air and has dismissed the entire history of contemporary dance for remaining stuck under the iron thumb of gravity.

His solution? In 1988, the helium-voiced former reindeer rancher sank 600 bucks into building the prototype of what's variously been called the "Strong Partner," the "ES dance instrument," or simply "Sven's flying machine." Attached to a 14-foot levered arm that's manually controlled by a stagehand, dancers can perform zero-G spins and Peter Pan twists as they glide over the stage. So far the instrument has been used mostly for theatrical special effects, cheap crane shots in films, and a dance tool for the physically disabled. But now Sven's touring his choreographic Canadarm around the world (including a stop at the 1999 Prague Biennale) to prove that space really is the final frontier — even for ballerinas.

Langham Court Theatre

Where: a converted carriage house
A stable of amateur and student actors horse around at western Canada's oldest community theatre.
805 Langham Ct., 384-2142

Phoenix Theatres

Where: university campus
One of Canada's top theatre schools runs a full season at its suburban campus. *University of Victoria, 721-8000*

Shakespeare Festival

Where: a reformed Catholic girls' school
Every summer, the Bardolators of Theatre Inconnu free their Willy in the auditorium of St. Ann's Academy.
835 Humboldt St., 360-0234

Kaleidoscope Theatre

Where: in limbo
After over 25 years producing professional drama for kids and adults, Kaleidoscope lost its Herald Street home but still puts on its original shows in various local schools. *383-8124*

Victoria Fringe Festival

Where: downtown, anywhere and everywhere
This unjuried festival of anything-goes theatre is one of the last stops on the North American Fringe tour. *383-2663*

Theatre SKAM

Where: where not?
While these theatrical innovators — who never met a loading dock or Plymouth Volare they couldn't turn into a stage space — have gone on to bigger things and cities, they still return for an annual Summer Kamp of dramatic derring-do in unexpected venues. *386-SKAM*

Shopping

Victoria offers a plethora of shopping choices, from padded snowboarding shorts, to chi-chi dog biscuits and wares from a napping seamstress. New, used, high-end, or budget, Victoria will show your shopping dollar a good time.

Freefalling

Victoria resident Dave Citra demonstrates the cushioning in his padded snowboarding shorts by filling a coffee can with eight pounds of pennies, sliding his hand under the shorts, and smashing the can on his hand. He breaks tables this way. A long-time windsurfer who got a sore behind when he converted to snowboarding, Citra took to wearing his windsurfing shorts under his boarding pants. A little sewing, some padding at the hip points and tailbone, and Freefall Gear (www.freefallgear.com) was born. His line has now expanded into compression shorts with Lycra down the back of the legs for warmth, and a hard-shell vest made from a polycarbonate that withstands a beating by an eight-pound sledgehammer. The shorts are sold throughout B.C. and in eastern Canada, and for those days when the hill is bulletproof, the $90 price tag seems worth it. They're available via special order from ThreeSixty (504 Herald St., 382-0360).

Now Boarding

HtO (1314 Broad St., 920-5511) is a good source for Frisbee discs and has the best selection of bathing suits. Coastline (152-560 Johnson St., 382-2123) offers a myriad of skate, surf, and snow gear, and ThreeSixty (504 Herald St., 382-0360) offers the same, along with a good selection of wakeboards.

super markets

These ethnic and specialty markets feature items you won't find at your local Safeway.

B & V Market

B & V could pass for any corner store, but past the worn display of girlie magazines is an excellent selection of Indian spices and condiments presented in an innovative retail display method: a half-moon cut out of the front of a cardboard box.
3198 Quadra St., 380-1455

Holland Specialty Deli

Look for the Dutch boy signboard on the sidewalk. Toothpicks with all the flags of the European Community, tea biscuits, and, of course, zout droppies.
4468 West Saanich Rd., 744-1295

Italian Food Imports

At Italian Food Imports, find bocce balls, Bialetti espresso makers, and the Marcato atlas and pasta bike. There's a large seating section for eating the big sandwiches made on the spot.
1114 Blanshard St., 385-7923

Ploughshare

Don't be intimidated by the chickens loitering out front. The cluckers belong to Ploughshare owner John De Medeiros and they're harmless unless he forgets to feed them. Like his rooster, De Medeiros is of Portugese descent and stocks his deli with European favourites such as squid ink pasta and exotic olive oils. Out back is an impressive display of indoor/outdoor pots, along with goats, rabbits, and other things that need feeding.
4649 West Saanich Rd., 479-2322

Vintage Clothing

There are bargains to be had at these vintage outlets, where you can transform yourself into Grandma in her heyday (if that's what you want).

Bachelor's New and Vintage Men's Clothing

National soccer team jerseys, polyester sports jackets, and rugby shirts. Grade eleven and twelve boys can bring in stylish shirts, pants or jackets to exchange for the basketball rookie card of their choice. Staff known to attempt spot removal by licking their finger and rubbing furiously.
2340 Douglas St., 381-7927

The Patch

Located in a cavernous space on Yates Street with a volume to rival Value Village. Specializes in brand-name (Gap, Guess) recycled clothing.
719 Yates St., 384-7070

Retro Wear

That familiar second-hand smell greets you at the door, but press on to find leisure suits, Wardair handbags, and some of the friendliest staff in the city.
202-610 Johnson St., 384-9327

Second Hand Rose's Originals

Women's vintage in an inviting shop on the lower level of Market Square. Check out the lamps made out of recycled toasters and hubcaps, and soup tin lids turned into a mirror frame.
45 Market Square, 386-3440

Side Show

Need a PVC corset in a hurry? Latex socks? Suzanne does custom work on a machine in the corner of the store, sometimes while you wait. She stocks vintage clothes and the occasional local designer. Also sponsors seasonal fetish shows (dress code enforced).
43 Market Square, 920-7469

Still Life

Located in the Grand Central building since the early 1980s, Still Life carries new and hand-picked vintage, putting Vancouver designers Black Hole and Allison in Wonderland on a rack next to $300 Betsy Johnson dresses. Select retro chic items, and Blundstone boots.
551 Johnson St., 386-5655

Seven Valleys Nutrition Centre

Seven Valleys is in the Leland Building at Bay and Douglas and offers a good selection of Persian sweets, cucumbers in brine, and teas from all over the Mediterranean. Sit in the front window under the $300 carpets. The store is named for the steps to spiritual growth in the Baha'i faith – knowledge, universal love (very difficult), unity, etc.
2506 Douglas St., 382-9998

10,000 Villages

This international chain was recently acquired by the Bridgehead catalog and offers Café San Miguel (coffee with a conscience), handmade paper from Vietnam, painted wood children's toys from El Salvador, and fairly traded footballs from Pakistan, all of which are products made not-for-profit. The tiny shop in Oak Bay has a reduced selection but wonderful smells from the bakery next door.
#30-777 Royal Oak Dr., 727-7281;
2030 Oak Bay Ave., 598-8183

Wooden Shoe Dutch Groceries and Delicatessen

Over 50 varieties of salty licorice, ceramic tiles and crockware, horsemeat, jellied eel, and shelves of Indonesian food (hauled back from the colonies), and of course, wooden shoes: open-backed, $99; closed, $109.
2576 Quadra St., 382-9042

East Coast Chic

When Pearl Jung closed her shop in Torbay, Newfoundland 14 years ago and moved out to Victoria, she told the knitters in English Harbour West to keep sending the sweaters. She named her new shop Heart's Content *(18 Fan Tan Alley, 380-1234)* after the town on Newfoundland's east coast, and stocked British donkey jackets, Ben Sherman, and Doc Martens before anyone else in town. The first year she had to blow bubbles to convince people to walk down the derelict alley, but now the store has a following that stretches across the country (including loads of bemused east coasters). Don't miss the row of wooden folding chairs in the back – they're straight out of a public school auditorium – with hat racks underneath.

Screening Room

Back in 1995, Trish Tacoma and Julie Higginson needed a roommate. Instead of placing an ad, they silk-screened a bug design onto a scarf in the spare room of their house and called the enterprise Smoking Lily. They sold their scarves and T-shirt designs at a stall in Market Square for a few years before renting a 44-square-foot shop across the street *(569 Johnson St., 384-5459)*. Then when Lily started to take over the house, they moved the manufacturing to a warehouse space on Wharf Street and started to screen medical instruments, hydro towers, and (anatomically correct) hearts on everything from pencil bags to tea cozies to footstools. They now have retail distribution from coast to coast (at Wenches and Rogues in St John's, NF) and a mail order business *(382-5164)* that keeps their seamstress sewing full-time. They recently started working with vinyl for handbags and wallets, finding it an entirely practical material for the moist west coast, and they hold sample sales at their warehouse every three months to correspond with a tax payment coming due (or when the big trunk in their workspace is full).

Record Deals

For anyone visiting from out of the country, Canada's west coast offers some of the cheapest prices for recorded music on earth. A Goldie CD that costs 12 pounds in the U.K. and 12 dollars in the U.S., will be 12 Canadian dollars in Victoria. Take advantage of our anemic currency at these fine stores:

Boomtown
Ambientechnobreakbeatjazzyacidhouse-type music. Boomtown offers mostly new imported vinyl, with some CDs by local DJs.
102-561 Johnson St., 380-5090

Ditch Records
College alternative vinyl and CDs. There's a rack of fanzines at the front of the store, and wacky album covers along the ceiling, including *How to Strip for Your Husband* and *Bill Cosby Talks to Kids About Drugs*. The crates of jazz 78s on the floor were procured from a naked guy on his deathbed.
635 Johnson St., 386-5874

Endangered Species

Moved from its Fort Street location to the former home of Sweet Thunder Records on Johnson. New and recycled vinyl and CDs, especially jazz, blues, and vintage rock.

575 Johnson St., 995-0099

Lyle's Place

Lyle's offers CDs in every genre, including sub-genres the larger stores don't (e.g. Punk/Alternative). It also has a good selection of blacklite rock posters and expensive T-shirts, and cool rotating jewelry cases at the front counter. Lots of used CDs.

726 Yates St., 382-8422;
711 Goldstream Ave., 478-9272

Roger's Jukebox

Good collection of Bob Masse's psychedelic posters. Mostly used vinyl.

1071 Fort St., 381-2526

Stylus

This tiny shop on Johnson Street offers a selection of electronic music for the DJ aesthete.

645 Johnson St., 383-7529

The Turntable

Need a pressing of Donovan's *Barabajagal*? This venerable shop in Fan Tan Alley specializes in '60s vinyl.

#107-3 Fan Tan Alley, 382-5543

sweet things

Candy treats (some with an Old Empire flair) for your own sweet heart.

British Candy Shoppe

The place to find *Coronation Street* fridge magnets, sexist English postcards, and Batchelors peas. All their candy is imported from England and not as sweet as the North American variety (they still use cream). Dog-eared "There will always be an England" sticker on the wall.

635 Yates St., 382-2634

English Sweet Shop

In the same location since 1910, claims to have the largest selection of English sweets, toffees, groceries, and chocolates on the west coast. Mail order shipments are available to anywhere in the world. There's a ten percent discount if you buy five pounds of bulk candy. Order online at www.englishsweets.com or call for a catalog.

738 Yates St., 382-3325

London Sweet Shop

Imported sweets, Celtic jewelry, Walker's crisps, and curled postcards of the Queen.

109-1644 Hillside Ave., 592-0101;
109-2250 Oak Bay Ave., 598-4106

Sidney Candy Man

Row upon row of candy in a crowded shop on Beacon. Sample gourmet jelly beans in flavours like golden pear or strawberry cheesecake or any of their other treats, which include ice cream, licorice, mints, and sugar-free candies.

2446 Beacon Ave., Sidney, 656-1333

offbeat, Victoria-style

Carnaby Street

Natural fabric clothing, rugs, and jewelry in a shop decked out like a Mideast bazaar. Head to the cordoned-off area of the shop in the back; most afternoons you'll find the resident seamstress sleeping in the bed to the right. She sews nights and sleeps in the shop during the day.
538 Yates St., 382-3747

Custom First Aid Systems

Headed for Mauritania next week and concerned about getting ill? Custom First Aid can whip together a kit of syringes, antiseptic towelettes, and other prophylactics to keep you alive during your travels. They also make all types of emergency preparedness kits – 72-hour survival, workers compensation, household first-aid, and watertight wilderness – and offer some of the best prices on solar powered radios in the city.
2047 Oak Bay Ave., 595-0744

Frontrunners Footwear

The knowledgeable staff insist you take the shoes for a spin. Owner Rob Reid also serves as race director of the Royal Victoria Marathon.
#182-911 Yates St., 382-8181

Pop Culture

Manager Harry Roet looks you in the eye and says, "There is nothing that you need in here," but still manages to sell over 100 sets of chili pepper Christmas lights over the holidays. He's run these kitsch shops in the city for over 17 years, and his store remains the shopping destination for typewriter-shaped greeting cards, rubber chicken key chains, and books on cooking in the nude.
#9G 1001 Douglas St., 386-8280

Choco-a-Bloc

Chocolate lovers: enter with caution.

Bernard Callebaut
Victoria locations of this award-winning chocolatier from Calgary.
632 Broughton St., 380-1515;
#620-777 Royal Oak Dr., 244-1596

Hill House Belgian Chocolate and Dessert Café
Enter this shop in the middle of Saanich farmland and let the smell of chocolate overpower the smell of horses outside.
6991 East Saanich Rd., 652-8171

Rogers' Chocolates
What more can be said about the chocolatier that receives praise from the White House and Buckingham Palace? Charles Rogers used to make his legendary Victoria Creams while wearing his bathrobe. The factory outlet *(4253 Commerce Circle)* sells "imperfect" creams at half-price.
913 Government St., 384-7021

Village Chocolatier
Tucked away in Athlone Court in a cavernous retail space.
2187 Oak Bay Ave., 592-2023

Feed Your Head

The best head shop in Victoria is Off the Cuff *(587 Johnson St., 386-2221)* where you'll find Freak Bros. rolling paper and three-foot bongs. "Restraint gear" hangs throughout the store and there are displays of clay figures in amazing states of copulation. The window displays rival anything on Madison Avenue — last December saw a tableau of an overdosed junkie and his weeping mourner. Off the Cuff Too *(589 Johnson St., 386-2285)* next door is less intense. The nude statues and bondage gear are replaced by "thank-you for pot smoking" stickers, non-permanent hair dye, and Scooby Doo patches.

Sacred Herb: the Hemp Shop
Look for the plant-sprouting bicycle on the sidewalk, and then head down the narrow arcade to find Victoria's oasis of sanity in the war on drugs. Pipes, bongs, papers, hemp clothes, underground literature, and a whole wall full of the latest news. (For more on marijuana politics, see the Living chapter.)
#106-561 Johnson St., 384-0659

Satin Moon

Quilters are a difficult bunch to please but this shop in Market Square gets rave reviews.
517 Pandora St., 383-4023

Soap Exchange

Ninety percent of the soap products in the store are manufactured in western Canada, and not paying for the packaging means they cost about 50 percent less. They also offer the "jentle" line of glycerine soaps in flavours such as luffa, cool cucumber, and caramel apple pie.
1393A Hillside Ave., 475-0033

Starfish Glassworks

Located in the old Bank of Toronto building, this glass gallery and studio opened in the spring of 1997. The gallery upstairs has displays of handmade glass and a catwalk with interpretive signs explaining the shaping of glass happening below.
630 Yates St., 388-7827

Zydeco

Asian tourists come specifically for the hot sauces, but this is a good source for Ganesh lunch boxes, Superman T-shirts, and even more stuff you don't need.
565 Johnson St., 389-1877

skin trades

Given the number of erotic shops for a city of its size, Victorians, it would seem, ain't lackin' in the lovin' department. Either that, or we're not afraid to ask for a little ... assistance.

Fantasy Fashion Lingerie Boutique

Chrome racks and exposed pegboard give this Douglas Street shop a temporary feel, but it offers an impressive selection of thongs, corsets, and thigh-high vinyl boots. The next time you're in the market for an orange tasseled bra with clear vinyl sides, try here.
1736 Douglas St., 382-7574

Garden of Eden

Push past the warning signs on the frosted glass door and enter the home of the Handyman Potent Developer Pump and orange "no-penishead" baseball caps, plus two racks of pantyhose and a small section of rent or buy videos in back. The phallus rack by the register is a crass example of "impulse purchase" retailing strategy. Obligatory secret: the Eden is also a sloop piloted by Charlie, the manager.
106B-1483 Douglas St., 385-3523

Fiber Options

West coast environmental products and hemp and organic cotton clothing, all in the former location of Robinson's Dry Goods (note the original tin ceiling) and Earthenware, a militant hemp store that battled with the city's heritage-design police. The new owners are more clear-eyed about their vision — they were nominated for a 1999 business ethics award — but their store's still got a woodsy, comfortable vibe.
642B Yates St., 721-3263

Hemp and Company

A smart, upmarket shop, featuring 100-percent, Canadian-made hemp clothing. It looks like the Gap, but it's politically much wiser.
547 Johnson St., 383-4367

Health Food-Plus

Capers

Victoria location of a health-food supermarket chain.
109-3995 Quadra St., 727-9888

Grass Roots Health and Natural Foods

Located in a huge space in Brentwood, with the Fresh Approach Café and Bakery in the front. Offers the usual health stuff plus beer and wine-making kits, and Grass Roots Peanut Butter (no sugar, salt, or preservatives).
7060 West Saanich Rd., 652-1211

Higher Ground Natural Foods

A tiny shop in Oak Bay featuring protein powders and walls of vitamins.
2033 Oak Bay Ave., 370-1055

Lifestyle Markets

Health food, books, and more, in a strip mall off Douglas.
180-2950 Douglas St., 384-3388

Seed of Life

Started as a co-op 27 years ago, the aromatic waft upon entry could knock you on your ass, but persevere. This is a good place to find unsulphured molasses, exotic teas, and beekeeper honey nut squares.
1316 Government St., 382-4343

Self-Heal Herbal Centre

The front windows of this tiny shop on Blanshard Street are painted blue and gold. Inside are dozens of jars containing dulse powder, Crystal Dragon, ginger capsules, and other natural remedies to fix what's broke.
1106 Blanshard St., 383-1913

Kiss and Tell

You could mistake Kiss and Tell for an aromatherapy shop – fancy soaps and a tea-bar front the store. But this upscale erotica mart, subtitled "the Art and Science of Love," carries an extensive line of Ben Wa products and prosthetics. The domination gear is made in Canada, and the love boat display offers non-latex condoms for people with allergies. A sample basket on the counter allows you to give the vibrators a buzz. Kiss and Tell also claims to be the first in Canada to offer the "bungee harness." Open late on weekdays, with discreet wrapping.
531 Herald St., 380-6995

Photo: Ross Crockford

The Romance Shop

Claims to have Vancouver Island's largest selection of sex toys, and there's no shortage of phallic devices in blister packaging. Over the past five years Ms. Romance has sold her wares at over 600 sex education home parties, which she attends for free. The Douglas Street store and sister shop in Duncan offer the usual apparatus plus an abundance of goofier products – honey dust, Belgian chocolate body paint, and satin g-strings decorated with embroidered tigers.
2022 Douglas St., 380-0069

flower power

You can find unusual bouquets and great selections at these selected florists.

Ballantyne's Florist

Owner Joyce Fairbairn has worked under the funky neon sign for 26 years, and fills the empty space with cardboard cutouts of butterflies, snowmen, or whatever the season requires.
900 Douglas St., 384-0555

Bloomfield's Flowers and Pottery

A huge selection of precariously balanced garden containers and pretty flowers.
938 Fort St., 382-4747

Flowers First

Fancy flowers and stained glass from local artists.
1025 Cook St., 384-2251

Flowers on Top

Fancy flowers displayed on the street or the stairs in the atrium of the Counting House Building.
1005 Broad St., 383-5262

Harry's Flowers

Good source of Oriental orchids and cracked-glaze glass vases.
1817 Oak Bay Ave., 598-3911

Integrity Sales and Distribution

Looking to match that wildflower mix that emerges along the highway every spring? Integrity's Pacific Northwest flower mix is the very same, and features over 20 varieties including: catchfly, blueflax, Siberian wallflower, batchelor buttons, bird's eye, dam's rocket, and five spot.
2180 Keating X Rd., 544-2072

Coffee, Tea, or...?

Not surprisingly, Victoria has some fine outlets where you can purchase an exotic blend or two of tea (and coffee, for that matter) to take home and try.

Cairo Coffee Merchants
Beans are roasted weekly in the roaster in the front window.
744 Fort St., 386-3937

Murchie's Tea and Coffee
Providing Victorians with liquid stimulants since 1894. Some of us never get tired of playing with the tea granny display.
1110 Government St., 383-3112

Silk Road
Blended teas, aromatherapy, and all manner of drinking vessels. They run weekly workshops on tea, aromatherapy, and other healthy living matters. Extensive pampering in the spa downstairs.
1624 Government St., 382-0006

Special Teas
The only shop in the city serving exclusively tea. Flavours include China Chum Mee, Marakesh Mint, and Rooibos Vanilla.
711B Broughton St., 386-8327

China Syndromes

Cracked Grandma's flatware and need a replacement in a hurry? Try one of the following.

Avenue China and Chintz
1465 Hampshire Rd., 595-1880

China Cupboard
1507 Wilmont Pl., 598-3858

Robert James Fine China
1005 Broad St., 386-4588

Sydney Reynolds
801 Government St., 383-2081

home furnishings

Look closely to find these funky places.

Chintz and Company

A big, sensual store filled with bedding, towels, dishes, glassware, and much, much more. Be sure to bring your credit card – this place is made for shopping sprees. *1720 Store St., 381-2404*

Clicks

Smart, simple goods at discount prices. Students and apartment-dwellers will like the futons and office desks; families on a budget will appreciate the sturdy sofas and dining room sets. *517 Herald St., 360-1100*

Design House

Stylish stuff for postmodernists with money. Specializes in sculpted chairs and tables by trés-hot Canadian designers like Karim Rashid and *Generation X* author Douglas Coupland. *616 Yates St., 383-3569*

Magpie

Find Noguchi's Akari light sculptures and Zen Sand Gardens in this tiny shop in the middle of Chinatown. *556 Fisgard St., 383-1880*

Romana Deco

Signature pieces of elegant yet functional Italian furniture, straight from high-end companies like Cassina, Futura, and Zanotta. The place to go when outfitting a power office, or a penthouse. *1696 Douglas St., 385-3336*

Ruby Road

Cool kitsch crowded in a shop in Cadboro Bay Village. Coloured glass, arborite tables, and diner dishes from the 1940s. *2573 Penrhyn St., 477-4057*

Surroundings

Kristiane Baskerville and her assistants take old pieces too damaged to be resold as antiques, and recondition them into beautiful new works: cupboards become bookcases, dining room sets are cut down to coffee tables. Affordable prices, and new home accessories as well. Be sure to say hi to Bentley, the big cat. *249 Cook St., 380-0324*

smokes stacks

Long gone are the halcyon days of John Kurtz's cigar factory at Government and Trounce Alley that kept 37 workers producing Havanas for Victorians, but there are still a few places to find a decent stogie. Just don't bring it to the nightclub.

Cabin Fever

A cedar-wood canoe, trout rod and loads of Cubans, Dominicans, and Hondurans (cigars).
2G-1001 Douglas St., 385-3744

Casa de Malahato

Cigar-store Indians, stuffed dead animals, smoking rooms, and other politically disagreeable vanities.
1-1441 Store St., 383-0812

Goodfellas

Located off the parking lot for the Bird of Paradise pub.
4291 Glanford Ave., 744-2772

Old Morris

The focus in this stately shop on Government Street is the *electrolier* (the old name for street lamp) made from Mexican onyx and installed in the shop in 1910. It serves as a cigar-lighter and has twin flames burning steadily all day. Long the favourite of U.S. celebrities looking to circumvent the trade embargo against Cuba. Mark Twain once smoked a cigar in the store; so have Bob Hope, Bing Crosby, and John Wayne. Rumour has it John Travolta likes to stop by during one of his regular flights up the coast.
1116 Government St., 382-4811

Army Surplus

With Esquimalt the western home of Canada's naval fleet, there is no shortage of military goods in town. Some of it ends up in these stores.

Badge Kingdom
Wall plaques, license plates and spent bomb shells.
1322 Government St., 385-7522

Capital Iron
Where you can also find hardware, camping gear, and other assorted goods.
1900 Store St., 385-9703

Command Post of Militaria
1306 Government St., 383-4421

Harreson's Military Shop
555 Pembroke St., 388-7733

John's Military Surplus
The army often produces unexpected extras (linen table-cloths and silver servers to name a few). Anything in the box on the landing of the stairs is free, and always worth a look.
704 View St., 360-2772

Thrift Stores

Can't wait for the half-price sale at Value Village? Some other places to find that 65-cent T-shirt.

Good Neighbours
103-721 Station St., 474-6788

Hillside
999A Hillside Ave., 389-1911

Royal Jubilee Hospital Auxiliary
585 Johnson St., 386-7111

Saint Vincent De Paul
2784 Claude Rd., 478-0282

9788B-2nd St., Sidney, 655-3188

6750 West Coast Rd., Sooke, 642-7846

840 View St., 382-3213

Salvation Army
7177 West Saanich Rd., 652-4622

123-777 Goldstream Ave., 478-6933

3948 Quadra St., 727-3853

9775-2nd St., 656-1732

3-6686C Sooke Rd., 642-3612

525 Johnson St., 384-3755

Women in Need
1803 Cook St., 389-2203

4-3475 Quadra St., 480-1802

785 Pandora St., 361-9303

You don't have to live with a TV set that's just a factory-made box. Victoria artist Peter Andringa transplants the guts of new TVs into space-age fibreglass bodies of his own design, creating fun and functional custom appliances that look like they'd belong on *The Jetsons* – in fact, they've already turned up in Austin Powers movies and Lenny Kravitz videos, and on the pages of *Time*, *I.D.*, and *Wired*. But such style doesn't come cheap: one of Andringa's limited-edition Orbit sets retails for $1,695 US. For more info, call 385-3920, or check out www.islandnet.com/~mercury7.

(Looking for some cool decor to go with your new TV? Try Lido, the virtual store run by Peter's partner Carmen, who specializes in stylish home furnishings. See www.thelookofmodern.com or call 480-0589.)

Gathering Places

by John Threlfall

Despite its Tetley reputation, few Victoria residents ever actually gather
in the nearest tea room to gab over a cuppa. More likely you'll find
them zipped into latex, grooving at a rave, stirring it up at a multicultural
coffee house or circling under a full moon. Victoria's biggest secret?
Big-city multiplicity packed into a small town's space.
By foot or by car, nothing's ever too far.

Night of Dreams

As the sun sinks behind the Sooke hills, you wander your way along Esquimalt's ocean seawalk, your path lit only by the soft light of candlelit paper bags and the ornate lanterns of your fellow revellers. At various unexpected points along the winding two-kilometre route, musicians serenade from rocky perches, and occasional breaks in the arbutus canopy afford you tantalizing glimpses of your destination: Captain Jamison's Park at West Bay, filled to glowing with a veritable amphigory of lanterns. A Maxfield Parrish tableau come to life? Nope, it's the Esquimalt Lantern Festival where, each May long weekend since 1996, the community comes ablaze with this soft parade. Lanterns range from the simple (brown bag over a flashlight) to the simply extravagant (a seven-foot schooner that takes two to carry). Little more than a community parade gone beautiful, participating in this annual illuminated procession may be one of the best ways to enjoy the multifaceted warmth of a summer night in Victoria.

Victoria Lights

In 1999, it was Solstice in the Square; Y2K saw Luminara 2000. No idea what the City has in store to celebrate the summer of 2001, but it's a sure bet it'll have something to do with lanterns. It seems City Hall was so impressed with Esquimalt's efforts that it decided to sponsor its own night of dreams, to great success. High points of the 1999 downtown event was a Centennial Square parade led by a 60-piece samba band; Luminara took the glow to Beacon Hill Park, filling the garden paths with all manner of flickering beauty. Eight weekends of pre-festival lantern-making workshops ensured a healthy turn-out, so there seems little doubt this lantern fest too will become an annual tradition. Will the venue and theme shift yearly as well? The only way to know is to attend.

lost subdivisions

While it may seem like the southern tip of Vancouver Island is one great Victoria sprawl, it is in fact a maze of smaller regions and neighbourhoods. Some distinctions are obvious – like Oak Bay, Esquimalt, Sooke – but where's the fine line between Fernwood and Fairfield, and what the hell is Spring Ridge? Here's a rundown on some of Victoria's lesser known districts.

Fairfield

"Fairfield" was originally simply the name of civil engineer Joseph William Trutch's manor house (built, appropriately enough, at 601 Trutch St.) Fairfield the neighbourhood took off after 1912, when the demand for more housing resulted in the draining and settlement of a swamp that turned into James Bay; hundreds of houses sprang up in Fairfield in a remarkably short time, providing new homes for the new century's emerging middle class.

Fernwood

Fernwood, which centres around Fernwood Road, was originally just the name of the enormous manor house built by Benjamin William Pearse on the corner of Begbie and Vining. Named for the surrounding flora, "Fernwood" was Victoria's first stone home, a 15-room monster house with a commanding view of the straits of Juan de Fuca and Georgia, Mt. Baker, and the Olympic range; it stood for a century until being bulldozed in 1969, a victim of the city's development boom. Yet parts of "Fernwood" still live on: the day before its destruction, a group of urban preservationists (or opportunists) descended upon the crumbling manor and took whatever could be dismantled – including the entire fireplace and mantelpiece.

Another Fernwood footnote in history: it was the site of the first flight by an all-Canadian airplane in 1910 (200 feet over a grassy field at Shelbourne and Lansdowne in a plane built by James Bay resident William Gibson).

Cafés & Societies

Since the death of Java, Victoria's most notorious bohemian café, and its subsequent reincarnation as Willie's Bakery (a reconstruction of the original building that's more fanciful than factual and a constant source of confusion for infrequent visitors trying to relive those hazy Java nights), local funksters have gone to seed, spreading out across the city in search of new sources of caffeine and culture.

Mocambo Café

Probably the busiest café in Victoria, this little spot and a half (go for the loft) hosts a wide variety of evening events, from the occasional '80s music nights to such weekly gatherings as the Mocambopo literary nights and Saturday improv comedy by The Impromaniacs. Surely the most likely inheritor of the Java spirit.

1028 Blanshard St., 385-4646

Fisherman's Wharf

Perhaps more a found subdivision than a lost one, Fisherman's Wharf has been home to Victoria's principal floating community since it was created in 1948. Linked by harbour ferry to both downtown and the other float community (Esquimalt's West Bay), as well as sporting this unique transit system, Fisherman's Wharf is also home to some of Victoria's most beautifully eclectic houses, its own restaurant (Barb's, a.k.a. "the floating fish 'n chip shop"), a fresh seafood store (the crabs live underwater and can be accessed via a trap door), and a park of the same name (home to the annual Pride Festival).

Harris Green

Stand on the corner of Pandora and Cook and ask a passerby where Harris Green is; odds are good they'll have no idea, even though you're standing on it. Named for Thomas Harris, Victoria's first butcher and mayor, Harris Green is actually the long grassy strip that parallels Pandora Avenue from Chambers to Quadra. Established in 1920, Harris Green was originally designed to be reminiscent of the wide European boulevards; but the only formal mention you'll find of it is on a small white memorial stone that's aging rather badly on the corner of Pandora and Cook.

Recently reclaimed by developers ("Harris Green" is now the name of the London Drugs plaza on Yates), Harris Green is more often used by longtime Fernwoodians to describe the neighbourhood that runs between View and Balmoral and Cook and Vancouver. The boulevard itself acts as a park for local residents, as much a place to walk your dog or play ball with your child as to hold political rallies and urban protests – much like Fernwood itself.

Songhees Point

Prior to the Hudson's Bay Company setting up shop in what would later become the heart of downtown Victoria, southern Vancouver Island was home to the Straits Salish or Songhees people, whose diverse population included the Kosampsom, Chilcowitch, Chekonein, and Swengwhung. Before Douglas and company arrived, the major Songhees village was located in Cadboro Bay – now home to the Royal

Victoria Yacht Club – which they called *Camoson* ("place of gathering camass"). With the arrival of the HBC and the development of a whole new trading economy, the Songhees up and moved their village (population 600) to across the Inner Harbour from the Fort, to Songhees Point (currently the site of the Ocean Pointe Resort and, until it was shortened to accommodate harbour air traffic, the world's tallest totem pole).

The Songhees did have use of the land prior to this business move; the region had long been known as "The Place of Cradles" (outgrown cradles were hung in the trees) where young people would participate in a coming-of-age ritual by diving into the water and retrieving a stone from the bottom of the Inner Harbour.

While they did a brisk trade selling clams, salmon, and potatoes to Victoria's residents, once the gold rush began, concerned citizens started demanding action against "the proximity of this wigwam settlement, with its possibilities of depravity and vice being injurious to the appearance, morals and business of the city." After 50 years of haggling, the Songhees agreed to sell the land to the province in 1911 for $755,000 – at the time the highest amount paid to any B.C. First Nations people for their land – resulting in their relocation to a new reserve in Esquimalt, and the end of their traditional way of life.

Fairfield Community Place

Like Little Fernwood, the FCP (or FCA for "Association," depending upon whom you ask) is home to more local groups than you could shake a talking stick at. Dances and workshops, meditation seminars and spiritual retreats, film screenings and political rallies, health clinics, yoga sessions, full kitchen facilities – it's everything you'd ever want your community centre to be. *1330 Fairfield Rd., 382-4604*

Ukrainian Cultural Centre

All things cultural happen here, and they don't have to be centred upon anything Eastern European. Dances, meetings, dinners, presentations, and Victoria's longest-running sports card show. *3277 Douglas St., 475-2585*

The Downtown Community Activity Centre

Downtown residents have their own refuge from retail and ruckus in this almost unnoticed but always busy place which hosts everything from dance and yoga classes to Qi Gong practice, childcare, psychological seminars, and the weekly Pandora Patio Café, a merry musical open stage. *755 Pandora Ave., 383-0076*

Gone to the Dogs

Dogs are a mixed blessing in Victoria. Reportedly sporting the highest dog adoption rate in Canada, during the 1998 Winnipeg floods the local SPCA flew lost dogs in for easy resettlement in the Garden City. The best places to play? The doggie playground on Dallas Road is the hands-down winner, although the daily battle between pups and bladers, joggers, strollers, kite flyers, model airplaners, and the occasional errant cyclist continues inside the Mile Zero-to-Clover Point leash-free zone. Another high point of Doggie Playground is June's annual Basset Hound gathering: you ain't seen nothing till you've seen a 10-Basset sprint.

On the other side of town, Rover can chase seagulls while you admire Mt. Baker down at Cattle Point, where the wave-free side of the Island means surf-shy dogs get to make their own splashes. Another plus to Cattle Point is the haunting Oak Bay War Memorial, just a quick

Spring Ridge

The original name of the Fernwood region, Spring Ridge was the source of both the Fort and City's water supply. Colonial Surveyor Joseph Despard Pemberton noted in his June 1852 HBC report that, "the well or rather spring, which applies the Fort with about 1,000 gallons per diem, lies high in the top of a gravel hill or bank. The head of the water (raised there by capillary attraction) seems to vary but little during the year ... [and would be] capable of affording considerably more than 100 times the supply at present required ... There are also some other springs of a similar kind in the neighbourhood as yet untried." Piped to downtown Victoria via bark-covered logs hollowed out and laid end to end, Spring Ridge was the principal source of water until 1875 and the establishment of the Elk Lake reservoir.

The springs, once located at Ridge and Spring Roads and Princess and Pembroke Streets (near the Jewish Cemetery), were declared a public reservoir by Governor Douglas in 1858 – but in 1861, the HBC sold them to a triumvirate of local water barons who quickly fenced the springs off and posted armed guards. George Hunter Carey, one of the principal owners, was also appointed the fledgling colony's first Attorney General in 1859. But rather than preserve the water for the public, Carey stepped in and cut a backroom deal with the HBC. When ownership of the springs became public knowledge, the uproar was such that in 1861 *The Colonist* condemned Carey "for violating what every citizen must consider a public duty. He deserves the full weight of public odium. Was there ever such consummate duplicity?" A series of water riots followed, resulting in burned fences and Carey's resignation from office; he returned to England and, just five short years later, died insane at the age of 34.

But it wasn't just Spring Ridge's water that was plundered; much of the neighbourhood's abundant sand and gravel was also made use of by the growing city, keeping Spring Ridge (and later Fernwood) constantly at the bottom of the civic improvement list. One glaring and lingering example can be found in Victoria's favourite photo opportunity: before the Empress Hotel could be built, a large part of the Inner Harbour needed to be filled and solidified. Where did it all come from? One of the ridges of Spring Ridge was levelled and excavated for fill; the resulting pit still lives on, now a basketball court behind the Fernwood Community Centre on Gladstone Avenue.

Vic West

Originally called Gorge Inlet, Vic West started out colonial life as an "attractive recreational amenity" for wealthy families – the sole intact survivor being the 1861-constructed Point Ellice House *(2616 Pleasant St., 380-6506)*. After the 1911 Songhees resettlement, the land was thrown open as an industrial precinct as a balm for Fernwood's increasingly resentful residents. Once the number of gravel piles started increasing, however, the larger estates were quickly subdivided and built up, thanks to a new streetcar link to Victoria and Esquimalt (see Transportation).

Really Lost Subdivisions

Despite the city's penchant for history, some of Victoria's early residential attempts have been all but lost to the past. Little more than location is known about Garden City (Burnside Road to Carey Road, near the Colquitz River), and even that is lost when it comes to Panama Flats – which apparently slipped underwater somewhere to the east of Victoria. As for Cadboro Lawn and Queen's View, they too have slipped away behind Oak Bay's tweed curtain.

dash across Beach Drive; behind it lies the Robin Hood beauty of a vast Garry oak grove, with small hills and enough space to let your pup mix and mingle with the more urbane Oak Bay barkers. Arf!

UVic's Mystic Vale is another great doggie secret, filled with long trails, winding streams, and open fields – but few garbage cans and a whole lot of winter mud. Over in Esquimalt, you can wander along the water from Saxe Point Park to Macauly Point, but no fair letting your pup chew on the ropes dangling from the climbing wall.

(See Living for more stuff on dogs.)

film nuts

Even though Victoria loses out to Vancouver in the world of film production, we're not without our own cinematic sensations.

CineVic

Hosting a variety of bimonthly screen events is the society's mandate, from the Speaker's Nights – featuring film professionals from all aspects of the industry – to their infamous Pizza & Discussion Nights (a typical tasty example was the recent double bill of dinner and a movie about notorious cannibal Alfred Packer).
#101-610 Johnson St., 389-1590

getting together

Hempology 101

While it's never a good thing to stereotype, when the Hempology class is in the students are sure to be high. Such is their *raison d'être*: since 1996,  Hempology has been sponsoring weekly smoke-ins at prominent locations around town. Aimed at raising awareness of the decriminalization of pot and the necessity of medical marijuana, Hempology regularly attracts crowds of more than 100 on Wednesdays at 7 pm during the summer. But bring your own smoke; remember, this stuff costs money *(381-3262)*.

Phile It Under Philosophy

There may indeed be stranger things in heaven and on Earth than in some philosophies, but they're sure to be discussed at Salon Philosophy, which meets to ponder both Eastern and Western ideas weekly at the Pyro Philosophy Shop *(3rd floor, 565 Fisgard St., 385-4646)*, or the Diotima Philosophy Society, which features more obscure mythopoetic musings, also weekly *(#213-932 Balmoral St., 595-5097)*.

South of the Border

Victoria's links with Latin America are remarkably strong, thanks in part to a number of flourishing groups in town: The Central America Support Committee *(Carlos, 598-7690)* sponsors Café Simpatico, a monthly get-together of music, dancing, and education seminars at the Fernwood Community Association *(1923 Fernwood Rd.)*; Club Café Merengue is another monthly Latin social, with DJ Roberto and a rotating series of bands keeping the focus more social than political at the Ukrainian Cultural Centre *(3277 Douglas St., 361-9433 ext. 212/215)*; meanwhile, CommonBorders keeps a close eye on the politics of Central America and offers seminars for people interested in serving as electoral observers in Mexico and all points south *(Steve, 388-0936)*. Then there's Sabados Tropicales, a weekly Latin dance night featuring DJ Loco, Saturdays at Café Ritmo Latino *(544 Pandora Ave., 384-2759)*.

Old and in the Gay

What if you've seen the downhill side of 40 but still want to keep up with what's up and out in the gay community? Check out Prime Timers Victoria, a social, educational and recreational group for gay and bisexual men 40+. As well as monthly events, you can read *Vintage Views*, the chapter's newsletter *(995-3190)*.

Scooters 'n' Ska

The local skanksters of the Capital City Scooter Club keep the mod dream alive via monthly meetings at the George and Dragon Pub *(1302 Gladstone Ave.)* and by hosting the annual May long weekend Garden City Scooter Rally, which attracts scooter devotees from up and down the west coast Throw in the occasional ska gig, a few fezzes, the mandatory checkerboard suit with a skinny tie and you've got a thriving subculture – no points for renting a scooter from one of the downtown vendors, though *(383-4045)*.

The Green File

Since 1983, the Local Exchange Trading System (LETS) has been promoting its "green dollars" as a way of increasing community self-reliance, well-being, employment, and a better standard of living. This alternative to the federal economic system operates out of CEDCO *(#100-703 Broughton St., 360-0852)*, and hosts frequent seminars, workshops, and monthly potlucks where you can connect with other users and access the ever-increasing list of goods and services you can buy with your green bucks.

One venture of note was its June 2000 pitch to buy the then-up-for-grabs *Times-Colonist* "at any fair price" using its green dollars. In exchange for ownership of his local fishwrap, newspaper tycoon Conrad Black was offered equal value in goods and services, including lawn cutting, organic soap, shiatsu massage, genealogical research, life transition rituals, use of a food dehydrator, and Reiki treatments. Had Tubby Black taken them up on it, subscriptions to *The New Times* would then have cost 75 percent green and a mere 25 percent federal – to pay for printing costs.

Let's Talk About Sex

Ever wonder what lurks beneath all that ivy all over town? Just like the Victorian-era Britain that local tourism apes, peel back the vines and you'll find a thriving fetish scene. Local fetish shows happen bimonthly at shifting venues across town (Evolution, The Icehouse). Similar to the rave scene, Victoria's relatively small population limits the cliquey nature of the larger fetish towns like L.A. and Toronto; here you'll find rubber boys back-to-back with leather girls, cross-dressers, PVC clad dark ravers, extreme piercers, gay leather daddies, dyke dominatrixes, buff bi's, gloomy goths, uniform fans, naughty schoolgirls (and boys), wrestling masks ... the list is as long as anyone's imagination.

Participation at the fetish nights is usually expected, if not mandatory, in the form of a "savagely enforced" dress code, but if you haven't got anything too kinky in your closet, you're always welcome to strip down to your undies or wrap yourself in the provided cling-wrap. Once through the door, expect to see folks whipped while chained to the ever-present St. Andrew's cross, spanked in a set of authentic stocks (both courtesy of Wicked Woodworks) or indulging in hot-waxing demos, pony acts, and liquid latex demonstrations. This is all on the surface, however; what goes on under the covers and behind closed doors is yours to discover. Stay current by checking in with Suzanne at Side Show in Market Square.

PEERS

The Prostitutes Empowerment & Education Resource Society (#414-620 View St., 388-5325) does exactly that: help prostitutes to help themselves. Staffed by those formerly in the business, they offer outreach services, counselling and retraining to those seeking a new life off the street. They even organize an annual picnic just for the families of sex-trade-workers.

Yacht Yoks

In and of itself, there's nothing too unusual about a yacht club; besides the obvious ones (Capital City Yacht Club, Royal Victoria Yacht Club), Victoria sports the Pacific Rim Yacht Club, a boating bunch specifically for local gay and lesbian boat owners. In addition to offering monthly boating and social activities, Pacific Rim also hosts outings, camping trips, and power boat events for their southwestern B.C. membership (595-5314).

Found in Space

There's long been a suspicion that residents of Mile Zero are a bit spaced out. Now it has been confirmed by an expert: not only is our place in space guaranteed by the fact that some of the moon's craters are named for local astronomers, but we also have David Balam, the man who one day might just save the earth. UVic astronomy professor Balam sits 140 nights a year as a member of Space Guard, an international association of professional and amateur astronomers who watch the skies in case an unexpected astral body suddenly makes a rush at us. Until that day occurs, however, Balam puts his time to good use discovering asteroids (35 so far) and, after 23 years of searching, a comet (Comet Zhu-Balam). His work with the stars isn't limited to the night skies, though; Balam was also technical advisor for the meteoric Hollywood film *Armageddon*.

And while we're on our star trek, did you know that Victoria's Dominion Observatory was once the world's largest operating telescope? Okay, so that was in 1917 and it was only for six months, but still....

Duck!

Right at the spot where Government Street meets Dallas Road rests Harrison Pond, a tiny concrete lake that seems like Victoria's most elaborate duck pond. But to most members of the Victoria Model Shipbuilding Society, "duck" is a dirty word; waterfowl notwithstanding, the VMSS are the main users of Harrison Pond, as they should be – it was made for them. Built in 1953 with a $50,000 provincial grant, the concrete pond was dedicated by then-mayor Claude

Harrison specifically "for the fun and enjoyment of model boating." After falling into disuse between the '60s and '80s, the ducks took over and made the pond their own, much to the annoyance of current society members who struggle with constant technical difficulties due to the, er, duck poop.

Model power boating and sailing demonstrations happen most Sundays, with competitive regattas (also known as Fungattas) happening at least twice a year.

Go Towards the Light

Given Victoria's quirky nature, it should come as no surprise that it would offer a support group for those who have managed to make it to the other side ... and return to tell the tale. The local chapter of the Near Death Experience Society meets monthly to share stories and experiences; open-minded guests are always welcome to join them (391-0700 or 389-0067).

Barbie Grrrls

Did you know Barbie turned 40 in 1999? Neither did we, but it's a sure bet the members of the First Victoria Barbie Doll Club, a club for adult collectors, did. They're dead serious about their Barbies, Kens, and Skippers; current president Debbie Peterson says that since they started in 1997, they've gathered more than 14 members and, via the different topics of their monthly meetings ("Barbie Travels," "Collecting & Collectors"), they've increased Canadian Barbie activism. Club successes include the production of the Hudson's Bay Barbie, an exercise in nationalistic splendour complete with the HBC's trademark red, green and yellow-striped blanket coat. Coming soon: Canuck Ken!

How's About a Pint, Guv?

More than just tweed, ivy, and readily available British candy, Victoria also boasts the *Coronation Street* Fan Club, where displaced Brits and indigenous fans can meet monthly to catch up on all the *Coronation Street* to-ings and fro-ings. Only in Canada, you say? Pity. They've been meeting for more than a decade the third Wednesday monthly at the RCAF Association Wing building (105 Wilson St., 544-1163 or 382-4382).

Love to Love You, Baby

Getting too much of a good thing? In a town like this, where "escorts" are welcome to do their business anywhere but on the city streets, it may be possible to over-indulge in the finer things of life ... like sex. If you're one of those people who just can't say "No" then drop by a meeting of the local Sex Addicts Anonymous chapter (592-1916) and join others who share your interest in curbing their overwhelming appetites. Curiously enough, the same organization also offers a separate Love Addicts Anonymous group, proving once and for all that love and sex are two entirely separate things.

Kiss and Tell

The city's newest sex shop is turning out to be much more than just somewhere to pick up lube; on top of their continuing art shows, in the summer of 2000 the good folks at Kiss and Tell (531 Herald St., 380-6995) began working with local counsellors to host a series of sexual health awareness nights for youths 16-24. Entitled "Can you say 'Sex'?", the workshops so far have been segregated to encourage openness and honesty amongst participants, rather than somewhere to practice pick-up lines.

NAKED BUNCH

The place to see and be seen — with no tan lines — in the summer is Prior Lake (also known as Upper Thetis Lake). Sporting the warmest water in the CRD, if you don't get there early enough to get one of the little islands to yourself, the best tan can be had by floating around the lake on an air mattress. Most people know it's nude and avoid it if they don't want to show off, but the reactions from the occasional teenage gawker or shocked canoe paddler are always good for a laugh. Thankfully, the CRD has yet to try to force people to put their clothes back on, so Prior Lake remains the first and last refuge of the cheeky and streaky.

not for heterosexual men only

Few present at the Friends of Dorothy's café on Johnson Street a few years back will forget the day when a gay traveller stepped through the door and asked the waiter where he could find a map outlining Victoria's pink zone. A collective guffaw escaped from the café's clientele as we all said the same thing: "Well, there's BJ's across the street ... and here!" He stared, not sure whether we were kidding or not. We weren't.

Despite our sizeable gay and lesbian population, official gathering places have always been few and far between. Back in '74, local queer Randy Notte wrote a pamphlet declaring that, "In Victoria ... gay people have few places to be with one another. If such places are not basically straight, they are patrolled extensively by the police. As a result, most gays in this city are lonely and isolated." While things have certainly changed — today it's the panhandlers keeping the police occupied, and gays are now only lonely and isolated by choice — the list of closed queer establishments is longer than the open.

Hot spots of gays gone by are now either straight (Garrick's Head, The Forge, The Bengal Room) or non-existent (The Bastion Inn Pub, Sappho's, Pals, Rumors, The Queen's Head Pub, Skybar, Everywoman's Books). What's left? Not much, but you can keep up on what's coming out via either the annual Vancouver Island Pink Pages (727-6669), the Vancouver-based *Xtra! West* or *Lavender Rhinoceros*, Victoria's lesbian, gay, and bisexual news magazine.

The G-Spot

From coming-out support groups to Sappho's Salons, women's coffee talks, dyke dances, video nights, Qi Gong practice and more, The G-Spot predominantly serves the needs of Victoria's lesbian community, but gay men, bisexuals, and the transgendered are also welcome for specific events. Home to the Women's Creative Network, you can join and become a member or pay the small drop-in fee to attend their events, held at a variety of venues around town. Call 382-SPOT.

Friends of Dorothy's

Easy to spot: look for the Oz-esque graffiti mural or the big-ass rainbow arching across its front window; step in and grab some lunch in the Emerald City, complete with gleaming towers and a fine selection of Dorothy collectibles. *615 Johnson St., 381-2277*

Steam Works

Victoria's only surviving bathhouse can be found in the alley that leads up to Urge Tattoos (follow the oh-so-subtle big red arrow). It's open 7 pm-9 am daily and is one of the few places in town to still allow smoking, so try it if you're desperate for an indoor butt. *582 Johnson St., 383-6623*

BJ's Pub

Looking for the perfect place to do some Streisand karaoke? BJ's is the place. Although they've got a small and quickly packed dance floor, there's no question this is a pub, not a club. More a place to hang with your friends than to dance the night away, you can find BJ's down the stairs under the awning with the pink triangle. *642 Johnson St., 388-0505*

Musaic

Victoria's chorus of lesbians, gays, and their allies is committed to creating musical bridges between both the gay and lesbian communities and the community at large via public concerts, special performances, and weekly Wednesday night rehearsals at the Church of Truth. *111 Superior St., 360-1966*

Shall We Dance?

From Morris dancing on Solstice dawns to traditional barn dancing, Victorians like to salsa, swing, and tango with the best of them. Put your best foot forward at any of these gatherings:

Salsa: weekly at Ukrainian Cultural Centre (3277 Douglas St., 592-8216).

Israeli Dancing: weekly at Burnside Lawn Bowling Club *(274 Hampton Rd., 595-6473 or 384-6055).*

Swing City: popular weekly big band jive dancing, lessons, contests, all-ages workshops and socials at the Edelweiss Hall *(108 Niagara St., 744-3666).*

Tango Vita: Tango lovers unite in a variety of weekly and biweekly dances at the Fairfield Scout Hall *(459 Chester St., 592-5207).*

VIP Friday Dances: near-weekly dances for singles and couples over 30 at the Freemasons Conference Centre *(638 Fisgard St., 370-9515).*

Pride Week

Depending on the year, number of volunteers, and general level of organizer burn out, the annual July 1st Pride Week has also occasionally been downscaled to Pride Weekend or simply Pride Day. Highlights include the Government Street Parade and the events which follow, including the Fisherman's Wharf party, the Marcus Tipton Memorial Drag Ball game at Beacon Hill Park, Urge Studios' annual Tattoo-a-Thon, the Queerly Incorrect roundtable discussion forum, and the obligatory Pride dance (one recent host was Canadian pop gender-bender Carole Pope). Organizers shift from year to year, so it's best to ask the good folks at AVI (see below).

AVI

A non-profit, community-based organization, the professional staff and 200+ well-trained volunteer force of AIDS Vancouver Island offer a wide variety of health, lifestyle, education, and street outreach services. As well, their offices also host the Men's Wellness Program which aims to improve sexual health while at the same time reducing HIV infections among gay and bisexual men. Men's Wellness also hosts youth programs and community events, such as Queerly Incorrect. *#304-733 Johnson St., 384-2366*

Campus Pride

Like most progressive academic institutions, both the University of Victoria and Camosun College offer their own associations helping to improve the lives of their gay, lesbian, bisexual, and transgendered campus populations. UVic Pride can be reached at their office in the Student Union Building *(472-4393)* and the Camosun College Pride Collective can be reached at *370-3429.*

Norwegian Folkdancing: weekly at Norway House *(1110 Hillside Ave., 595-3556).*

Gum Boot Dancing: no boots required at these South African high-energy dance classes at the Downtown Community Activity Centre *(755 Pandora St., 383-0076).*

Dance of the One Heart: last Saturday monthly alcohol-free all-ages good-karma worldbeat dances held by Dancing Wolf, White Crow and the rest of the One Heart community at Fairfield Community Place *(1335 Thurlow St., 477-1164).*

Let's Dance: John and Vicky Ward's weekly social ballroom dance at Oak Bay's Monterey Centre *(1442 Monterey Ave., 370-7305).*

Victoria Ballroom Dance Society: quarterly events, not always strictly ballroom but usually held at Saanich Commonwealth Place *(3636 Elk Lake Dr., 721-JIVE).*

final gatherings

Victoria has more than its fair share of cemeteries, and not all from the latter half of the unofficial "newly wed and nearly dead" motto. Here's a brief rundown on our necropoli, but for the real skinny on the skeletons in our closet, call the Old Cemeteries Society (598-8870) or catch one of the weekly $5 tours they run nearly year-round starting from Fairfield Plaza. *1516 Fairfield Rd.*

Pioneer Square

Victoria's first cemetery, Pioneer Square, served as the final resting place for residents from 1858 to 1873, until the encroaching population of an ever-expanding city resulted in the establishment of Ross Bay Cemetery. Found on the corner of Quadra and Meares, you're now more likely to see people using Pioneer Square as a place for lunch on a sunny day than the site of any mourning rituals. Living as it does in the gothic shadow of Christ Church Cathedral, however, there's an inescapable eeriness to Pioneer Square that has survived residential encroachment. The best way to see it? At night, during the summer lantern tours.

Ross Bay Cemetery

Featuring some of the nicest statuary in town, Ross Bay Cemetery is probably Victoria's worst-kept secret, more popular as a place to walk in the sun than mourn a passing shade. Back at the turn of the century, before Dallas Road existed to stop waves from pounding the shore, coffins were often unearthed by the storms that decimated Ross Bay; *The Colonist* newspaper often featured letters from citizens outraged at the disrespect and shame they felt towards their city for letting the dead litter the beaches and float out to sea. These days, the cemetery retains much of its glory through the efforts of the Old Cemeteries Society, which conducts weekly tours eight months of the year, as well as helping with both the upkeep and renovation of the site.

Within the walls of Ross Bay are such B.C. luminaries as Judge Matthew Begbie, Governor James Douglas, Emily Carr, Richard Blanshard, Joseph Trutch, the Dunsmuirs, and Billy Barker (after 100 years in an unmarked grave, it was the Old Cemeteries Society

Spiritual Quests

Be Witched

Ever since *Michelle Remembers* put Victoria firmly on the world occult map back in the mid-'70s via the imaginative exploits of an alleged population of devil worshippers (see Notoriety), the spotlight on Victoria's witches has only gotten brighter. While it's true that Victoria does boast Canada's largest per capita population of Wiccans, pagans, and Goddess worshippers, the closest thing you'll find to a satanist here is the heavy metal graffiti on any high school.

What's that in absolute numbers? Hard to say, since a lot of witches aren't exactly eager to stand up and be counted, but if you include the Gulf Islands, estimates for the southern Vancouver Island region have ranged as high as 5,000. Being a witch in Victoria is like being gay in San Francisco; there's just so darn many that it's no longer a big thing. It just is, even in the books.

If you can find a copy, take a gander at *Witches, Pagans & Magic in the New Age*, Kevin Marron's exploration of Canadian witchcraft; in the chapter "The Public Witches of Victoria" he writes, "Fears about satanism and its supposed links with witchcraft are deep-seated in Victoria ... this satanist scare has tended to colour local reactions to the city's flourishing and unusually public Wiccan community. The witches of Victoria have had to struggle to overcome negative public perceptions of their beliefs and practices. In doing this they have established good communications with churches and other community groups ... These efforts have made the Victoria witches leaders in the attempt to achieve public acceptance of Wicca in Canada."

Since the release of Marron's book back in '89, the witches of Victoria have flourished, offering pagan pub nights (at Christie's Carriage House, 1739 Fort St.), coffee houses, youth groups, classes both basic and advanced, legally recognized marriages and burials (via the Aquarian Tabernacle Church), ministers that offer spiritual outreach services to both the William Head Prison and the Greater Victoria Hospital Society, a university student group with a court-sanctioned presence in UVic's Interfaith Chapel, a pagan publishing house (Horned Owl Press), two completely separate stores (Triple Spiral in Fan Tan Alley

that provided a headstone for this gold rush legend and Barkerville namesake). Looking for something more than a rest in peace though? Check out the annual O-bon Festival held by Japanese Buddhists at the Kakehashi Monument each August.

Chinese Cemetery

Tucked away at the end of Crescent Road on the eastern curve of Gonzales Bay is the Chinese Cemetery at Hartling Point. It's hard to find and there's not really much there, but for those with an interest in the dearly departed, it's worth a trip nonetheless. Final resting place of the "celestials" who came from China for the gold rush and ended up helping to build the roads and railroads that made this province great, the Chinese Cemetery may look like little more than a park full of holes. Far from being plundered for hidden gold, however, there's little left here, thanks to the Chinese practice of digging up their dead and reinterring them overseas. Your best bet for learning more is to take one of the tours given by the Old Cemeteries Society.

Christ Church Cathedral

What's at the bottom of those red-tiled steps leading down into Christ Church's basement? Well, dead people. Below Victoria's most scenic church rests a peaceful columbarium, a room with niches that house the ashes of somebody's dearly departed. Named for St. Columba (but guarded by a statue of St. Michael), there's room for 1,800 niches, with about 700 still available. More than that, however, there's seating for around 50 mourners, plus a spot for plants. No worries about rain or headstone-tipping here, but there is one catch: you have to be Anglican.

Jewish Cemetery

Like Victoria's Jewish community itself, the Jewish Cemetery often gets overlooked. Tucked away where Fernwood Road meets Hillside Avenue at the corner of Ryan and Acton, the Jewish Cemetery is the final destination for most of Victoria's Jewish population. Since Temple Emanu-El was built in 1863 to serve Victoria's roughly 200 families, the cemetery has continued to grow, despite the fact that the count is now closer to 125. Still, the cemetery is worth a visit, being the only surviving natural beauty in the deeply suburbanized neighbourhood that was once Spring Ridge, home to Victoria's first water supply — and, somewhat ironically, its first slaughterhouse.

Veterans' Cemetery

You can find another unusual graveyard behind CFB Esquimalt — and in the middle of the Gorge Vale golf course. The Vets' Cemetery was created when the British high command instructed Admiral Hastings to purchase a piece of ground for deceased officers and sailors; he bought the land from a nearby farm, and the ground was consecrated in 1868. One of the first people to

and Avalon in Market Square) and, until it fell to the great Canadian magazine purge of the late '90s, *Hecate's Loom*, Canada's only international Wiccan and pagan magazine — the only pagan magazine, in fact, to ever be reviewed in *The Globe and Mail*.

Of all the myriad covens, study groups, moon circles, community organizations, and solitary practitioners, the busiest groups are the Thirteenth House Mystery School, which offers classes, training, theory, and private rituals under their artistic mandate, and The Temple of the Lady, a province-wide multi-tradition umbrella organization that made headlines by publicly opposing the 1994 NDP shutout of Matsqui candidate Sam Wagar.

Just how big is Victoria's witch community? Big enough that writer, poet and academic Robin Skelton, the most famous Victoria witch of them all, has to fit in a different chapter of this book.

Rave New World

After San Francisco, Victoria is fast becoming the second best west coast destination for DJs, raves, and the whole electronica scene. Why Victoria? Reports have ranged from the beauty of the Island, the hotbed of homegrown talent (pick up a copy of *Garden City Dubs*, if you can find it) and the overall positive nature of the scene here, where the PLUR motto (Peace, Love, Unity and Respect) still applies. Like so much else, the rave scene here is smaller than Vancouver, but for once that works in our favour; in Victoria, it seems, people come to dance rather than just pose or cause trouble. Add to that the fact that the segmenting characteristic to most larger parties (glam, candy raver, cyber, industrial) just doesn't happen here. A small scene means more fun, more diversity and more space to dance.

Hot locations for one-off parties have included Memorial Arena, the Salvation Army, CHEK 6 TV, White Eagle Hall in Duncan, Island View Beach, various basements of various Victoria businesses (The Patch, Ocean Island Hostel), the laser tag court on View Street, an

be interred was Frederick Seymour, a governor and commander-in-chief who died (his memorial says) "while in discharge of an important official duty" in 1869; a few years later, the graves of some 36 men were moved there from Brothers Island in Esquimalt Harbour, which the navy was using as a firing range. The farmland surrounding the cemetery was later sold, and the golf course opened in 1931. The cemetery was recently declared to be a national historic site. It certainly is an interesting place – look for the old monuments, for example, to the sailors who "fell from aloft" – and not too hard to locate. Just turn off Colville Road at the yard for the motor pool, and drive up the hill. It's best to park at the gravel lot and walk in; you can drive right to the cemetery itself, but the road cuts across the 12th fairway, and a screaming tee shot might dent your car.

Hatley Memorial Gardens

This more recent resting place was established in 1932 on the grounds of Hatley Castle and houses some notable Victorians who chose not to spend eternity in Fairfield. Hatley Castle is now part of Royal Roads University at 2005 Sooke Rd. *(478-1754)*.

St. Andrew's Catholic Church

Got 15 minutes to kill before your movie goes in? Hop across the street to the corner of Blanshard and View for a small collection of interesting and well-preserved Catholic tombstones dating back to Victoria's original settlement in the 1850s.

nine unusual places of worship

Victoria Conservatory of Music

At 907 Pandora Avenue stands what was at one time one of Victoria's most gothic churches. With its enormous circular stained glass window, ornate interior woodwork, and the towering spires surmounting its massive stone walls, it doesn't take much to imagine consumed students of classical music scurrying about what was, since 1890, the Pandora Avenue Methodist Church. Also worth a look is the art deco façade of the original Conservatory building on Convent Place – but see it before the wrecking ball does.

The Church of Truth

One of Victoria's many self-styled "new thought" churches, the distinct pyramid-peaked James Bay building (111 Superior St., 382-5412) has become something of a centre for non-dogmatic worship. The building is used by a wide variety of community groups, offering facilities for yoga practice, solstice ceremonies, sound healings, and vibrational therapy to those who are looking for a more inclusive, community-based spiritual following.

James Bay Labyrinth

To find the labyrinth, simply walk up to the park at the corner of Menzies and Michigan in James Bay and look around. You won't see it. Nobody does until they actually walk into the park and stand on top of it. Neither a maze nor a raised knot garden, the labyrinth is simply a collection of smooth white stones laid out at ground level into an ornate blossoming design ancient enough to pre-date written history. Built in 1999 by the James Bay Labyrinth Society and jointly funded by the

unidentified elementary school on an unnamed Native reserve, a patch of old growth forest, and a windy west coast cove accessible only by boat. Featured performers have included John Digweed, Sasha, Juan Atkins, Kevin Saunderson, John Debo, the folks at Moontribe, plus local spinners Brent Carmichael, Jimbo, Spencer, Liam Lux, Dub Gnostic, the Stir Fry Crew, Velvet, and many, many more.

Also catch the Johnson Street stretch of turntable stores (Boomtown, Stylus, Complex) plus Whitebird Studios for DJ lessons and studio time; up in Duncan, check out Area 51. While the word itself may now be unfashionable, "rave" fashions can still be found all over the city (Off the Cuff, Side Show, Retro Wear, Funkytown, Still Life, Complex). Local promoters include Noble House, Atomique, Digniti, and the Alien Mental Association. There's also Electrix, the internationally-demanded company that makes electronic music gear, based out of Sidney.

Keep up with what's going down via the Rave Victoria website, which is probably the Island's most comprehensive listing of whos, whens, and whats in the local electronica scene (www.rave.victoria.bc.ca).

More? Check out *Rave Culture: An Insider's Overview*, written by local author Jimi Fritz.

Ethnic Festivals

Victoria is more multicultural than the official propaganda may lead you to believe; just like ye olde Englande, Victoria is now (and has always been) filled with colonials from across ye olde empire (and then some).

The Celtic Festival

Take an incredible line-up of the best in Canadian and international Celtic bands, add a whole lot of Guinness and shake up and down for two days. The result? Three years of Celtic festivities, late May annually in Market Square.

Chinese New Year

Given the age, history, and pride of Victoria's Chinatown, it's no surprise that there is a celebration of note each February, when you can watch the lion dancers roam down Fisgard Street as the lion's snapping jaws gobble up the lettuce and little red envelopes that hang from every building; don't forget to rub Buddha's belly while wishing the latest animal year well.

Photo: Stewart M. Wood

James Bay Community Project (547 Michigan St.) and the City, the labyrinth actually required more than two years of planning; despite the simplicity of its design and layout, City engineers had to level the ground and literally pound sand so the grass would live up to the labyrinthine wanderings of its users. While walking labyrinths on your knees was all the rage of Middle Ages penitents, contemporary designers encourage you to do it on your feet — seven times, though. Our recommendation? Try it when the moon is full.

The Yurt

Speaking of things labyrinthine, don't worry if you get lost on your way out to the Yurt on Old West Saanich Road — everyone does their first time. Tucked away on some backwoods acreage and marked only by a small roadside sign that simply reads "The Yurt," this modern adaptation of an ancient Asian shelter is a beautifully designed and constructed New Age retreat centre, home to monthly healings, channelling sessions, rituals, dances, solstice celebrations, and numerous workshops. Much more elaborate than anyone ever expects, this yurt has foregone the traditional thatched roof and mud floors in favour of an oiled pine, hardwood floor, and woodstove aesthetic, complete with a canvas ceiling spiralling up to a planetarium-esque peak, with a string of tiny white lights simulating the stars. Not to be outdone, they also have their own labyrinth on the grounds. (CorUnum One Heart Centre, 652-6558)

Sufis

Faith of the beloved poet Rumi and the mother religion from which Islam split, Sufism is still going strong after 1,000 years, even in Victoria. In addition to interfaith work and the occasional weekend workshop, local Sufis sponsor monthly Dances of Universal Peace that are simple, joyful meditations of the heart. Learn some of their beautiful chants, try your hand at a diad or get the knack of whirling like a dervish when they meet the first Tuesday monthly at 1831 Fern Street. (385-3378)

Theosophical Society

Still around after 125 years, the Theosophists continue to promote their central premise of perennial wisdom, that we are all one. Prominent elements of the incredibly welcoming Theosophical philosophy are a reverence for life, compassion for all and respect for every religious traditions. They seek to understand our place in the universe, as well as the purpose and meaning of our lives, by meeting monthly in the Windsor Park Pavilion's Pine Room *(2451 Windsor Rd., 655-9471)*. They also sport a 78-acre retreat just east of here on Orcas Island. Founded in 1927, Camp Indralaya (a Hindu word for "a home for the spiritual forces in nature") is an ongoing practical experiment in applying Theosophical principles to daily life.

Temple Emanu-El

At the time of its 1863 construction, Temple Emanu-El (or Emanuel, depending on where you look) was only the third synagogue in Canada, built to offer services to Victoria's tiny Jewish population (only 200 families). Even though the number of Victoria's Jewish residents has steadily declined, the Temple is still going strong, and has received a handsome heritage restoration. By-donation tours run Tuesdays and Thursdays during the summer months *(1461 Blanshard St., 382-0615)*.

First Church of Christ, Scientist

When the Women's Infirmary and the original Royal Hospital were demolished in 1890, few expected to see mighty Corinthian columns and an enormous stark white dome rise from the dust, but that's exactly what happened. Built in 1919 by the Christian Scientists as a glorious companion to their humble downtown reading room, this Grecian-style church dominates Fernwood's view of Harris Green. The oversized architecture is a favourite of local skaterboarders, who get great air from the top of the front steps. Whatever would Mary Baker Eddy say?

St. John the Divine

Not that there's anything unusual about Christianity, but worth noting is that at 9:00 pm on the four Sundays preceding Christmas, this church burns incense, swaps electric lights for candles and offers simple Gregorian chants as a refuge from the Christmas hubbub, at 1611 Quadra *(383-7169)*.

Dahliwal

This East Indian festival of song and dance happens each fall, bringing Victoria's surprisingly large East Indian community together for a weekend festival up at UVic.

Francophone Festival

A francophone population in ye olde Victoria, you say? *Mais oui!* La Société francophone de Victoria *(388-7350)* estimates there are 6,000 francophones and nearly 30,000 bilinguals in the Capital City, 10 percent of our total population; on top of that, some 40 percent of Victoria's original settlers were French (no surprise to the one-time residents of the Catholic St. Ann's convent). La Société does their best to accommodate these unheard masses with their own 3-week annual festival in late February-early March, and by manning the Quebec tent at the annual Canada Day festivities.

street festivals

Highland Games

Prepare to hoist yer kilt and toss that caber at the annual Gathering of the Clans. While it's billed as a highland fling, lowlanders and fans of all things Scottish are more than welcome to come try their hand at these ancestral games that have been an important part of Scots culture for centuries: the games kept them battle-fit and ready for war, as well as increasing clan *esprit de corps*. The year 2000 saw the 63rd annual gathering, where clans from across Canada and the US converged on the grounds of Royal Roads University to participate in dance contests, sheepdog displays, drumming, piping, and (of course) the mighty caber-toss. Och, aye!

Latin-Caribbean Fest

Each July, Market Square comes alive with food, arts and crafts, and a visual art show all aimed at celebrating the diversity of Caribbean culture; the real highlight, however, is the music festival that goes along with it. Given the common denominators of sun, sand, and ganja, doesn't an Island celebration of reggae only seem natural, mon?

Most residents of Victoria love any excuse to get out and mingle, so it's a good thing we've been blessed with both an affable climate and population. Where to go to meet and greet? Here's a few ideas.

Art in Bloom

A celebration of the natural art found in flowers. Where else but in the Garden City? (June, 953-2033)

Art on the Fence Festival

Given the number of artists living and working here, art festivals in Victoria are about as common as political protests in Ottawa. This one happens annually in Belleville Park, and it's really as simple as it sounds: artists gather to hang their work on the fences of the park. (October, 381-3456)

Bike-to-Work Week

Given our reputation as Canada's cycling capital, something cycle-ish was bound to happen – besides the Galloping Goose, that is. This week-long pedal-fest features a number of events that prove just how much faster, cleaner, healthier and better it is to ride rather than drive around Victoria. (June, 413-8000)

Burnside Gorge Community Festival

A true community family fun fair, the Burnside Gorge fest has been bringing the people of the Selkirk waterfront together since 1990. With a celebrity dunk tank, whaling canoe rides, barbecue, clowns, games, contests, climbing walls and yearly surprises, it's always great fun and always absolutely free. *(June, 388-0223)*

The Classic Boat Festival

Celebrate the tall ships (and wooden boats) in the style to which they've become accustomed, each fall in the Inner Harbour. *(September, 953-2003)*

The Cobble Hill Fair

The calendar may say "fall" but it's always still warm and sunny by the time the Cobble Hill Fair rolls around. Bring in the harvest without worrying about wearing a sweater, just over the Malahat on the way to Duncan. *(August, 743-2453)*

Esquimalt Buccaneer Days

Shiver me timbers and walk me plank! Hearken back to the days of yore with this annual Vic West pirate fest. Highlights always include a parade, rides, an arts and crafts show and enough skulls and crossed bones to keep Roger jolly all year. *(June, 414-7104)*

Fernwood Day

Funky Fernwood may not have the splash of Fairfield or the dash of Oak Bay, but it does have a unique style all its own. More like Vancouver's Mt. Pleasant district, Fernwood features a number of spontaneous ad-hoc fests throughout the year; this is the planned one, though, a day of Fernwood fun that usually happens just around Labour Day on Gladstone Avenue. *(September, 381-1552)*

Kidding Around

Everyone knows Victoria's a great town for raising children, but here are a few things the kiddies can do that you might not have known about.

Running of the Goats

The Beacon Hill Park petting zoo is no real secret — drive into the park and there it is — but what many people don't know is that around 5:15 pm each day you can watch the "Stampede of the Goats," when the staff encourage visitors to line the route from the petting area to the barn and help chase the goats into the barn. Clap your hands and try your lungs on some of those great herding yells you've been working on; anything just to get them little kids a-runnin'. Hmmm, maybe it'd work at home, too *(381-2532)*.

Hilarious Hillside

At 10 am each Wednesday, Hillside Centre mall gives its food court over to the Children's Fun Hour for 60 minutes of no charge children's entertainment. Jugglin' Jay, Fizzlepop, Mr. & Mrs. Tiggy Winkle, Sparkles the Clown ... each week a different performer keeps your child entertained, and that's one more hour you don't have to worry about. Find out who's on this week by calling the mall at 595-7154.

Once Upon A Time

Tell Me a Story bookstore on Oak Bay Avenue features tales for tykes *por nada* (10:30-11:30 am Tuesdays weekly), just as Annabelle's Books in Market Square does (2 pm Saturdays). Chapters and Munro's Books (ask about the story fairy) also offer free story times, but not with the same regularity.

Garden City Walkfest

See the city in a way you can really appreciate it – on your feet! The Garden City Walkfest highlights just that, Victoria's gardens. Internationally known and attended, pre-planned routes take you from the Inner Harbour through each neighbourhood in town. Wear comfy shoes and leave the umbrella at home ... and don't forget to bring water. *(May, 477-5207)*

The Harbour Street Festival

For two days, Government Street in front of the Empress gives over to a full-on street party featuring bands, buskers, balloons, and the boating beauty of the harbour ferry ballet. *(May, 472-1690)*

Lavender Harvest

Since 1988, the good folks at the Happy Valley Herb Farm have been inviting the city to swim in their sea of blue scent, by participating in their annual Lavender Harvest – one of the sweetest ways we know of to spend a weekend in Victoria. And while you're not able to spend the night sleeping in a field of lavender, we're sure no one would mind if you caught a quick afternoon nap. *(July, 474-5767)*

The Moss St. Paint-in

On a normal Saturday, the biggest action along Fairfield's Moss Street is the Moss Street Market; but once a year, those crazy kids at the Art Gallery of Greater Victoria bust loose from the gallery walls and spread their art from Fort Street to Dallas Road, filling both halves of the sidewalk – and then some – with everything from printmaking and performance art to sculpture and soundscapes. But that's only half the fun: in addition to meeting and mingling with more than 70 artists producing works-in-progress right before your eyes, local residents turn Moss Street into one big fair, with garage sales and home-made treats galore. Truly one of Victoria's finest events, it's only once a year and not to be missed. *(July, 384-4101)*

Oak Bay Tea Party

Since 1962, the people of Oak Bay have been coming together for their own neighbourhood celebration at Willows Beach. Never ones to do anything small, the Oak Bay Tea Party regularly features an airshow, fireworks display, parade, midway, two days of entertainment and, oh yes, tea. *(June, 388-4457)*

The Pacific Classic

Another recent Victoria cycling tradition, the Pacific Classic offers competition cycling to both serious competitors and the greater community, with a number of events both gregarious and gruelling. While the Bastion Square Grand Prix may be the most exciting (speed cycling through downtown!), the Mt. Tolmie Hill Climb is without a doubt the most exhausting (34 km. up and down!). *(June, 360-BIKE)*

Pride Parade

Who's the real queen of Victoria? Find out each year when the reigning monarch takes her place of pride as the head of the Pride Parade, Victoria's annual gay, lesbian, bisexual, and transgendered community celebration that's always a surprise to unsuspecting tourists ("Why Henry, they're having a parade! Look, they all seem so happy, so ... gay!"). From Centennial Square down Government Street, past the Empress Hotel and the Legislature and on to Fisherman's Wharf park, it's the perkiest parade you'll ever see. And the best coordinated, to be sure. *(July, 384-2366)*

Cadborosaurous Climb

Is your child's heart set on climbing on giant sea creatures that are outrageously cartoony? Then fun awaits down at Cadboro Bay's Gyro Park, where Victoria's best oversized concrete critters can be found — including the beloved Caddie. This seaside stopover also features some of the city's sandiest beaches and loveliest views, especially when the moon rises over the bay. Sigh.

Girlfutures

A great program based in James Bay that works to improve both the self-esteem and life skills of pre-teen and teenage girls, Girlfutures is run for girls by girls and often features such sessions as rock climbing, belly dancing and self-defence. It's all completely free, but it's just for girls and it's not every week at the James Bay Youth Centre *(521 Superior St., 386-1179)*.

Birds and Bees

There are few organizations as busy as the folks at the Capital Regional District parks program, who offer weekly year-round outdoor activities that are for the most part as free as the birds you'll see and learn about. With a focus on both education and adventure, many of the local parks feature fun naturalist programs that will expose you and your kids to the west coast rainforest environment in which we all live. Give 'em a call at 478-3344 and see what's happening.

The Swan Lake Christmas Hill Nature Sanctuary (3873 Swan Lake Rd., 479-0211) is another popular learn-and-look destination that also features year-round and seasonal-specific activities. Around for 25 years and just a five-minute drive from downtown, the Swan Lake Nature Sanctuary is a guaranteed good getaway for your family.

The same can be said for the Goldstream Park Visitors Centre (478-9414), which offers weekend walks and workshops just twenty minutes up Highway 1 at the base of the Malahat. Seasonal treats include the famous Goldstream salmon run (spawning so thick you could walk across their backs) and the annual eagle fly-in that follows (gulp!).

Saanich Summer Sunfest

Cross Bay Street and you may think you're still in Victoria, but when the street signs change colour, you know you're in Saanich. See all that downtown's northern neighbours have to offer at this multi-venue, fortnight family festival featuring more than 50 events up and down the Saanich peninsula. *(July, 595-7121)*

Summer in the Square

The City's annual summer gift to the city, Summer in the Square features a full eight weeks of music, dancing, film, workshops, concerts, and celebrations in Centennial Square, right next to City Hall on Douglas Street. *(July-August, 361-0388)*

Victoria Day Parade

Again, not much of a secret to this one. How could it be when most of the city turns out to line Douglas Street from Mayfair Mall to the Legislature each Victoria Day? Still, it's fun to watch a full-size viking ship sail through town as the Sons of Norway grimace and wave faux-swords at the smiling crowd. Authentic? Nah. Fun? You bet. *(385-5711)*

West Shore Summer Festival

This free outdoor family arts and crafts fest always features impressive children's music by the likes of Fred Penner as well when it rolls into Sidney's Juan de Fuca Recreation Centre. *(August, 478-8384)*

Victoria is a hotbed of movie locations, media scandals, magazine meccas, and outrageous rock bands – not to mention the hometown of an Oscar-nominated director.

Why Do They Call It Monday?

Back in the early 1970s, when ex-New Yorker Gene Miller got the idea of creating an alternative weekly in Victoria, there were two daily newspapers in town, the *Victoria Times* and the *Daily Colonist* (which merged in 1980 to become the fine product we know today). Since the employees of the dailies were God-fearing union folk who did not toil on the Christian sabbath, neither paper published a Monday edition. And so, on July 13, 1975, Miller stepped into the breach with *Monday Magazine*. Soon, however, Miller realized that no one wanted to read an arts-oriented paper at the beginning of the week. He kept experimenting with the publication date, and eventually settled on Wednesday. But he'd built up a lot of goodwill in the original name (and was stuck with all that *Monday* letterhead) so he kept it, and ever since, *Monday* employees have had to retell the story you've just read.

Campus Controversy

The University of Victoria's student newspaper, *The Martlet*, was raided by Victoria police in October 1970 when the newspaper was about to publish the manifesto of the Front de Liberation du Quebec, in defiance of the War Measures Act. *Martlet* staff showed the police some galleys with offensive sections temporarily removed, then used a different printer to do the run. It turned out to be one of the newspaper's best-read issues. Another controversial issue was published on Valentine's Day, 1992, under then-co-editor James MacKinnon (who later edited *Monday Magazine*), dedicated to gay and lesbian issues: the cover art included detailed pictures of genitalia. Although unofficial censors collected all the newspapers on campus and trashed them, *Martlet* staff dug them out of the garbage – and ended up on the national news.

Victoria on film

The 1930s saw a boomlet of "quota quickie" films made in Victoria, which qualified as British productions and could therefore be sold into the protected UK market. Most of these were shot by Central Films, a company set up by Columbia Pictures in Canada. In 1938, the special treatment for films made in the Dominion was lifted, and the companies quickly pulled out of Victoria. Things were quiet on the Victoria film scene until the Canadian dollar tanked in the 1980s. Now Hollywood is again transforming Vancouver and Victoria into cities like New York and Paris.

P o i s o n (filmed 2000)

A multimillion-dollar mansion in Deep Cove was used for this mother-daughter psycho-thriller starring Rosanna Arquette and Jurgen Prochnow. Homeowners used the filmmakers' hydraulic cherry picker to get some painting done.

S c a r y   M o v i e (2000)

Vic High (with an added fountain) appears in numerous exterior shots in Keenan Ivory Wayans' bad-taste blockbuster.

D o u b l e   J e o p a r d y (1999)

A distaff version of *The Fugitive* recast in the Pacific Northwest. Ashley Judd drives a car off a Gulf Islands ferry to elude Tommy Lee Jones.

T h e   G u a r d i a n (1999)

Esquimalt's Carleton Club Cabaret becomes a biker bar for this feature by Gerry Lively, known for his work on *Hellraiser 4: Bloodline*. Also features gunfights and a vehicle explosion on Hillside Avenue.

FIRST SCREENS

Although the first film to be shown in Victoria was at the Searchlight Theatre on Fort Street in 1897, the first permanent theatre was the Avenue, built in 1913 on the south side of Oak Bay Avenue at Foul Bay. In 1936, the theatre went up for sale as part of a commercial block, and in 1943 the Avenue was converted to a 10-suite apartment block that is still there today.

Masterminds (1997)

Patrick Stewart (a.k.a. Jean-Luc Picard of the Starship Enterprise) installs a security system at Shady Glen School (Royal Roads Academy) and proceeds to kidnap 10 of the world's richest children. BCTV news anchor Pamela Martin has a cameo as a news reporter, and in an ironic turn of events, Stewart ends the movie in a sewage outflow pool. Worth renting to hear him say, "You little bugger."

Excess Baggage (1996)

One-time Batgirl Alicia Silverstone gets kidnapped and her dad throws the ransom money off the Johnson Street Bridge — the highlight of this bomb also starring Chrisopher Walken and Harry Connick Jr. The replica of a parkade was built behind Chintz and Company. The city depicted is somewhere in Washington State, not necessarily Seattle.

Little Women (1994)

Lots of heaving of chests and braiding of hair in this adaptation of the Louisa May Alcott novel starring Winona Ryder (who was nominated for an Oscar) and Susan Sarandon. Humboldt Street becomes Greenwich Village, Royal Roads becomes Nice, and Cobble Hill becomes Concord, New Hampshire.

Intersection (1994)

Victoria plays Vancouver in this remake of the French film *Les Choses de la Vie* starring Richard Gere, Sharon Stone, Lolita Davidovich, and Martin Landau. Climactic scene filmed at the Royal Jubilee Hospital.

Knight Moves (1992)

Hatley Park is the exterior and the Empress is the interior of the fancy hotel chess-champion Christopher Lambert stays at while visiting an island near Seattle.

Bird on a Wire (1989)

Mel Gibson and Goldie Hawn rob a bank at the old Carnegie Library (ironically now a real bank), and ride a motorbike through Fan Tan Alley and into a hair salon in Bastion Square.

Hot Pursuit (1987)

John Cusack flunks his chemistry exam at a school looking suspiciously like St. Michael's University School so he can't join his rich girlfriend and her family in the Caribbean. But thanks to a generous professor, he's free to chase them, only to find Ben and Jerry Stiller in the way.

Year of the Dragon (1985)

The sub-basement of the Empress Hotel is transformed into a bean sprout factory where Mickey Rourke discovers two corpses. Empress staff were not amused when the filmmakers headed back to the States and left behind a ton of rotting bean sprouts.

The Glitter Dome (1983)

Victoria stands in for Los Angeles as two cops investigate the murder of a pornographer, starring James Garner, John Lithgow, and Margot Kidder. When an extra at the Oak Bay Marina complimented Lithgow on his role as Roberta, the transsexual fullback in *The World According to Garp*, the actor reportedly replied, "I wish I could do all my parts in a dress."

Harry Tracy (1982)

Gordon Lightfoot (yes, *that* Gordon Lightfoot) is a U.S. marshal trying to track down Bruce Dern, the last member of Butch Cassidy's Hole-in-the-Wall Gang, who falls in love with Helen Shaver, the woman of his dreams. Johnson Street gets covered in a layer of dirt and gravel to become turn-of-the-century Portland.

Secret Magazines

Although *Monday Magazine* is the source for news and entertainment in the Garden City, there are a few other magazines of note that call Victoria home.

Lavender Rhinoceros

The *Lesbian News*, started in 1988 by Debby Yaffe, morphed into the *LNews*, which became the *Lavender Rhinoceros* in February 1999, edited by Barbara McLauchlin (follow that?). Created for Victoria's "lesbigay" community. For more information, write P.O. Box 5339, Station B, Victoria, V8R 6S4.

Harry in Your Pocket (1973)

This drama about pickpockets stars James Coburn and Michael Sarrazin.

Son of Lassie (1945)

Lassie chose not to stay with the crew at the Empress during the filming this sequel to *Lassie Come Home*. Peter Lawford is a World War II RAF navigator who parachutes over enemy territory with his dog Laddie (Lassie's son) in his arms. When he sends Laddie to get help, the pooch mistakenly returns with two Nazis.

The Commandos Strike at Dawn (1942)

Saanich Inlet is transformed into Norway for this film about a resistance fighter battling the Nazis. After missing the bus to the shoot one morning, actor Alexander Ross terrified denizens of the Empress by striding through the lobby in full Nazi uniform followed by a contingent of Wermacht troops.

Manhattan Shakedown / Murder is News (1937)

Victoria plays Gotham in this story of a newspaper reporter who investigates a psychiatrist suspected of blackmailing his patients. In the sequel, the reporter thinks a wealthy industrialist has murdered his wife.

Death Goes North (1937)

Rin Tin Tin Jr. stars in the story of two Mounties who find love (not with each other) while investigating a murder.

Across the Border / Convicted (1937)

Two films Rita Hayworth did for Columbia Pictures in Victoria. In the first, whose working title was *The Devil in Ermine*, a customs officer falls in love with her character, Patricia Lane, but in the process gets in trouble with a bunch of fur thieves. In the second, a detective is entrusted to solve the case of a strangled woman. *Convicted* is the only "quota quickie" shot by Central Films still in circulation.

Lucky Fugitives (1935)

This is the story of well-known author who escapes from prison and causes no end of havoc. The author gets handcuffed to an unlucky woman and as the two of them become fugitives, an unintentional romance develops. The Crystal Gardens' pool becomes an ocean liner's swim tank and the fugitives jump from a train on the E & N Railway line near Langford.

HIGHER POWER

CJVI plays dreaded "oldies" today, but the city's first licenced radio station had very different origins. In 1922, the Reverend Dr. Clem Davies, a charismatic preacher from southern California, was appointed as the pastor of Centennial Methodist Church (now Centennial United) on Gorge Road. Davies knew the power religious radio stations had in the States, and he pushed his congregation to build one in the church basement — telling them one morning, "We are going to broadcast over our own radio station, and you are going to pay for it, thank you very much." The 500-watt station, CFCT ("Calling Friends of the Christian Temple"), went on the air just in time for Davies' 1923 Easter Sunday address, the first broadcast of a church service in western Canada. A year later, Davies split from the church (he later went back to the US); in 1926, CFCT went commercial, changed hands, and in the 1940s became CJVI — a training ground for broadcasters who later became national TV personalities, such as CHEK's Ida Clarkson and the CBC's Ted Reynolds.

Victoria plays London in this film (which was retitled *The Black Robe* in Victoria and Vancouver so as not to offend members of the Chinese community). The plot revolves around the efforts of the police to track down a group of opium smugglers operating in Victoria's Chinatown. Donegal Dawn, a private detective, is commissioned to assist the police and manages to enter the smuggler's hideouts at will. This is despite the fact that he's curiously disguised as a Hindu.

Crimson Paradise (1933)

Based on Alexander Philip's book, *The Crimson West*, the film starred and was bankrolled by Kathleen Humphreys (daughter of James Dunsmuir) and filmed at Craigdarroch Castle and Hatley Park. When it premiered at the Capitol Theatre in Victoria, theatre manager Ivan Akery had 20,000 promo leaflets dropped from an airplane that read "COME TO THE PREMIERE OF THE FIRST ALL CANADIAN TALKING PICTURE MADE IN VICTORIA." The opening was attended by Victoria's plutocracy, including then-premier T.D. Pattulo and mayor Victoria David Leeming. Ivan Akery, resident manager of the Capitol at the time, is reported to have said, "It was a real turkey. So lousy it was good." It ran for only three days after its premiere before moving to the Pantages Theatre in Vancouver for a week's run. The production company went bankrupt within two months.

WHALE MUSIC

The Taj Mahal, the Great Pyramid at Gizeh, Beijing's Temple of Heaven, the Garden City.... Okay, so Victoria isn't usually catalogued among the world's most profound spiritual centres. But in 1970, when New York-born jazz star Paul Horn discovered Transcendental Meditation in India and became disillusioned with the Hollywood music scene (where he swung with the likes of Miles Davis and Tony Bennett), the Grammy-winning flautist, saxophonist, and clarinetist chose Victoria (which he'd visited while on tour with Donovan) to make his spiritual retreat, eventually building a house stuccoed with 20,000 oyster shells. Widely acknowledged as the "godfather of New Age music," Horn recorded his *Inside* series in such sacred locales as the Taj Mahal, Gizeh, and Vilnius's Kazamierus Cathedral. Canadians know him best for his 1973 *Paul Horn Show* on CTV, but the meditative musician made his biggest splash locally when he brought his flute to Oak Bay's now-defunct Sealand and serenaded Haida, a killer whale in mourning for its mate, back to health.

great moments in media

Howie's Pyjama Party

Ebullient restaurateur Howie Siegel has done film reviews on CHEK TV and a phone-in show on CJVI, but his most famous foray into broadcasting was *The Pyjama Party*, a live, no-holds-barred chat show that ran Sunday nights on Rogers community TV in the early '80s. In one notorious episode, Howie got naked under the sheets on a waterbed with his wife Marion, a "sexual astrologer," a realtor, and Nikki Killer Snot (a lesbian "funster" into leather and piercing), and for a full half-hour they regaled Victorians with frank talk about sex and birth control, while Howie wielded a cucumber and quizzed Marion about which condoms she wanted him to wear. Deluged with complaints, Rogers cancelled the show soon afterward, claiming it had "run its course." If you want to see what the fuss was about, you can rent a video of the show from Pic-A-Flic *(382-3338)*.

Mayor v. Monday

Combative Victoria mayor Peter Pollen was one of the original investors in *Monday Magazine*, but that didn't deter him from suing the weekly for libel. In 1983, *Monday* ran a two-part series claiming, among other things, that Pollen had speculated in land and altered development contracts, told bare-faced lies about a restaurant-jetfoil proposal for the Inner Harbour, and "held women in scorn and contempt." The B.C. Supreme Court ordered *Monday* to pay the mayor $25,000. The magazine was "bent on producing a sensational story regardless of the facts," the judge said, but the damages were reduced because Pollen was "no stranger to discord and hostility, and so his reputation [did] not have as long a fall."

Gorde's Last Gaffe

Times Colonist typist Gorde Hunter was already the butt of jokes and angry letters for the factual errors and regurgitated right-wing invective in his "One Man's Opinion"

FANCIFUL FILM

Tragically, Victoria is not a movie town. Like the greasy golden topping that drowns their bland popcorn, most local silver screens persist in bringing in the worst that Hollywood has to offer. Independent films, foreign films, documentaries, great B-movie cheese — little of it crosses the water with any regularity, and those films that do rarely last more than a week. Hope, in the way of short-run alternate titles, is kept alive thanks to UVic's Cinecenta *(721-8365)*, The Vic *(383-1998)*, and occasionally, the Roxy CineGog *(382-3370)*, or catch free screenings at Movie Monday in the Eric Martin Pavillion at the Royal Jubilee Hospital (Eric Martin is the city's psychiatric ward, and many of the patrons of Movie Monday are the patients themselves) *(595-3542)*, or in the summer, at Starlight Cinema on the Ocean Pointe Resort terrace *(360-5914)*.

Hope also lingers on in the form of small, genre-specific film fests. Two such gold mines of quirky gems are the Victoria Independent Film and Video Festival *(February, 389-0444)* and the Antimatter Film Festival *(September, 385-3327)*. Both offer local and international indie filmmakers a chance to screen their work to receptive audiences at reasonable prices. Mini ethnic film fests are also a cure for Victoria's white-bread movie malaise; recent two- or three-day screenings have included Jewish, Francophone, and East Asian film festivals. Usually at the UVic campus, these mini-fests serve Victoria's often-invisible ethnic communities and complement Cinecenta's theme programs, which showcase the work of a given country (Iran, China, Cuba, Tibet, Germany) over a few days.

column, but in October of 1992, he outdid himself. A *T-C* editor yanked a Hunter column justifying Montreal police harassment of black residents (Hunter said black immigrants were "riff-raff" and "gangsters") and Hunter was so enraged that he reportedly threatened to "pop" the editor. Then, three weeks later, an economics "expert" from Montreal named Fred Aine sent Hunter a letter claiming that Quebec families had received $4,000 each in federal money; Hunter reprinted the letter verbatim without doing a simple fact-check, and it turned out the letter was a hoax (*fredaine* means "prank" in French). Hunter was cut loose from the paper a few months afterward.

News for Sale

Deciding what to cover on the TV news often involves hard decisions, but local station CHEK made it easy in 1997: if a business wanted coverage of their latest widget on the show *CHEK at Noon*, they'd have to pay for it, up to $500. CHEK's news director defended the practice by comparing it to "advertorials" in newspapers, even though the show was considered part of the channel's required weekly news content. As one UVic journalism prof observed: "It's not 'news' if you have to pay to get on it."

Shaw's Christmas Log

Over the 1999 Christmas holidays, Victoria's community TV channel suddenly ended up on the national news. Shaw 11 had temporarily replaced its programming with a cozy around-the-clock scene of a roaring fire, and as the holidays came to an end, "Save the Log" fans held a protest in front of the station, demanding that it keep the fire burning all year long. Alas, though the log was real, the demonstration wasn't: the protesters were Shaw employees and their friends. The station did get many phone calls in support, but that wasn't surprising – after all, a chunk of flaming wood has more snap and crackle than what's usually on community TV.

Secrets of the Atom

Certainly the most famous filmmaker to ever come out of the Garden City is Atom Egoyan, the cerebral writer and director of eight art-house features including *The Sweet Hereafter*, which was nominated for two Oscars (including best director), and won the Grand Prix at the Cannes Film Festival in 1997. Born in Cairo, Egoyan's artistic Armenian family (father Joe is a painter, mother Shushan is an interior designer, sister Eve is an accomplished pianist and composer) moved here when he was two. Young Atom worked as a houseboy at the Empress Hotel, and made his first film (an 8mm effort called *Lusts of an Eunuch*) while in high school at Mount Douglas. After graduating he moved east, and made films at the University of Toronto, where he studied international affairs and classical guitar; one of those films got broadcast on the CBC, kicking off his brilliant career.

Egoyan's life has certainly informed some of his art: his 1991 film *The Adjuster*, for example, was inspired by a chance meeting after a fire destroyed his mother's business (Ego Interiors, at 1028 Fort St. 382-3200). (The fire had been set by an arsonist who was angry about being alone for New Year's Eve.) So what are viewers to make of the kinky goings-on in his movies? Tough to say … Egoyan simply could be articulating the muffled passions of all Anglo-Canadians, or there may be something more personal involved. As he told one interviewer about *Exotica*, his 1993 film of murder, smuggling and voyeurism: "These are people who are doing things I would like to do sometimes." Egoyan lives in Toronto, but he's pondered returning here to work; he was hoping to shoot *Felicia's Journey* (1999) in Victoria, but author William Trevor insisted that the movie of his novel remain in England. Too bad, because Victoria would've perfectly captured the sense of disorientation that permeates Egoyan's films. "There is that sort of idea of a fake attachment to an England that doesn't really exist except in people's imagination," the director said recently of his home town. "The whole idea of an England that's created for tourist culture that has very little to do with what that city actually is about." Atom Egoyan knows: Victoria is a city of secrets.

SPREADING THE GOOD NEWS

"There are two world class things in Victoria," opined one local jazz buff, "Butchart Gardens and Louise Rose." Audiences can thank the good Lord that this sweet-sounding Rose fell in love with the Garden City and decided to transplant herself here. The woman who prefers to describe herself as a "music-maker" rather than confine her playing to any one genre, was born in Norristown, Pennsylvania, studied piano with Canadian jazz legend Oscar Peterson, and performed with Duke Ellington and other musical luminaries. While this ordained Baptist minister may have foregone the bright lights of a big-city jazz career when she settled into the Fairfield home she calls "Strawberry Roost", that hasn't kept her music from moving the masses: still a regular on the festival circuit, Rose hosted for several years *Let's Sing Again*, Vision TV's sing-a-long show, which 300,000 viewers crooned into every week (it continues in reruns), and leads the 200-strong Good News Choir, an all-ages, all-abilities community chorus always willing to throw open its songbook to new members (call 658-1946 for details).

bands on the run

Victoria boasts a colourful roster of homegrown bands, many of whom poke outrageous holes in Victoria's staid image – but not all of 'em (see below).

Candy

Marilyn Manson, what have you wrought? Onstage crucifixions and genital piercings, simulated abortions and axe-whackings, and more pigs' intestines than a Chicago abattoir – at their infrequent live shows, local shock rockers Candy offer a tour through all the sublevels of Hell that Dante couldn't stomach. Mistress of the dark Mishelle L'Amour will do just about anything to get a rise out of the most jaded audiences, while her leather-faced band backs up her stage frights with a soundtrack of ear-jarring industrial metal – not that anyone comes for the music.

The Dayglo Abortions

Victoria's godfathers of drunk punk mayhem staggered into national notoriety in 1988 when the daughter of a Nepean, Ontario police officer brought home a copy of their *Feed Us a Fetus* album. Obscenity charges were laid against the band (then later dropped), their record label, and their distributor. Two years later, an Ottawa jury delivered a precedent-setting "not guilty" verdict in favour of Fringe Product and Record Peddlar, but the court case soured the Dayglos' relationship with label owner/distributor Ben Hoffman and nearly bankrupted the band. A decade and several line-up changes later, the punk rock reprobates who penned such immortal ditties as "Argh Fuck Kill" and "Fuck My Shit Stinks" are still making music to shock the cops. Lost your copy of *Here Today, Guano Tomorrow?* Then call Abortions founder Jesus Bonehead at his new indie label, God Records (592-2839) – if only to hear the Dayglo drummer reply, "God Records, Jesus speaking."

ROYAL PERFORMERS

Some of the people who've performed at the Victoria's venerable Royal Theatre over the years: Will Rogers, Fred Allen, Jimmy Durante, John and Ethel Barrymore, Bing Crosby, Bob Hope, Charles Laughton, Katharine Hepburn, Paul Robeson, Sarah Bernhardt, Jascha Heifetz, Ignace Jan Paderewski, Mikhail Baryshnikov, Rudolph Nureyev, Vincent Price, Shirley MacLaine, Mitzi Gaynor, Robert Wagner, Jill St. John, Tom Jones, k.d. lang, Melissa Etheridge, Bryan Adams, Harry Belafonte, Bob Newhart, Bruno Gerussi, B.B. King, Liona Boyd, Little Richard, Stompin' Tom Connors, Ray Charles, Nana Mouskouri, Marcel Marceau, Reveen, Victor Borge, Rich Little, Honor ("Pussy Galore") Blackman.

Carolyn Mark

Victoria's first lady of country heartache, the inimitable Ms. Mark has played in more bands than most musicians have had hot meals – the Vinaigrettes, the Fixins, the Corn Sisters (with alt-country goddess Neko Case), the Roommates, and the Metronome Cowboys among them. Now she's making a name for herself all on her lonesome as Canada's *Party Girl* – the title of her Mint Records solo debut of lovin' and leavin' tunes. When she's not on tour, the woman otherwise known as Miss Kitty Trousers (who also performs in the raunchy sketch comedy duo Chicks in the Nabe) plays hostess-with-the-mostest for various hootenannys around town.

The Moffatts

Victoria's reply to the boy-band phenomenon, the Moffatt brothers (eldest Scott and triplets Clint, Robert and David) were cutesy kidlets who crooned country pop for tourists in the Inner Harbour until their dad dragged them to Nashville and transformed them from chipmunky cowpokes into angst-rock teenybop idols. Now the Moffatts sell countless CDs to junior high panty-tossers and doff their T-shirts for sultry *Tiger Beat* spreads. But a backlash is growing against the teen stars: anti-Moffatt websites have proliferated, including "The Mo-Fart Page" and another which notes that *mofeta* means "skunk" in Spanish.

THE BLUES BROTHER

If you're wandering up Government Street and suddenly hear a rollicking whoop-up of country blues, don't be too surprised when you discover it only takes one man to stir up all that joyous noise. Dave Harris, the bushy-haired granddaddy of local buskers, has been taking his music to the streets for over two decades, and can often be found with his kit – kick drum and hi-hat, guitars, fiddle, and rack-mounted harmonica – parked in front of Munro's Books or the entrance to Bastion Square. Stop for a listen and Victoria's most conspicuously talented multi-instrumentalist will be happy to sell you one of his CDs or tapes of blues standards and snappy originals, recorded as a one-man band or with such local outfits as Slim and the Dusters and Barrelhouse (who hold down a popular Monday night house gig at Swans pub).

Victoria's been home to many media personalities, but one of the best-loved was CFAX radio commentator Ken Dobson, a cigar-chomping character as loud and outrageous as his checkered sports jackets. "He was a rascal," says veteran broadcaster Barry Bowman, who remembers "The Dobber" for his raucous "Legion-hall laugh" and his on-air antics. One famous story: Soon after Dobson arrived in Victoria in 1976 from Montreal, Bowman asked him what he'd be doing on the Expos' opening day. "I'd be in the stands with my can of beer in one hand and my penis in the other!" exclaimed the Dobber, into a live microphone. He thought he'd said "peanuts," but everyone knew what they'd heard — including the Dobber's wife, who called the station a few minutes later and said, "Tell Kenny he hasn't got enough to hold in one hand!" Ken Dobson died of cancer in April of 1995, but he lives on in the memories of sports fans. Sidney's Sandown harness-racing track runs the Dobber Memorial Pace, an annual event, and the broadcast booth at Memorial Arena has a sign forever designating it as "Dobber's Den."

NoMeansNo

Photo: Courtesy of NoMeansNo

Wright brothers Rob and John (later joined by guitarist Tom Holliston) launched this seminal Canadian hardcore act from the Kitty Hawk of Victoria in 1981. Punk purists with an anti-marketing aesthetic, NoMeansNo refuse to make music videos, have recycled the same promo photo of drooling blindfolded members for over a decade, and play fast and loose with the band's biography to throw intrepid reporters off the scent. Despite their limelight-dodging, the forty-something trio have built a devoted following in North America and Europe for the allusive lyrics and noise-core sounds of recordings like *The Worldhood of the World (As Such)*, *Why Do They Call Me Mr. Happy?*, *Oh Canaduh!*, and *Dance of the Headless Bourgeoisie*. Now based in Vancouver, NoMeansNo occasionally drop their musical gloves and play Ramones-y odes to beer, girls, and hockey as their "puck rock" alter ego, The Hanson Brothers.

Velvet

We still don't know whether Velvet will be the biggest local act to ever — or to never — break. Led by satin-voiced, bullhorn-wielding *fashionista* Ohani Küba (aka Kamal Kudra), this self-described "organic collective" of DJs, musicians, and visual artists creates a fusion of semi-improvised soul/R&B/electronica and psychedelic eye candy every Sunday night at Steamers (570 Yates St.) — no two jams are ever the same. They've been courted by major labels eager to exploit their timely marriage of radio-friendly grooves and rave nation sensibilities. But so far Velvet have played coy, still waiting for the right moment to go for the gold. Catch one of their legendary live shows before they explode onto the world's biggest stages — or implode under the weight of great expectations.

Nightlife

For insomniacs, night-shifters, and assorted "life-of-the-party" types: bingo halls, glow bowling, and 24-hour eats.

Cocktail Chic

Victoria's got an abundance of pubs offering fish and chips on the menu and Canucks games on TV. Fortunately, there are also a few swellegant places where you can sip your Cosmopolitans in style.

Cook's Landing

This room at the Laurel Point Inn has everything a lounge lizard requires: candlelight, a waterfront view of the Inner Harbour, and a padded baby grand especially designed for slurred requests of "Ebb Tide." *680 Montreal St., 380-8721*

Herald Street Caffé's Lounge

A long, softly-lit room suited for romantic evenings, with access to the same kitchen as the fancy restaurant beside it. A good place for desserts and liqueurs. *546 Herald St., 381-1441*

Polo Lounge

In the Executive House Hotel, an executive's dream: a well-serviced bar, free hors d'oeuvres after 5, and a steak joint next door. For more private affairs, meet downstairs at Doubles, a dark and cozy place with discreet booths and a fireplace. *777 Douglas St., 381-5111*

Süze

A true European bistro, popular with the local *fashionistas*. Inexpensive food done with flair, and a crowded bar offering 18 types of martinis, rare single malts, and numerous wines by the glass. *515 Yates St., 383-2829*

Tommy Bahamas

The restaurant on the ground floor keeps changing, but the subterranean lounge remains the same: live jazz, a fireplace, and dark corners for nuzzling with your sweetie. *#128-560 Johnston St., 386-1140*

Vista 18

This bar and restaurant at the top of the Chateau Victoria hotel has the best bird's-eye view of town and beyond, from majestic Mount Baker to the east, and the Sooke Hills to the west. Open 6:30 a.m. to midnight, it's also a great place to watch the sun come up after a night of carousing. *749 Burdett St., 382-9258*

drink, drink, and be merry

The following is a subjective and varied list of places to imbibe your favourite potions in Victoria, the result of a week-long survey in the spring of 2000. Remember that bars are notorious for closing arbitrarily, so keep this in mind while you are making your way through the list: the names may change, but the addresses usually won't.

Bartholomew's Bar/ Rockefeller Grille

Two venues located in the basement of the Executive House. Pub-like interior with sports photos and snug booths. Live bands.
777 Douglas St., 388-5111

Bengal Lounge

Sit back with your scotch and recall the glory days of the Empire at this, the Empress Hotel's signature bar, outfitted with potted palms, deep leather chairs, and a Bengal tiger skin over the fireplace. (The original tiger was stolen by UVic students in 1985 and later turned up, worse for wear, on the steps of the *Times Colonist*; the current tiger was purchased in 1989 from a Colwood missionary who'd shot it in India.) John Wayne, who used come up for fishing trips, often held court in the Bengal when his minesweeper was tied up in the harbour.
721 Government St., 384-8111

Krazy for Karaoke

Yes, even in Victoria, you can lip-sync with the best of them.

Paul's Upstairs
Sing "Brown-Eyed Girl" with drunk college kids, or choose from the 92-page songbook.
1900 Douglas St., 382-9231

Topaz Lounge
An intimate setting where one can belt out "Solitary Man" to a restrained crowd.
2915 Douglas St., 385-6731

Glow Bowling

Bowling alleys always look better in the dark. But it's one of the few nightlife activities where you aren't safe dressing in black.

Mayfair Lanes

The glow starts at 9 pm Wednesday and Friday and is complemented by cosmic murals on the walls. Victoria's finest alley, with 40 lanes of ten pin bowling, ten pool tables, a licensed bar and the Lane 41 lunch counter.
760 Tolmie Ave., 386-3461

Miracle Lanes

Five-pin glow bowling during the day. On weekends it starts at 1 pm, on Fridays at 4 pm.
2375 Bevan Ave., 656-2431

Town and Country Lanes

The laser bowling starts at 10 pm Fridays, a half-hour earlier on Saturdays. Five pins and packed with 12 year-olds.
3493 Saanich Rd., 475-1400

Blues House

An older crowd especially for the rare live shows by touring blues legends. 80s night on Wednesdays still attracts a huge crowd ($2 drinks).
1417 Government St., 386-1717

Boom Boom Room

Zebra-striped tables, leopard skin stools, and a very young crowd. Male strippers shake it at the atavistic ladies' nights. Don't forget your ID.
1208 Wharf St., 381-2331

The Brick Yard

Pizza, beer, and bands on weekends in a space the size of a boxcar.
784 Yates St., 995-2722

Bourbon Street

Too much neon gives this lounge in the basement of the Ingraham Hotel an ersatz N'Orleans feel.
2915 Douglas St., 385-6731

Cabo: a Mexican Bar

Sol cerveza flags, plastic plants, chili pepper lights. You get the picture.
759 Yates St., 384-7494

Carleton Club

The sign outside says "Always looking good" but not so during the 18-day shoot of the movie *The Guardian*, when the club posed as a seedy biker bar. Esquimalt's top-40 party machine.
900 Carleton Tce., 361-3666

Evolution

What's the latest evolution of this club on the edge of town?
502 Discovery St., 388-3000

Hugo's

DJ booth a full storey above the dance floor with a young, professional crowd. Dark club, dark clothes, a fine kitchen, house-brewed beer, and mock-bullet holes in the frosted glass windows.
625 Courtney St., 920-4844

Hunter's Pub Grill and Tapas Bar

Tuck in your shirt, settle into the huge, padded booths, and pretend you're at Le Cirque 2000.
759 Yates St., 384-7494

Hush

Collegiate crowd. A far cry from the gay Rumours at its zenith.
1325 Government St., 385-0556

Icehouse

The bar behind the Horizon West Hotel brings a wild mix of live acts, from fetish shows with porn star Ron Jeremy to indie rockers like the Supersuckers and Murder City Devils. Lots of mirrors in this strip club by day.
1961 Douglas St., 382-5853

Ingy Pub

A huge sports bar with terrycloth table-covers and shuffleboard. In the enviable position of serving the most Labatt's Blue draft in the world.
2915 Douglas St., 385-6731

Liquid

A DJ booth and dance floor replace the stage that once was home of the legendary Harpos, and paraded Victoria's best indie rock. Now a big beat nightclub crowded with tight, shiny shirts.
15 Bastion Square, 385-2626

Something's Brewing

Brew pubs are a local specialty: quaff a made-in-Victoria brew and pick your favourite.

Harbour Canoe Club
Claims to be Canada's only full-service marine brew pub, with a huge patio. The fancy décor attracts a business crowd and there's a Russian sub parked out front.
Number of Different Beers: 5
Biggest Sellers: Pale Ale, Davey Jones Locker, Springbok
450 Swift St., 361-1940

Spinnakers
Opened in 1984 as Canada's first in-house brew pub. Located on the edge of Lime Bay with a view of the Parliament Buildings, this is a real neighbourhood pub, with mugs behind the bar for regular customers.
Number of Different Beers: varies according to time of year, but usually 10
Biggest Sellers: Dunkleweizen, India Pale Ale, Extra Special Bitter, Spinnakers Ale
308 Catherine St., 384-6613

Mr. B's

Located in the quirky Cherry Bank Hotel, Victoria's best spot for off-track betting is in the Race Place where satellite TVs bring in the horse races from Melbourne and Hong Kong. Built when burgundy was the pervading aesthetic. *825 Burdett Ave., 389-9941*

Neptune Sound Bar

An electronic music venue for the serious connoisseur. There's a small dance floor, and it's too loud to talk. Instead, plant yourself on a chill-out couch and pretend you're in a jazz club. *1601 Store St., 388-5758*

The One Lounge

The soon-to-be hip set has a new, freshly renovated place to dwell. The pool table is just about the only holdover from the joint's concrete days as The Limit; now sensual red neon presides over deep blue walls, hardwood dance floors and cool electronic beats. *1318 Broad St., 384-3557*

Steamers

Once a strip bar, now filled with the sneaker-and-baseball-cap crowd. Pool tables, cigarette-scarred counters, and one of the few places in town that still has a rotation of live bands. Velvet, a collective of DJs, musicians, and artists plays every Sunday. *570 Yates St., 381-4340*

Swans

Developer Michael Williams turned this former feed warehouse into a fine brew pub with flower-filled patio and window boxes, a handmade bar, and walls filled with very expensive and truly unique Canadian art. Check out the stylized totem pole in the restaurant lobby. *Number of Different Beers:* 11 (8 core, 3 rotating) *Biggest Sellers:* Arctic Ale, Brown Ale *506 Pandora Ave., 361-3310*

Strathcona Hotel

Billed as a "complete entertainment centre," the Strathcona is a drinker's paradise, with access to seven drinking establishments in one building. Big Bad John's (see photo), the hillbilly bar, dates from 1962, decorated with bras hanging from the ceiling and peanut shells covering the floor. The Cuckoo's Nest is one of the few places in the city to dance to canned music with no cover charge. The music is radio top-40 and the DJs are old school, but the price can't be beat. The Sticky Wicket has a bar from a 19th-century trans-Atlantic ocean liner owner John Olson found in Belfast. The Games Room attracts a shockingly young crowd for pool and beer; the opposite of the Maple Room upstairs. Legends nightclub in the basement was a bowling alley years ago and is really the only downtown venue for larger acts. Permanent vinyl sign outside says, "Welcome US Navy." They also have what they claim is the world's only roof-top beach volleyball court.
919 Douglas St., 383-7137

CAFÉ PHILOSOPHY

Is God dead, or is he just nodding off in an Oak Bay retirement home? That's one of the subjects that could come up at this provocative salon, held every Wednesday in the civilized, caffeinated setting of Torrefazione Italia *(1234 Government St.)*. Michel Picard, who did his Ph.D. in philosophy at MIT, directs the proceedings, dealing with such big themes as Meaning, Sustainability, Wisdom, and Evil. The evenings start with a 6:30 "food for thought" session of small table coversations over Italian pastries and panini, and then evolve into an open-room discussion ($4 cover) at 7:30. For further enlightenment, call *385-4646*.

Sugar

Notwithstanding the present incarnation, one of the best nightclub spaces in the city, with huge disco balls, an iconic DJ booth, and a long flight of stairs for stumbling down at 2:30 in the morning.
858 Yates St., 920-9950

Sweetwaters

Stuck in the 1980s, this paean to neon will take you back to 1989. So throw on a slip dress and mouth the words to "It Takes Two."
27-560 Johnson St., 383-7844

Thursdays

An intimate setting for live music and home to an insurgent country-folk scene.
1821 Cook St., 760-2711

Yukon Jack's

Located in the Douglas Hotel, this venerable watering hole (c. 1912) is all brass and wood and triviaoke. More serious drinking occurs around the corner at the Douglas Pub, the toughest bar downtown.
1450 Douglas St., 383-4157

ALONG FOR THE RIDE

One of the best views onto Victoria's nightlife is a tour with the police in the Ride Along program. Although much of the evening consists of answering noise complaints, ferrying drunks to the tank, and taking other disturbed types to Eric Martin, they really get busy after 2 am when the bars close and the fights start. In fact, police usually do a "knob patrol" early in the evening and identify potential troublemakers (revealed by a hunched back and furrowed brow). They also visit notorious party houses on a regular basis (the apartment block at Bay Street and Esquimalt Road for one), and, of course, the night isn't complete without a stop at Smitty's. But unfortunately, since the advent of *COPS*, everyone wants to ride in a police car, and the Ride Along program is now restricted to doctors, social workers, and other people seen as resources to the police.

neighbourhood pubs

With its like-the-English pedigree, it's not surprising that Victoria has more than its share of neighbourhood pubs.

Bird of Paradise

Located in a 1914 Royal Oak farmhouse, but there's no oak or brass. Santa Fe style rather, with terra cotta walls and hand-painted ceramics.
4291 Glanford Ave., 727-6466

Christie's Carriage House

Built in 1898 by Elbridge Christie, local carriage-maker, this house was long known as Sandolphon. Opened as a pub in 1986. One of the two carriages out front is a 1905 Rockaway Coupe.
1739 Fort St., 598-5333

Four-Mile House

The fourth-oldest building still standing in the city, dating from 1858. Jake is the resident ghost, and often spotted in the dining room, but he disappears before servers can take his order. *199 Island Hwy., 479-3346*

Garrick's Head

The original Garrick's Head opened in 1867, selling whiskey to men condemned to death in the old courthouse across the way. Now it's a neighbourhood pub in the core of the city. *69 Bastion Sq., 384-6835*

Loghouse

Built in 1988 entirely of logs stripped of their bark with power hoses to avoid scarring.
2323 Millstream Rd., 474-1989

Ma Miller's Goldstream Inn

In the 1930s and early 1940s, Mary Miller kept miners, loggers, and working-class drinkers in line. Twenty years later she died, and the pub was named after her. *2903 Sooke Lake Rd., 478-3512*

Bingo Dreams

Bingo Bingo
Smell the smoke from the parking lot. See the dauber-pocked tables through yellowing blinds. Sit on the orange plastic chairs. Listen to the distracted caller. But don't follow the advice on the cafe's whiteboard: "Try our Deep Fried Foods."
820 Esquimalt Rd., 381-4499

Seven Eleven Bingo Emporium
A huge heated smoking tent out back, and on Saturday night the caller sometimes wears a metallic silver shirt. It doesn't really liven up the party.
713 Johnson St., 381-0711

Victoria Bingo Palace
This is the mother of all Victoria bingo parlors.
3400 Tillicum Rd., 384-8770

Maude Hunter's

Opened in 1986, the original Maude Hunter's was a turn-of-the-century corner store and gathering place for the neighbourhood. Ironically, the original Maude was a fierce prohibitionist. *3810 Shelbourne St., 721-2337*

Monkey Tree

Also in the class of 1986, at the top of the hill next to the Monkey Puzzle Tree. Patrons include sports teams, students, and the rest of us.
4025 Borden St., 727-3550

Prairie Inn

Opened as a hotel in 1893, this joint has been a store, rooming house, café, and a pub for the last 25 years. *7806 East Saanich Rd., 652-1575*

Seventeen-Mile House

The name refers to the distance along the old stagecoach route out to Sooke. "Ma" Wilson ran the pub for 30 years starting in 1940. A firm supporter of family values, she would reportedly shut down during the supper hour, and allowed family men a maximum of only two beers. *5126 Sooke Rd., 642-5942*

Six-Mile House

The province's longest-running pub license. Some of the tables have life-sized, five-globed lamp standards arising from the centre. *494 Island Hwy., 478-3121*

Stonehouse

Located around the corner from the Swartz Bay ferry terminal, this Tudor-style home was built in the 1930s by boat builder Hugh Rodd with such features as leaded windows. It's also got some excellent food.
2215 Canoe Cove, Sidney, 656-3498

late night nibbles

The clubs have closed, and you've got the munchies. Where to go?

Café de la Lune

This café is part of the Douglas Hotel entertainment complex. Choose the loft upstairs unless you like dealing with weird late-night traffic.
1450 Douglas St., 361-1450

Denny's

While ubiquitious throughout North America, this is the only Denny's outlet on Vancouver Island, believe it or not.
3100 Douglas St., 382-3844

QV Bakery and Café

This one-time gas station outside the gates of Chinatown is a favourite during the summer, thanks to its large outdoor patio.
1701 Government St., 384-8831

WHERE THERE'S SMOKE

Smoking is verboten in Victoria — at least, it is on paper, if not in practice. At the beginning of 1999, a new bylaw came into force making it illegal to combust the foul-smelling weed in any bar or restaurant in the capital region, and over the course of that year bylaw officers slapped $100 and $50 fines on 208 establishments and individual patrons in the city, despite occasional drunken threats of violence. (Twenty smokers disputed the tickets, but all of them ended up getting convicted — including the wit who asked the judge, "How did you know it was tobacco?") Now many Victoria smokers dutifully head for the exits whenever they feel the urge.

But indoor smoking is tough to snuff out. The Capital Health Region has used up all the heart and lung association cash it got to enforce the bylaw, and though it still comes down hard on a few openly defiant establishments like the country-fried Esquimalt Inn and its happy "freedom fighters" (see photo), it's still possible to sneak a few puffs in many Victoria bars. When downtown or in Saanich, where most of the anti-smoking zealots live, discreetly ask for a saucer or a "mint dish" and head for a darkened corner. Things are more relaxed out in Victoria's blue-collar districts: In certain pubs in Sooke or Langford, you can tug on your Export A's till the fire alarms go off and still not raise the bartenders' eyebrows.

The Ins and Outs of "Escorts"

Just as they did a century ago, Victorians like to believe that their sons are decent, upstanding gentlemen who only engage in conjugal relations with women they intend to marry — or at least take out for pizza and a six-pack. But as the ads in the back of *Monday Magazine* prove, even that degree of commitment is more than some men have in mind.

There are four agencies in town (three of them owned by women) that arrange sessions between sex-trade workers and their paying clients, and a number of self-employed working boys and girls. Most are based in Saanich (except for a few who advertise that they're "only five minutes from the legislature!") because escort agency business licences are only $65 there, compared to $1,500 in the City of Victoria. But even though they're tax-paying businesses, many are located in houses and apartments — apparently our municipalities are not so tolerant that they'll let escorts rent commercial spaces.

Who's their clientele? Escorts say their business increases during the summer tourist months and whenever a U.S. warship's in town, but during the rest of the year it's a mix: students, lawyers, bus drivers, Viagra-popping senior citizens, journalists, salesmen, and not a few politicians. And the ads in *Monday* help, as much as some readers hate them: as working girls and common sense will tell you, it's safer doing business in a bordello than it is walking the street.

Notoriety

by Ross Crockford

"That's the thing about polite English society – behind closed doors there's always a lot of *spanking* going on." – film director John Waters, offering an explanation for Victoria's scandalous history

John Waters' mom grew up in Victoria. Sure, we are amused. But are we surprised? Victoria's always been home to oddballs. After all, the founder of the *Daily Colonist* newspaper and the second premier of our province was a guy named Amor de Cosmos, "Lover of the Universe" (see photo). So if you're a substance-abusing movie star, a tax-dodging preacher, or a slimy sea monster, Welcome! You've come to the right place.

Photo: Courtesy BC Archives C06116

Crime by the Numbers

Sleepy? Forget it. Victoria has the highest per capita crime rate in British Columbia: 232 Criminal Code offences per year for every 1,000 residents, compared to Vancouver's 146 and a provincial average of 122. The cops blame it on geography. Only 75,000 people live in Victoria proper, but another 29,000 come into town every day from surrounding municipalities to work, and even more arrive with the tourists on weekends to get loaded in the downtown bars. That's why Victoria topped the capital region in 1999 when it came to per capita rates for assault, robbery, break and enter, theft, and vandalism. But other municipalities are more prone to particular types of crimes that are arguably in keeping with their character....

Homicide: Langford and Saanich (tie). If you lived in a sprawling suburb where there was nothing to do but watch Shaw Cable all day, you'd probably want to kill someone, too.

Sexual offences: Esquimalt. Home to the biggest naval base in western Canada. What more do you need to know?

Offensive weapons: Esquimalt. Again, blame the military. Handle guns all day, and you're bound to take some of your work home with you.

The Bank, The Thief, His Wife, and His Novel

Robbing banks is as addictive as heroin – just ask writer Stephen Reid. On June 9, 1999, addled from a two-week binge on booze and smack, Reid walked into the Royal Bank in the Cook Street Village wearing a fake Mountie uniform and brandishing a shotgun. He threatened the staff and the customers, bundled $92,924 into a duffel bag, and ran to a waiting sedan. After a wild chase and shoot-out with a motorcycle cop in Beacon Hill Park, Reid and the driver abandoned the cash and the car in James Bay and fled on foot. Reid ran into an apartment building, and holed up in the suite of an elderly couple for several hours before the police stormed in and found him passed out behind a sofa bed.

It was a humiliating downfall. In the 1970s, Reid was a member of the notorious Stopwatch Gang – so named because he wore a stopwatch to make sure their heists took no more than two minutes – and ended up on the FBI's most wanted list for stealing more than $15 million from over 100 banks across the U.S. and Canada. But Reid's creativity extended beyond crime: While serving a 14-year sentence in Ontario, he wrote a novel called *Jackrabbit Parole*. His editor was B.C. poet Susan Musgrave (see photo with Reid), and through their mutual love of words, they fell in love. They got married in 1986, the same year

Famous Haunts

With its stone houses and oak trees, Victoria looks like a place that would be home to many ghost stories, and indeed it is. Many of these tales you can hear on tours run by John Adams (Ghostly Walks, 384-6698) or the Old Cemeteries Society (598-8870), but these ones are Victoria's most famous.

Tod House

At 2564 Heron Street, a quiet lane in Oak Bay, sits Tod House, one of the oldest continually occupied homes in western Canada. Not all of its occupants have been alive, however. In 1944, a retired colonel and his wife purchased the house, and soon discovered that a benign but tempermental spirit had taken up residence with them. A door leading from the kitchen to a cellar would not stay shut, even after it was carefully latched, and objects suspended from hooks in the kitchen began rocking on their own. One Christmas morning, the colonel found all the decorations had been pulled off the walls and the tree and placed in a neat pile on the living room floor. On another night, two young airmen who'd stayed over fled from an upstairs room, claiming they'd seen a Native woman in chains, pleading for help.

That story led some people to wonder if the ghost had been a victim of the house's first owner — a mystery that deepened in 1947, when the colonel was digging beside the house and came upon the remains of a headless skeleton. The house had been built in 1851 by John Tod (see photo), one of first retirees from Hudson's Bay Company, who'd served the HBC for more than 37 years. He was famous for his explosive temper: one story had it that he'd saved Fort Kamloops from marauding Indians by holding a lit match over a keg of gunpowder, and threatening to blow up the fort and them with it. He'd also had at least five wives, and several of them had been Natives. Tests proved that the bones belonged to an Asian or Native woman. Had she been a victim of Tod's fury? No one ever found out. After the remains were removed, the ghost disappeared and never returned. (P.S. People still reside in the Tod House, so don't go poking around. Unless you want to become its next ghost, that is.)

Reid's novel was published to critical acclaim. When Reid was paroled in 1987, he and Musgrave moved to Vancouver Island. Reid became a dedicated father and dabbled in teaching and acting, but he never caught the same literary fire he'd had in jail. So while building a new house for his family in 1998 he started messing with dope again (he'd been an addict as a teenager), commencing the downward spiral that ended with his desperate Cook Street robbery.

Reid pleaded guilty to armed robbery and attempted murder. Many of Victoria's poets testified in defence of his character, but it didn't make much difference to the sentence: Reid got 18 years. He seems to be recovering, though. He's writing again, and his work often appears in Canada's national newspapers.

Reid's Getaway Route

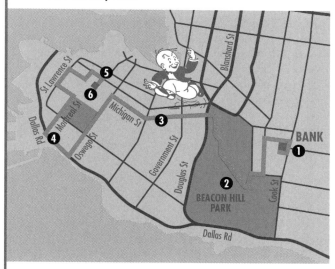

1. Reid and an accomplice rob the Royal Bank at 304 Cook Street at 9:40 am.
2. Fleeing in an old sedan through Beacon Hill Park, Reid fires a shotgun at a pursuing motorcycle cop, forcing passers-by to dive for cover.
3. Flagrantly ignoring several traffic control devices, Reid and company careen through James Bay and head for the beach.
4. Angry that they can't stop for carrot cake at the Ogden Point Café, the robbers fire again at police.
5. The suspects abandon their car (and the cash) and run, shooting at the police. The officers return fire — the first time that's happened in Victoria in two decades. The driver is arrested.
6. Reid flees across a yard and into an apartment building at 235 Michigan. Police raid a second-floor suite and arrest him at 3:45 pm.

No Justice for Molly

On the night of January 18, 1943, 15-year-old Molly Justice stepped off a city bus and started walking toward Swan Lake. Skaters were playing on the ice, but the city had dimmed the streetlights out of fear of a Japanese attack. No one saw what happened. A few hours later, Molly was found in some snow-covered bushes, stabbed to death with a pen knife. The public was horrified.

A city-wide manhunt began. The crime became an international incident when Victoria's mayor blamed it on the nightly dim-out, which B.C.'s premier had ordered at the request of the U.S. Army. In February, detectives found a pair of men's gloves near the crime scene, and went to the trouble of tracking down the owners of 96 similar pairs that had been sold in Victoria that winter. But the big break in the case came in May, when police arrested Frank Hulbert, a 15-year-old delinquent who'd assaulted a girl near Swan Lake and threatened that she'd "get the same as Molly Justice." Hulbert denied he'd had anything to do with the murder. He said he knew who did it, though. The cops arrested a 50-year-old logger, but later ended up dropping the charges for lack of evidence. The case remained unsolved for over 50 years.

Then in July of 1996, detectives announced that they'd cracked it. Hulbert was guilty, they said. In fact, documents indicated that he'd confessed to the killing, but his stepfather — B.C.'s deputy attorney-general at the time — had declared the documents "confidential" and thwarted the prosecution. A retired judge appointed to investigate the claims concluded that there was no evidence of a cover-up. Maybe, but that still didn't answer the big question. Did Hulbert do it? We'll never know. Hulbert died with his secret in Port Alberni in March of 1996, just a few months before the detectives announced that he was the murderer.

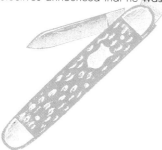

Phantom of the Links

Every spring at dusk, local students make a pilgrimage to the seventh fairway of the Victoria Golf Course to look for one of the most frequently sighted ghosts in North America. Doris Gravlin, a young nurse, was senselessly murdered there by her estranged husband (a sports editor at a local newspaper) in 1936, and ever since the 1940s people have claimed to see her apparition, sometimes wearing a white dress or just as a floating ball of light, gliding over the bushes and along the shoreline. One of the most detailed accounts was given by a pack of high school students who said they saw Doris's ghost on two consecutive nights in April of 1968, which gave rise to several local folktales. One says that the ghost will come out if you ring a bell on the night of a full moon; another says the spirit is seen only by young couples. But don't go with your true love: the tale also says that couples seeing the ghost will never marry.

Point Ellice House

Likely the most haunted home in Victoria, the Point Ellice House still seems to be occupied by several long-dead members of the O'Reilly clan that built the house in 1865 and owned it for over a century. Strange events have been reported in the house as recently as 1999, but one of the most unusual occurred soon after it opened as a museum in 1967. A mysterious woman in an old-fashioned blue dress gave a visiting family a tour of the place, and then vanished. The family ran into a guide and inquired about who the woman was, but the guide said no one else was in the house at the time. They checked around, and in one room they found the blue dress laying on a bed – a dress worn by Kathleen O'Reilly, who had died in 1945.

St. Ann's Academy

When plans were drawn up in the early 1990s to turn the gorgeous cloister into a shopping mall, stories started to circulate that on certain nights at dusk, the face of painter Emily Carr would appear in the cupola atop the building. (When asked how they knew it was Carr, witnesses said it was because they saw her pet monkey Woo sitting on her shoulder.) Many took this as a sign that Carr wanted St. Ann's to be protected. It eventually was, and today St. Ann's is home to government offices. Carr, by the way, is probably the most pervasive ghost in the city: she's also been spotted in Beacon Hill Park, at her house on Government Street, and at the James Bay Inn, where she died.

Goodbye, Sailor

Homosexuality was still a crime in Canada in the 1950s – and in one famous case in Victoria, it was a crime that carried the penalty of death. On September 6, 1958, the men in Cabin 150 of Esquimalt's HMCS Naden naval base awoke to horrible screams. When they turned on the lights, 23-year-old Able Seaman Bud Jenkins was dead at their feet. His throat had been cut, and a bloodied knife was on the ground beside him. The navy doctor said it was suicide. But in Jenkins' locker, detectives found religious books, a pair of women's earrings, and postcards signed by Leo Mantha (see photo), 30, a former navy officer living in James Bay. When confronted by the detectives, Mantha confessed he'd fallen in love with Jenkins, but after a few torrid months together, Jenkins dumped him, called him a "sucker" and announced that he was going to get married. The next night, Mantha consumed a twenty-sixer of rye, sneaked onto the base, and killed Jenkins in his bunk.

At the trial, Mantha's lawyer argued that his client had committed a crime of passion, and got a psychiatrist to testify that the devoutly religious Mantha suffered from "Kemp's disease," a mental disturbance caused by the repression of desire. Unimpressed, the judge convicted Mantha of first-degree murder and sentenced him to death. The Roman Catholic Church and even members of Jenkins' family lobbied the federal government to spare Mantha's life. They had reason to hope: Prime Minister John Diefenbaker had spared the lives of 21 convicted killers since he'd been elected in 1957. In fact, four days before Mantha was scheduled to die, the feds commuted the death sentence of a B.C. farm boy who'd shot his own brother. But Mantha got no such reprieve. The Navy's image had been sullied, and Mantha was expendable. On April 27, 1959, he was hanged in Burnaby's Oakalla prison. Leo Mantha was the last person to be executed for a crime in British Columbia.

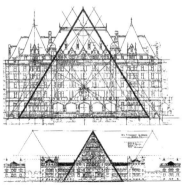

Francis Mawson Rattenbury, the designer of the Empress Hotel and the legislative buildings, is Victoria's most celebrated architect. He's also its most famous murder victim. At a glamorous dinner at the Empress in 1923, Rattenbury met Alma Packenham, a beautiful young flapper. A brilliant but cruel man, he started flaunting her around town, much to the torment of his wife, who eventually sued him for divorce in 1925. There were more scandalous rumours, including one that Alma had gotten Ratz hooked on cocaine. So they fled to England in 1929, and holed up in a villa in Bournemouth. Rattenbury became besotted by drink, demoralized by impotence, and impoverished by failed land deals. Alma started sleeping with their 18-year-old chauffeur. When the chauffeur believed that Alma and Rattenbury were reconciling, he became enraged – and on March 24, 1935, bludgeoned the architect to death with a mallet.

That's the official version. But Chris Trenholm, a Victoria stone mason, has another theory. He notes that the design of the Empress Hotel forms a perfect equilateral triangle, and that the path in front of the legislature to the statue of Queen Victoria follows in a direct line to Mount Douglas. These prove, Trenholm says, that Rattenbury adhered to principles of "sacred geometry" to tap into a higher cosmic order – the same order followed by the mysterious society of men known as the Freemasons. Rattenbury was a Mason from 1893 to 1898, when he was suspended for failure to pay his membership dues. Did he reveal the society's great secrets? Did he monkey with the cosmos? We don't know, but Trenholm says Rattenbury was killed in a manner suspiciously like the Freemasons' initiation ceremony, in which the apprentice is knocked on the head and then falls back into the arms of his comrades. Is there a connection? The Masons won't say.

Shelbourne Street

The late occultist Robin Skelton said that on Sundays in October between two and three am, Shelbourne (just south of Hillside) reverts to what it was nearly a century ago: a gravel road with grass growing down the middle, fringed by trees and bushes instead of houses and shops. Skelton ascribed this to an "energy memory" of the old street, which apparently is so strong that it continues to appear. The pints at Maude Hunter's Pub, a few blocks further south, have got nothing to do with it.

Among the Stars

Every city can lay claim to having family connections in Tinseltown. These are some of ours.

David Foster

This songwriter and Grammy-winning producer put together some of the biggest records of the 1980s and '90s for Lionel Richie, Neil Diamond, Kenny Rogers, Barbara Streisand, Whitney Houston, and Celine Dion, proving that no one knows their cheese like a Canadian. Foster still returns to his home town every year to host a celebrity-studded benefit show (and occasional softball game) to raise money for his foundation for children in need of organ transplants.

Here Caddy, Caddy, Caddy

"Men really need sea-monsters in their personal oceans ... An ocean without its unnamed monsters would be like a completely dreamless sleep." – John Steinbeck

Not many aspects of Native mythology have become part of modern pop culture, but one legend that certainly has is the belief that a sea monster lurks around Victoria. Over the past century, hundreds of people have claimed to have seen a creature with a head like a horse, a mane of seaweed, and a body like a snake, slithering through our waters.

The first recorded observation of this creature occurred in 1881, when a 12-year-old boy claimed he fired a slingshot at it from a canoe off William Head. But sightings of it really didn't take off until 1933, when the first reports came in of a similar monster in Scotland's Loch Ness. On October 1st of that year, a lawyer and an employee of the provincial archives were out rowing near Chatham Island when they saw the monster, "nearly 80 feet long and just about as wide as the average automobile." The *Victoria Daily Times* ran their story on the front page, and within a few days more reports came in, including one that the creature had been seen in Cadboro Bay a week earlier. That led a cheeky letter writer to suggest that it should be called Cadborosaurus: "Besides, the name is euphonious, and, if too long, can be shortened to 'Caddy' as a pet name, especially for the lucky ones who see him from the nineteenth hole at [the] Oak Bay [golf course]."

The new monster excited world-wide interest, and delighted Victoria's chamber of commerce. The sightings grew in number and in detail, from places all along the Straits of Georgia and Juan de Fuca, and from as far away as California and Alaska. The reports dropped off in the '60s and '70s, when Caddy mainly became a subject of photo-contest hoaxes. But the sea monster seems to be resurfacing. In August 1999, the *Times Colonist* reported that Caddy was seen by a family in Mill Bay, and over the past two years a team of "cryptozoologists" have been setting up video cameras at strategic points along Victoria's coastline to try and capture pictures of the elusive beast.

Marlene Dietrich called her "the most immoral woman who ever lived," but actress Tallulah Bankhead (1903-1968) found a home away from home in quaint Victoria. The chain-smoking, hard-drinking, "ambisextrous" (her word) daughter of a powerful Alabama family (her father was the speaker of the U.S. House of Representatives from 1936 to 1940), Tallulah stormed the London stage in the 1920s, and later American movie screens in such films as Alfred Hitchcock's *Lifeboat* (1940). While in London, she won the attention of Dola Dunsmuir, the shy youngest daughter of Victoria coal baron James Dunsmuir. Dola frequently travelled to London to see Tallulah perform, and their friendship continued right up until Dola died in 1966. Whenever Tallulah visited Victoria, she would stay at Dolura, the home Dola had built on the edge of Hatley Park (now home to Royal Roads University). During World War II, the two women hosted extraordinary booze-fueled events for officers from the Esquimalt naval base, and even into the 1960s the pair threw marathon dinner parties and hosted bridge tournaments for prominent figures from Victoria's arts community. After both women died, Dolura fell into disrepair; the house was demolished in 1997.

Many people speculated that Dola and Tallulah carried on a lesbian relationship, something neither of them directly denied. (Tallulah said, "I know what people say, but I've never seen Dola in a slip." For her part, Dola remarked to a friend: "In our way, you know, we really love each other.") That wouldn't have been the most scandalous chapter of the actress's sexual history, however: recently the British intelligence agency MI5 revealed that it tried to get Tallulah thrown out of Britain in 1932 because she had indulged in "indecent and unnatural practices" with several Eton schoolboys.

Meg and Jennifer Tilly

Perhaps most famous for wrapping herself around William Hurt in *The Big Chill* in 1983, Victoria-raised Meg Tilly went on to be nominated for an Oscar for her role as a tormented nun in 1985's *Agnes of God*. (Perhaps overly confident, she also turned down roles as Mozart's wife in *Amadeus* and the lead in *Flashdance*.) Meg and her film-exec husband now own a waterfront mansion in the Uplands. Her younger sister Jennifer is still on the silver screen: she was nominated for an Oscar in Woody Allen's *Bullets Over Broadway*, and played the mate of a murderous doll in 1998's *Bride of Chucky*.

Pamela Anderson

She's not really from Victoria, but the star of the world's most famous home movie grew up just over the Malahat in Ladysmith. She still shows up in town from time to time to visit her folks.

THE RIPPER'S WEST COAST TOUR

On September 29, 1899, Agnes Bing closed her bakery on Store Street and walked home across the Johnson Street bridge. The next day, her naked body was found near the tracks of the E&N Railway. She'd been strangled to death, and her purse and her rings were gone. But the most appalling detail was that the killer had disembowelled her corpse, and spread her entrails in a circle around the crime scene. Panic ensued. Blame was put on the Songhees natives who lived nearby, then on escaped mental patients. But no killer could be found. The police chief resigned in disgrace a few months later.

The case is still unsolved. That may have been because the killer was too experienced to get caught. Some local historians have noted that his gruesome *modus operandi* was much like that of Jack the Ripper, who had been at large in England a decade earlier. (Several people affiliated with a prime suspect in the Ripper case also turned up in Seattle in the late 1890s, during the Klondike gold rush.) The suggestion that the killer was a tourist was reinforced when the police hired a psychic to find the culprit's trail. The psychic reportedly led the officers down to the pier where the ferries to Seattle boarded — and told them, "The trail ends here."

King of the Boondoggles

Maybe it's our heritage as a frontier town or our population of trusting seniors, but Victorians have always seemed more susceptible than most to the charms of snake-oil salesmen. (And women: police are currently investigating several local tea-party societies which purport to "empower" ladies by giving them $40,000 if they invest $5,000 and find new paying members. Can you say "pyramid scheme"?) Perhaps the most grandiose con artist of them all was a German businessman and former used Mercedes dealer named Frank Hertel (see photo), who blew into town in 1984 boasting that he would turn Vancouver Island into a high-tech centre, thanks to his fantastic plans to triple the output of oil wells and generate thermal power from water. Hertel's International Electronics Corporation took over a monumental downtown office building (see photo below), and he was feted by every politician in town and named "Citizen of the Year" by Victoria's Chamber of Commerce. But less than two years later, after his complex network of research investment-credit deals collapsed, Hertel disappeared — only to resurface in Venezuela, beyond the reach of pending charges of tax evasion.

The Fight of Her Life

Many courageous people have lived in and around Victoria, and probably the most famous of them is Sue Rodriguez. In the late 1980s, Rodriguez was diagnosed with amyotrophic lateral sclerosis, an always-fatal illness (also known as Lou Gehrig's disease) that robs every muscle of the ability to move. Instead of suffering a slow death connected to respirators and feeding tubes, Rodriguez wanted a doctor to help her kill herself. But assisted suicide was illegal, and in 1993 she went all the way to the Supreme Court of Canada to fight the law. The nine judges ruled 5-4 against her, reasoning that the constitutional right to life and liberty doesn't include the right to choose how and when to die. "It has been worth it," she told reporters. "I'm pleased that people are looking at this and thinking about the issue." Five months later, on February 12, 1994, she died at her home in Sidney at the age of 43. Svend Robinson, a member of parliament who championed her cause, said he was with Rodriguez when she died, and that a doctor had helped her. To this day, he refuses to give any more details.

Exit Strategy

Unfortunately, Sue Rodriguez's fight to change the euthanasia laws wasn't entirely conducted with dignity. In March of 1993, John Hofsess, the executive director of the Victoria-based Right To Die Society of Canada, held an unauthorized press conference announcing that Rodriguez would die publicly with the society's assistance. Angry and embarrassed, Rodriguez left the organization, but Hofsess didn't give up: in newsletters and on the Internet, he ghoulishly documented and took credit for Rodriguez's legal battle, even after she'd died. Hofsess has been laying low lately, but in November 1999 he reappeared at a euthanasia conference in Seattle to show off the "DeBreather," a device he helped develop which he claimed had already been used by 10 people in the U.S. to kill themselves.

Just Passing Through

Victoria's always been a tourist town, but some tourists leave a bigger impression than others.

John L. Sullivan

Back in the days when Victoria was a gold rush boom-town, the famed bare-knuckle prizefighter would often stop here for exhibitions. According to one account, the Irishman shocked the locals at a dinner by refusing to toast to the health of the Queen. But the incident he's best known for is threatening to "eat" the mayor, who voted against giving Sullivan a permit to fight in November of 1886. Sullivan was persuaded to abandon the idea after his friends convinced him it would have "serious international complications."

Scott of the Antarctic

In the 1890s, Robert Falcon Scott was a lieutenant on the HMS *Amphion*, which was stationed in Esquimalt, and spent much of his time here dining and dancing with Kathleen O'Reilly, the beautiful daughter of the Point Ellice family. Scott and Miss O'Reilly continued to correspond over the years as he advanced up the chain of command

and, eventually, led an expedition to the South Pole. Tragically, Scott never reached his historic destination; he died during his second attempt to the reach the pole in 1912.

Winston Churchill

Even in 1929, 11 years before he became Prime Minister, the British statesman had a famous reputation as an orator, and more than 800 people crammed into a hall in the Empress Hotel on September 5 of that year to hear Churchill hold forth on Victoria's importance to the Empire. "Your green lawns and sturdy oaks, and hearts as British as the oaks, all remind me of the Mother Country," he told the audience, which greeted him with five minutes of thunderous applause. He wasn't entirely at home, however: B.C.'s bizarre liquor laws made it illegal to drink in public at the time, so the Empress staff had to serve Churchill his whisky in a china teapot. Just before he left town, the man who later led the war against Nazi Germany planted an English hawthorn in the "mayor's grove" of Beacon Hill Park. His tough little tree is just northwest of the baseball diamond, toward the park's Quadra street entrance; look for the plaque hidden in the tall grass.

Yes, Minister

Casinogate, Bingogate, Hydrogate – there are so many scandals involving British Columbia's politicians that it would be impossible to recount them all here. (In fact, by the time this book sees print there's sure to be a few more to add to the list.) But the provincial capital's most famous government intrigue began in 1954, when "Honest Bob" Sommers, the minister of lands and forests, was rumoured to be taking loans and favours in exchange for licences to cut trees on vast territories of public land. The accusations grew louder, several witnesses to the deals came forward, and Sommers resigned from the cabinet in 1956, claiming he'd been defamed. But the police laid criminal charges against him, and after the longest trial in B.C.'s history (76 days), he was convicted and sentenced to five years in prison. Sommers went down in history as the first minister of the Crown in the history of the British Empire to serve time for bribery.

Photo: Nov. 2, 1958 Colonist

One Pursuit Too Many

Charles Barber had many talents – born in Victoria, he started the Victoria Kool-Aid youth hostel, served on several government boards, played the piano and violin, conducted a local orchestra, and at the young age of 25 was elected to represent Victoria in the B.C. legislature, a seat he held from 1975 to 1983. But for every hero there is a tragic flaw, and in Barber's case, it was his appetite for young boys. In 1985, he was sentenced to 45 days in jail for commiting "gross indecency" (while he was still in office) with a 15-year-old. Barber moved to California after that, but he wasn't able to escape his past: in May 2000, he returned to Victoria to plead guilty to another charge of gross indecency, for fondling and having oral sex with a 15-year-old street kid in 1978, and was fined $1,500.

ugly Victorians

As anyone who visits quickly notices, Victoria is whiter than a Klan rally in a snowstorm. The 1996 census showed that visible minorities make up only 7.6 percent of Victoria's population, while the provincial average is 18 percent. Could it be that several ugly aspects of Victoria's history have scared some people from moving here?

The Last Stand of Mifflin Gibbs

Photo: Courtesy BC Archives B-01601

Philadelphia-born Mifflin Gibbs arrived here in 1858 with 250 American blacks who'd been persecuted in California and sought refuge under a British flag. Gibbs opened a grocery business, and later became a popular city councillor, but he was also barred from sitting in the best seats of Victoria's concert halls. So one night in 1861, Gibbs and several black friends tested the colour bar by sitting in the "dress circle" of the Victoria Theatre. One performer refused to take the stage, and a storeowner handed out onions to throw at Gibbs' party. When a bag of flour was tossed on the black pioneers, Gibbs and a friend threw punches at their attackers. All involved were arrested, but the most significant result of the "riot" was the posting of official notices that blacks were welcome only in the gallery. After it abolished slavery in 1863, Gibbs went back to the United States.

Losing My Religion

A place blessed with the gifts of nature, Victoria's always been a mecca for spiritualists and mystics. But as our history proves, blind faith sometimes leadeth one right off a cliff.

The Satanic Verses

To this day, Victoria has a sinister reputation as a hotbed of crazed devil worshippers. Blame it on a book: *Michelle Remembers*, published in 1980 by the (devoutly Catholic) local psychiatrist Dr. Lawrence Pazder. *Michelle Remembers* told the story of Pazder's unearthing of a patient's buried "memories" of childhood abuse at Satanic rituals held in Victoria — including being lowered into a grave at the Ross Bay cemetery, eating the ashes of a dead woman, and stabbing a dead baby with a crucifix. The book became an instant bestseller, creating a nice career for Pazder and his patient (and soon-to-be wife) Michelle, who started appearing on talk shows as experts on the occult crime "epidemic" that was sweeping America at the time — an urban myth their book had largely created in the first place. Apparently no one bothered to figure out that if the events described in the book were true, they would have happened decades earlier in 1955, when Michelle was five years old. Pazder continued to hold himself out as an expert in "ritual abuse" for years afterward, despite the lack of supporting evidence that such rituals ever actually occurred. He continues to practice in Victoria today, and runs Anawim House, a live-in drug and alcohol rehabilitation centre. Michelle, meanwhile, has gained a new and far less scary reputation as a fabric artist.

Fall From Grace

"I believe God's people should be the most successful in the world," Brian Ruud once said, and he lived as if that were true. A former speed freak and small-time thief in Saskatchewan, in the late 1960s Rudd had a revelation in prison, converted to Christianity, and wrote a book. But his real talents lay in public speaking, and his tale of woe and halo of gold curly hair became trademarks on the Christian school lecture circuit in the 1970s. Gold was Ruud's colour. He took to wearing diamond-encrusted gold chains and parked a gold Lincoln out in front of Eagle's Nest, the grand Oak Bay mansion he moved into in 1971 (and decorated with frescoes depicting his life). But Ruud ended up being a fatted calf for the tax man: in 1981, Revenue Canada slapped him with a $1-million bill, and in 1984 they dinged him again for $1.7 million. Ruud sold his palace (asking price: $6.3 million) in 1989, but people say he's still around town.

Then We Take Berlin

Usually a restrained bunch, on May 8, 1915, Victorians became unhinged. The previous day, a German U-boat torpedoed the Cunard liner *Lusitania* off the coast of Ireland, and close to 1200 passengers lost their lives. Among them were over a dozen Victorians, including 21-year-old Lt. James "Boy" Dunsmuir, the beloved son of coal baron James Dunsmuir. Feelings were particularly bitter among James' regiment, and they took their revenge out on the bar in the German-owned Kaiserhof Hotel (see photo; now home to the Demitasse café), where they threw spitoons and smashed mirrors. The mob then moved on to the German club on Government Street and Simon Leiser's warehouse on Yates. (As a precautionary measure, Leiser's bust was removed from the Royal Theatre, but was never returned; its location remains a mystery.) The mayor read the Riot Act and called in the cavalry to quell the disturbance. Within a few nights, order was restored.

Photo: Courtesy BC Archives A-02709

Yellow Peril

Victoria's always been afraid that it's about to be overwhelmed by immigrants from Asia. In 1875, the B.C. premier passed an act declaring that neither Chinese people nor Indians could vote, and in 1885, the province imposed a "head tax" on every Chinese migrant entering the country. Between 1900 and 1908, Victoria's legislature passed a series of racist bills designed to keep Asian immigrants out of B.C. (placing requirements for everything from comprehension of English to the length of a migrant's hair) even though all such laws were repeatedly struck down by the federal government or the courts; undaunted, in 1909, premier Richard McBride told a convention of his party, "We stand for a white British Columbia, a white land, and a white Empire." Fears about Asian immigration started to subside when World War I broke out in Europe, but Chinese residents didn't get the vote in B.C. until 1947, and Japanese residents not until 1949. Some people wonder if local attitudes have improved that much: when four shiploads of Chinese refugee claimants arrived off Vancouver Island in August of 1999, the daily *Times Colonist* published the infamous headline "Go Home" on its front page, along with the results of a loaded phone-in "poll" showing that over 3,000 readers wanted the boat people deported immediately.

described in the Book of Revelation, and then tracked him down and decapitated him in the London brass shop. The Peace on Earth store was evicted from its Broad Street location, and Immel's followers scattered. Tiernan pleaded guilty to a reduced charge of manslaughter. He's been confined to a mental hospital in England ever since.

Bad Weed

One of the oddest trials in Victoria's history took place in 1988 when Lion Serpent Sun, a self-proclaimed Gnostic minister, sued the Christian TV program *100 Huntley Street* for defamation. The show ran an interview with Len Olsen, a Vancouver man who had attended one of Sun's nude, drug-filled rituals — and, he claimed, been offered by Sun for human sacrifice. For weeks the show's host referred to Sun as a Satanist, to which he took great offence. In the courtroom, however, it was revealed that Olsen seemed to have only suffered paranoid delusions brought on by strong marijuana and a profound flash of Christian guilt. The jury awarded Sun $10,000 in damages. If you want to ask him about the trial, he's still around town, providing tarot readings at the Avalon Metaphysical Centre on Johnson Street.

Mr. Christie, You Defend Bad Cookies

Known nationally as the defence lawyer for anti-Holocaust teacher Jim Keegstra and hate literature peddler Ernst Zundel, Doug Christie (photo below) has been the centre of controversy almost since the day he moved to Victoria in 1970. A strict vegetarian who neither smokes nor drinks, Christie still lays claim to a cramped office in a converted parking lot attendant's booth across from the downtown courthouse, and continues to be in the news as the force behind the Canadian Free Speech League, which draws protesters whenever it brings in speakers to denounce Canada's immigration policies.

(Want to know more about the influence the conquering British had — and still have — in Victoria? UVic history students have created a virtual "anti-imperialist walking tour" that reveals secrets behind several of the city's landmarks, including the faux-colonial brass clock that hangs from the roof of the Eaton Centre mall. Check out the tour at web.uvic.ca/~hist66)

Without a Trace

Every parent's worst nightmare became real for Bruce and Crystal Dunahee on Sunday, March 24, 1991. The Dunahees were getting ready to play some touch football on the grounds of Blanshard Elementary at the corner of Kings Road and Wark Street, when their four-year-old son Michael wandered away from them. When they turned to look for him, he was gone. An immediate police search found no trace of the boy. Several hundred volunteers combed the area over the next several days. Police interviewed several men who matched a sketch of someone seen lurking in the area; they also hypnotized a woman to find more clues, but ended up with nothing. National headlines and reports on the TV show *America's Most Wanted* brought in hundreds of tips, but no solid leads. The case is still unsolved; no ransom note or message from the kidnapper has ever appeared. To remind people about their son, Michael's parents maintain an annual Keep the Hope Alive Drive, and a fundraising run for missing children that's held every March.

Bad Girls

Sugar and spice and everything nice – no one in Victoria will believe that cliché again after the murder of 14-year-old Reena Virk. On November 14, 1997, Reena was lured to a party by a pair of girls who were angry that she'd stolen an address book and was spending time with one of their boyfriends. At the party, she was attacked by eight teens – seven of them girls – who beat her up. She escaped and ran to the Gorge inlet, near the Craigflower Bridge. But Warren Glowatski, 16, and Kelly Ellard, 15, pursued her, and when she told them that she'd turn them in, they beat her again. Ellard stood on Reena's back and drowned her in the waterway. The police didn't find Reena's body for eight days.

When it was discovered that nearly all the attackers were girls, the story went global, and UVic prof Sibylle Artz – who'd just published a book called *Sex, Power and the Violent School Girl*, about Victoria-area teenage girls who used fear to gain respect and attention – became the media expert du jour. Eventually six girls were convicted of assault. Glowatski and Ellard are in jail for second-degree murder.

$13 Million on Holy Spirit in the Fifth

What happens to that money in the collection plate? That's a question many Victoria Catholics started asking in the spring of 2000, when they learned that their beloved former bishop, Remi De Roo, had bet and lost millions of the church's dollars on a series of bad deals to build a horse race track in Washington State. After the diocese announced that it was paying $7,000 a day in interest on bank loans and that it might have to sell some of its numerous properties on Vancouver Island, it went begging to the flock – and the members of its 37 parishes broke open their piggy banks and bought $13 million worth of church-issued bonds to keep the creditors at bay.

X marks the oddball

Victoria's first mayor was a 300-pound butcher named Thomas Harris, who (according to one account) rode "a horse that was so swaybacked that [its] belly scraped" the ground. At the first-ever city council meeting on August 25, 1862, Harris lowered his bulk into the ceremonial seat of office, whereupon it shattered into pieces and dumped him on the floor. Since then, all sorts of other lovable oddballs have also tried to get elected mayor — and some of them have been as cracked as the chair itself.

Joe Richards

A retired stockman from the forest service, Joe's been a thorn in the side of every city council for decades; he still turns up at council meetings, sporting thick glasses and a grubby baseball cap and bristling with demands for more cops on the street or slashed admission fees at the Royal B.C. Museum. He's also run for high office numerous times

Who Shot JFK?

Did Ralph Simpson of Victoria shoot JFK? He claimed he did — with a wide-angle camera. Simpson is listed as a witness in a number of key Kennedy documents, including the controversial Warren Commission Report, which declared that the November 22, 1963 assassination was the act of a lone gunman. Simpson's involvement is also detailed in the 1967 conspiracy manual *Accessories After the Fact*, which states that his valuable photos were supposedly "lost in the mail" en route to Dallas, Texas.

So what's the real story? Simpson was actually Ralph Henry William Smele. He'd seen the assassination all right — on TV in his house at 1141 Caledonia Street. He later phoned Dallas cops with his bogus tale of wide-angle photos. In 1983, Smele died a lonely alcoholic living in the Douglas Hotel. Since he can't speak for himself, the words of one relative will have to do: "He was a rolling drunk."

Doctor of Psychedelia

Every college student who's experimented with anything stronger than lemon gin has probably read *The Doors of Perception*, Aldous Huxley's book about the mind-expanding properties of mescaline and LSD. But what students don't know is that Huxley's famous trip has a Victoria connection. In 1952, Huxley became friends with Humphrey Osmond and Abram Hoffer, two Saskatchewan psychiatrists who were doing research with LSD to understand schizophrenia (whose victims, they theorized, were constantly tripping on a chemical imbalance in their brains) and, later, to provide a possible cure for chronic alcoholism. During a visit to California, Osmond gave Huxley the mescaline which inspired his legendary book, and after it was published in 1963, Hoffer and Osmond (who were referred to in a footnote) became reluctant counterculture celebrities, lecturing at Berkeley alongside Allen Ginsberg and Timothy Leary. In 1967, the two shrinks also wrote their own clinical textbook, *The Hallucinogens*, which has since been stolen from practically every library that put it into circulation. Osmond is retired now, but Hoffer practices in Victoria — where he's still on the controversial fringes of psychiatry, curing (he says) schizophrenics with doses of Vitamin B-3. There has also been renewed interest in his early work in psychedelic therapies. For a BBC documentary on the subject, Hoffer is currently trying to track down the 2,000-plus alcoholics he dosed with LSD in the 1950s, 40 percent of whom (he says) subsequently swore off the hooch. It's too bad the recreational popularity of LSD made it politically difficult to continue such work, comments Hoffer today: "In its place, it was a very valuable treatment."

Montreux's Martyr

No one exactly knows why the sufferers of anorexia nervosa try to starve themselves to death. But it's fair to say that few people have lived more closely with this mysterious condition than Victoria's Peggy Claude-Pierre (photo left). When both her daughters became anorexic in the 1980s, Claude-Pierre dropped out of psychology at UVic and became a full-time counsellor to hospital patients and her own girls. She became convinced that anorexics suffer from a "confirmed negativity condition," a pervasive sense of worthlessness that can only be cured by constant love and attention. Whatever the reason, she had a healing touch: her reputation grew, and in 1993 she opened the Montreux Counselling Centre in a mansion in Oak Bay. (Claude-Pierre named it after the Swiss town because her daughter Nikki remembered a family visit there as the happiest moment of her life.) Appearances on TV shows like *Oprah* and *20/20* and her 1997 bestseller *The Secret Language of Eating Disorders* brought Claude-

in Victoria (he used to refer to himself as the "persistent candidate," then later threatened to sue anyone who called him that), and simultaneously in other municipalities as well. When asked by a reporter whether candidates should live in the municipality they're running in, he said that would be ridiculous: "For all you know, I could be shacked up with a woman in Oak Bay."

David Shebib

This self-proclaimed "holy man" first ran for Victoria's top job in 1981 as a candidate for the Chameleon Party, which claimed to have over 1,000 members, all spokesmen for the "Lord of Hosts." Shebib ran again numerous times after that, but in 1999 stayed out of the race to manage his "101-Candidate Campaign for Mayor of Victory City," threatening to overwhelm the ballots with people he recruited from his Vehicle for Democracy, a dilapidated schoolbus parked next to Centennial Square. Several people only slightly less unusual than Shebib took him up on the offer, bringing demands from incumbents to impose a $100 election deposit to deter "fringe" candidates.

Richard Olafson

Back in 1987, poetry publisher Olafson and his partner Carol Sokoloff (also running for mayor) threatened to put their child in front of the bulldozers to stop construction of the controversial Eaton Centre. When that didn't work, Olafson taunted the incumbents at town halls with verse: "Councilmen hang upsidedown like bats/marionettes of greed."

Jonathan LeDrew

A beatnik child of the TV generation, LeDrew unnerved other candidates throughout the 1996 election by videotaping their every move at town hall meetings. (He still has the tapes in his vast library, because he believes the media rigs all elections.) When asked about his own policies, however, he replied, "The *camera* is running for mayor."

Ian Hunter

Perhaps the most articulate candidate of the 1996 election, the then-owner of the Sacred Herb shop on Johnson Street got plenty of TV airtime for his promises to legalize marijuana, which he smoked with supporters at every all-candidates' forum. (A former resident of Vancouver, where he'd campaigned to give children the right to vote, Hunter said he moved to Victoria because of a particularly groovy magic mushroom experience he had here: "It's a city where even the psychos are pleasant.") Although denounced by established politicians, he pointed out that the winner usually only gets about 7,000 votes out of 70,000 residents, and far more people than that in Victoria smoke pot. So who's the "fringe" candidate?

Pierre even more clients, who paid up to $925 (US) per day to stay at the clinic. All was not well with Montreux, however. In 1999, former employees told Victoria's regional health board that they'd force-fed patients (including a three-year-old boy) and admitted people who were too sick to be without medical care. After a lengthy hearing that got national news coverage, the board revoked the clinic's operating licence. The clinic (photo below) closed its doors a few months after that. But Montreux may rise again: Claude-Pierre has had several offers to relocate the clinic to other countries.

Living

by Ross Crockford & John Threlfall

Photo: Kevin Barefoot

The good people from the Welcome Wagon can tell you where to buy toothpaste, but they're not quite as handy with the *real* info you need, like where you can renew a prescription for birth control pills, or whether it's safe to smoke pot on a street corner. No, for such questions, often you have to rely on word of mouth — and who knows where that mouth has been? Instead, try our own guide to some of the more unusual services in Victoria.

The Spa Life

The word *spa* comes from the name of a town in Belgium which, loosely translated, means "healing waters" — or, we suspect, "liquid assets." For centuries, well-heeled Europeans have visited opulent resorts like Baden-Baden to treat themselves to curative mineral baths and exotic massage treatments. Now the practice is catching on in Victoria, where you can drop hundreds of bucks in a single afternoon in one of the city's numerous day spas. (And the clientele isn't restricted to women: local spas claim that up to 40 percent of their clients are stressed-out men.)

Practically all of Victoria's spas offer seaweed body wraps and rosemary-pine pedicures, so choosing the right one for you depends on the particular services and ambiance you desire. The Spa at Ocean Pointe Resort (45 Songhees Rd., 360-5858) has several rooms with views of the Inner Harbour and offers such unique treatments as the "Lastone massage," a rubdown with warm volcanic rocks that's supposed to open up the chakras and release life-affirming chi energy; the spa also has gourmet lunches and a full fitness centre.

Another room with a spectacular view is the Features Penthouse Day Spa and hair salon (#1210-345 Quebec St., 388-8888), which looks out on the Olympic Mountains. For something more cozy, try the candlelit Spa 517 (#1A-1218 Langley St., 480-1517), which also has an invigorating, all-body Vichy shower, or explore the soothing charms of Silk Road (1624 Government St., 382-0006), an aromatherapy and tea shop specializing in herbal treatments, such as a detoxifying green tea facial for the bargain price of $35.

If you feel like blowing a bankroll, seek out Elaine Lesley Aesthetics, which has done so well at its Oak Bay location (1820 Oak Bay Ave., 598-4555) that it's opened the 7,000-square-foot Le Spa Sereine (1411 Government St., 388-4419) downtown, featuring a hypobaric (low-pressure) chamber and time-share accommodation for regular visitors who can't get enough pampering. Also, keep your eyes and facial masks peeled for Solace, a new spa expected to open soon in the Empress Hotel.

You step off the Clipper after a weekend in Seattle, and Canadian customs agents find a copy of the controversial lesbian magazine *On Our Backs* in your suitcase. They immediately charge you with importing pornography, much to the disgust of your gay partner, who announces that he's leaving you and going to sue for everything you've got. Depressed, you go for a walk downtown, and buy a joint from one of the dealers hanging out on Douglas Street. But the "dealer" turns out to be an undercover cop, and he chases you into traffic — where you get creamed by the lieutenant governor, driving back from an emergency meeting with several importers of rare Scotch whisky. As you lay bleeding on the asphalt, you realize that you need a lawyer, very, very badly. Who are you going to call?

Lawyer: Joe Arvay (388-6868)
Specialty: civil rights issues
Arvay has argued more than 20 cases before the Supreme Court of Canada, and is famous for representing little guys against big government: he's been the lawyer for APEC protesters at the RCMP complaints commission, and Vancouver's Little Sister's bookstore, which was charged with importing gay and lesbian "porn."

Lawyer: Alison Campell (380-6688)
Specialty: family law
To resolve the dispute with your partner, call Campbell, who specializes in same-sex issues.

Lawyer: Bob Moore-Stewart (380-1887)
Specialty: "street" issues
To beat the marijuana rap, retain Moore-Stewart, who's one of the most requested legal-aid lawyers in town. He's also well-known for defending environmental activists.

Lawyer: Deborah Acheson (384-6262)
Specialty: personal injury
For your claim against the lieutenant governor, try Acheson, who's one of the most experienced personal injury advocates in town.

Bylaws, Bylaws, Bylaws

The City of Victoria's motto is *Semper Libre*, a Latin phrase that means "ever free." However, that clarion call of liberty rings a little hollow when you consider the bylaws governing just about every type of activity in town.

Video Gaming

According to bylaw 89-15, you can't have more than four "amusement machines" in your place of business unless you're licenced to operate a bar or an arcade. (Possible penalties? A fine of $1,000 and up to 30 days in jail.)

Free-Range Dogs

Animal control bylaw 92-19 warns that your pooch can't run without a leash anywhere in the city, except in the designated turf of Dallas Road. Dogs are also completely banned from Gonzales Beach during the summer. Even if you've got a leash, it must not exceed 2.4m in length, although it can go up to 8m if it's retractable. ($50 fine — but if the authorities impound your pooch and you don't reclaim it within four days, they can sell it or have it killed.)

What's the Poop?

92-19 says Fido can't take a dump anywhere unless you immediately pick up the poop and dump it in a garbage can. ($50, but Fido gets a break if he's a guide dog for the blind.)

Other Critters

92-19 says you can't keep any farm animals in the city except for chickens, and even those are restricted to a "reasonable number" for your personal use. (No roosters, though: we like sleeping in.) Exhibitions of animals performing tricks or fighting "for the amusement of an audience" are also strictly *verboten* — as are leg-hold traps, according to bylaw 79-89.

Body Work

Escort agencies have to pony up $1,500 to ply their sinful trade in Victoria, according to bylaw 93-134. So too must body-painting studios, modelling studios (where someone exposes their "genital area or buttocks" for the purpose of being "observed, sketched, painted, drawn, sculptured [or] photographed") and counsellors who hold "encounter sessions" — defined as "a meeting for the purpose of relaxing, comforting, or similarly affecting a person." Presumably that definition doesn't apply to sessions between elected officials and enraged taxpayers.

Lawyer: Jane Morley (480-7477)
Specialty: mediation

If the lieutenant governor wants to avoid the spotlight of a nasty trial, call Morley Ross Lovett and Westmacott, an all-woman firm specializing in mediation.

Lawyer: Chris Considine (381-7788)
Specialty: high-profile cases

To handle the press, a guy to have on your dream team is Considine, who's always involved in the most sensational and politically delicate trials in town; discreet, articulate, and media-savvy, he's gone to bat for locals as diverse as death-with-dignity patient Sue Rodriguez, Montreux clinic founder Peggy Claude-Pierre, and Darren Huenemann, who was convicted of persuading two students to murder his mother and grandmother in 1989.

By the way, after your injuries mend, a few Victoria lawyers could help you profit from your story. Scott Hall (384-6600) could write your screenplay: although he does civil litigation now, in the 1970s he wrote TV scripts in Hollywood (David Soul of *Starsky and Hutch* was a next-door neighbour). And if your movie of the week gets produced, criminal lawyer Jim Heller (360-1040) could do the soundtrack: still shaking off the eight years he spent trapped in the cult of the boy-god guru Maharaji, Heller is now often found at night playing guitars very loudly in local clubs with his band, The X-Flies.

(Note: The above is for information only, and should not be considered an endorsement of the lawyers listed. No warranty as to the quality of their work is in any way expressed or implied.)

You can find organic vegetables in just about every supermarket in Victoria, but if you want to make sure you've always got some in your icebox, subscribe to one of several services in town that'll deliver the goods right to your door.

The blue ribbon for commitment to local farms goes to Saanich Organics (658-4921). For about $20 per week, they'll provide you with a box of certified organic fruits and vegetables from five farms right on the Saanich peninsula. You get what's in season – berries and figs in summer, leeks and king cabbages in the winter – but year round there's braising and salad greens, beets, carrots, potatoes, onions, and garlic. Fresh Piks (383-7969) has the greatest variety of organic goods: for $35 for a large box, even in mid-winter you can get things as exotic as grapefruit, strawberries, oyster mushrooms, pears, and roma tomatoes. Like Share Organics (595-6729), another good local organic company, they buy first from local and B.C. organic growers, and then import from elsewhere when necessary. For a complete list of other delivery programs, as well as organic farms, organic plant nurseries, and community gardens in the Victoria area, call Lifecycles at 383-5800.

By the way, going organic doesn't mean you have to be a raving vegan. Lee's Hill Farm (250/653-9188) and Moonstruck Cheese (250/537-4987), both on Salt Spring Island, respectively sell certified organic poultry and cheeses; Sidney's Kildara Farms (655-3093) deals in certified organic meat and eggs.

Bylaws, cont'd

Photo: Kevin Barefoot

Sandwich Boarders

Those poor folks on lower Government Street who wear billboards around their necks and woo tourists to nearby restaurants and attractions have their own rules to live by. Not only must they "continuously change locations" according to Victoria bylaw 97-91, they must also remain completely mute: a different bylaw against "audio advertising" prohibits them from announcing the wonders of their establishments to passers-by. ($85 fine.)

Skate Punks

According to 92-84, the mammoth Streets and Traffic Bylaw, it's illegal to ride a skateboard or roller skates anywhere in Victoria's downtown, even though you often see kids getting away with it. ($30 fine for a first offence, and the authorities can seize your board or 'blades.)

Poster Children

Though it probably violates the constitutional right to free expression, mighty bylaw 92-84 says it's illegal to stick posters on "any structure or fixture in or on any sidewalk or street." The only exceptions are the metal cylinders installed on downtown lampposts, which often sport a thick bark of accumulated advertising. ($200 fine.)

Street Kids

The most controversial sections of 92-84 were added recently, mainly to hustle our wayward youth out of the sight of middle-aged tourists. One rule prohibits anyone from obstructing downtown sidewalks by "squatting, kneeling, sitting, or lying down" during daylight hours; another bans "aggressive" panhandling, and begging near banks and bus stops. (The initial fine is only $5 — but tickets are never issued because civil liberties groups have promised to challenge the constitutionality of the bylaw in court.)

If it's any consolation, every municipality in greater Victoria has its share of odd rules. For instance, in tweedy Oak Bay, where appearances are everything, it's illegal to park a boat or an RV in your front yard, including on your driveway. And in Langford, which is trying to remake its rock-and-roll image, it's illegal to operate a store selling hemp goods — and bow hunting is restricted to a few far-flung corners of the district. Gee, what would Ted Nugent say about that?

To Market, To Market

Victoria abounds with local markets that feature home-grown, home-made, and home-cooked foods and organic vegetables, along with arts and crafts. Most markets follow the May to October growing season and sprout like weekend weeds in almost every neighbourhood across town. Local faves include: the James Bay Market, which runs 9 am-3 pm Saturdays at the corner of Menzies and Superior, just behind the Legislature; the Moss Street Market, which runs 10 am-2 pm Saturdays at the corner of Fairfield and Moss; the Peninsula Country Market, another 9 am-1 pm Saturday offering out at the Saanich Fairground (1528 Stelly's Cross Rd.); the Fernwood Community Market, running 11 am-3 pm Sundays in the village square in front of the Belfry Theatre where Fernwood Road meets Gladstone Avenue; and the Burnside Gorge Farmers' Market, which can be found 9:30 am-1:30 pm Saturdays at the Selkirk waterfront, off Jutland and Gorge Road.

Curry in a Hurry, Phad Thai on the Fly

You don't have to limit yourself to pizza or Chinese food if you're ordering takeout. Dine In (361-3463) will deliver meals anywhere in Victoria, Saanich, and Esquimalt from 29 different eateries in the city, from Dairy Queen milkshakes and White Spot burgers to Yoshi Sushi's B.C. rolls and sauerbraten from the Rathskeller. In fact, you could go completely postmodern and order all of the above for one big feast: Dine In will deliver it all for $4.50, as long as you place a minimum order of $10 with each restaurant.

bakin' whoopee

Victoria is blessed with dozens of bakeries. Here are a few.

Ada's Original Cinnamon Bun Café

This shop on Burnside Avenue has cinnamon buns in small, medium, and three-pound sizes, along with inspirational messages on the chalkboard in the window. There's lots of parking out back, but the café is closed on weekends.
1 Burnside Ave. West, 385-1570

Boland's

This humble bakery is located in a converted house in Oak Bay. The granola bars alone are worth the trip.
677 St. Patrick St., 598-5614

Bond Bond's

They don't put preservatives into their breads, and they don't sell day-olds. They do make their own mayonnaise and supply both the Empress Hotel and Butchart Gardens with baked goods.
1010 Blanshard St., 388-5377

Breadstuff's

Just down from the street from the Belfry Theatre. Try the sunflower seed bread and cinnamon knots.
1307 Gladstone Ave., 386-1199

Captain Cook's Bakery

Located in a Tudor building on Fort, and popular among the older set, the tearoom at Captain Cook's is decorated with an elaborate wall mural depicting Cook's arrival at the Sandwich Islands. Until recently, it showed a native with a bone in his hair sitting over a boiling pot saying "Stay fo' dinna?" but has since been painted over with a more politically agreeable grass hut.
1019 Fort St., 386-1020

DRINK, WITHOUT DRIVING

It may be the 21st century, but you can still get milk delivered to your door in old-fashioned glass bottles, thanks to Royal Oak Dairy *(479-5097)*. A family-owned and operated business for 13 years, Royal Oak turns raw milk from Abbotsford farms into one-litre bottles of skim, one percent, homo, and "standard" (pasteurized, with a layer of cream on top). They also deliver butter, cottage cheese, and yogurt they make themselves, along with cheese, eggs, and ice cream.

If you're the type who prefers to pour whisky on your corn flakes, there's a service for you, too. Dial-a-Bottle *(475-2797)* is open 9:30 am to 11 at night, and if you give them a ring they'll pick up a fifth of Old Crow and drop it off for a service charge of five bucks. (That includes up to three items; each extra item is another 25 cents.) Expect delivery to take a little longer on welfare Wednesdays, and be prepared to show some ID: too often, staffers say, they answer a call only to find out it's some kid hoping to bribe or sweet-talk a bottle out of the driver.

CRYSTAL BALL-GAZING

If you need a glimpse of the future – or some clarification of the present – the best psychics in town work out of Triple Spiral Metaphysical at 3 Fan Tan Alley *(380-7212)* and Avalon Metaphysical in Market Square *(380-1721)*. Thanks to Victoria's fascination with things mystical, you'll also find readers of all manner and type scattered in markets and cafés across town. Time-proven local favourites include tarot readers Lion Sun (read about his famous trial in the Notoriety chapter) and Allison Skelton-Faulkner (call Triplespiral, *380-7212)*, astrologer Jill Kirby *(388-7905)*, Diane the Ph.D. parapsychologist, and spiritual counsellor/channeler Lynne Shields *(598-2391)*.

Cascadia Wholefoods Bakery

They make their own granola and supply Re-Bar with goodies. Try the Chelsea buns.
1812 Government St., 380-6606

Dutch Bakery and Coffee Shop

This coffee shop attracts an older crowd with prices that have hardly changed since it opened in 1956. Everyone has their favorite, but some standout pastries are: dollar rolls, flying saucers, and the tiniest and tastiest cinnamon Danishes in the city.
718 Fort St., 385-1012

Italian Bakery

Providing Victorians with the finest cornetti, barchetti, and other Italian goods since 1978.
3198 Quadra St., 388-4557

Lunn's Pastries Deli and Coffee Shop

An award-winning chocolatier located on the main street in Sidney.
2455 Beacon Ave., Sidney, 656-1724

Ottavio Italian Bakery and Delicatessen

This is the sister-bakery to the Italian bakery on Quadra (the parents ceded management of the Italian bakery to their son Alberto, and sister Monica now runs Ottavio).
2232 Oak Bay Ave., 592-4080

Patisserie Daniel

Flaxseed muffins, biscotti, and truffle tarts can all be found in this shop on Fort Street. The Kitchen on Cook is Daniel's factory, filled with noisy machines and mountains of cardboard boxes, but you can also get pastries there.
768 Fort St., 361-4243; 1729 Cook St., 361-3234

Rising Star

The bakery started as a co-op in Vic West, and continues to provide various businesses in the city with fresh breads.
1320 Broad St., 480-0021; #1-313 Cook St., 360-1811

Village Patisserie

Award-winning pastries found behind the Tweed Curtain.
2217 Oak Bay Ave., 370-0766

Wild Fire

Organic breads like Spelt, Ciabatta, and Olive Fougasse are baked in the brick wood oven and displayed on pieces of slate.
1517 Quadra St., 381-3473

Willie's Bakery

Has been a bakery on and off since Louis Willie commissioned the building back in 1887. Roberta's Guest Rooms upstairs includes breakfast in the bakery.
537 Johnson St., 381-8414

home movies

What will it be tonight: Bergman's *Persona* or *Debbie Does Dallas*? You can decide at these specialty video stores.

Island Video

The videos are displayed on plain white wire racks, but this store offers a variety of services including movie conversions to and from all standards. The door that keeps slamming in the back leads to a long room of porn films. Head back outside and to the other half of Island Video in the corner of the strip mall and you'll find over a thousand South Asian titles from *Baadshah* to *Sarfarosh* and all the latest from Bollywood. The posters on the counter are free.
3388 Douglas St., 475-1212

WOMEN'S ISSUES

It still is a man's, man's, man's world, and that's why there are several busy women's organizations in town. The best-known is the Victoria Status of Women Action Group *(383-7322)*, which runs workshops and a court monitoring program, and can refer you to support groups, and woman-positive doctors, lawyers, midwives, and therapists. If you need shelter from a storm, contact the Women's Sexual Assault Centre *(383-3232 for its 24-hour crisis line, 383-5545 for regular business)*. Up at the university – where only 29 of 205 full professors are female, by the way – check out the UVic Women's Centre *(721-8353)*, where you'll find a library and an extensive referral service, and the office of the *Third Space* (née *The Emily*), English Canada's oldest university-based feminist newspaper.

MEN'S ISSUES

Life isn't always easier for men: they're more prone to stress-related illnesses, they're far more likely to commit suicide, and they often get the short end of custody battles for their children. That's why hundreds of capital-region males have banded together to form the Victoria Men's Centre *(370-4636)*, a group that holds regular meetings to discuss political and personal problems. For those who want to channel their energy into (literally) building a new home for men, an interesting group to contact is the health-oriented Well Foundation *(383-4001)*, which is constructing a rustic retreat facility on a lake about 45 minutes outside of town.

(Note: see Gathering Places for services aimed at gay men and lesbians.)

FAMILY PLANNING

We talk more about sex now, but that doesn't mean we're any wiser when it comes to contraception: in 1994 there were 48.8 unplanned pregnancies for every 1,000 women aged 15 to 19 in British Columbia, up from 41.1 in 1987. Those numbers would probably be even higher, though, if it weren't for the South Vancouver Island Family Planning Society and its clinics in Saanichton *(2170 Mount Newton Cross Rd., 544-4830)* and Victoria *(1947 Cook, 388-2201)*. Their friendly, non-judgemental staff offers referrals to doctors, tests for sexually transmitted diseases, and sells birth control at prices only slightly above cost, incuding the injection methods Norplant and Depo-Provera. (They also offer free condoms, but the rubbers don't get many takers; nearly all the clinic's clients are women.)

Pic-a-Flic

Pic-a-Flic is the beginning and end of cinephile video in Victoria. The Tillicum store offers more animation and wrestling videos; expect Bugs Bunny to be on the TV over the counter, so send the kids to the Mr. Vend machine with a quarter while you search for a copy of *Black Orpheus*. At the Cook Street location, you'll find more esoteric and foreign titles.

328 Cook St., 382-3338; 2967 Tillicum Ave., 361-4494

Make Your Mark

If you're looking to pick up a little local colour while you're in town, you can't do better than Urge Studios *(586 Johnson St., 380-2989)*, which has been fast gaining a reputation as one of the finest tattoo shops on the west coast of North America. In addition to supporting local causes (such as AIDS Vancouver Island's annual Pride Tattoo-a-Thon), Johnny and his team of internationally trained and travelled artists provide excellent custom work at prices that don't make you wince. But, given their reputation as a custom studio, they just might recommend you to another shop if all you want is something from the books. Other good places to make your mark include Tattoo Zoo *(1215 Wharf St., 361-1952)*, Universal Tattooing *(1306 Broad St., 382-9417)*, and the hard-to-find (but worth the effort) Stark Raving Tattoo tucked away in Fernwood *(1115 North Park St., 388-0136)*.

If you're looking to get a little metal under your skin, Urge also wins out as the best place to go. All their piercers must make the pilgrimage to San Francisco to be trained by Fakir, the godfather of modern piercing, and with four specialists on staff, you won't have to wait long to get a gleaming accessory that even your mother would love (or not). Urge also does professional branding and scarification, if that's your particular cup of tea. Tips from the pros? Ignore the "CRD Health Board Approved" notice on many ads for such parlours – which the CRD recently demanded be removed for fear of liability – and run from any place that uses a piercing gun. Like massages, the best pierces come from the hands of a caring professional.

The Dope on Marijuana

Most Victorians talk so nonchalantly about marijuana that you'd think it was legal here. Think again. In 1999, 334 people in the capital region were charged with pot-related offences, and most of them (251) were nailed for simple possession. So *discretion* is the watchword: defence attorneys say that whether you get busted for sparking a fatty in Victoria depends on where you are, the mood of the cop who catches you, and (of course) whether you're a clean-cut commerce grad or a teen with dreadlocks and a lip ring. In particular, lawyers suggest doing your doob away from the park on Wharf Street beside the Johnson Street bridge, a favourite ambush spot for stealthy bike cops. We also suggest that you never burn the stinky bud inside a car: cops don't like drivers who are under the influence of anything except coffee and doughnuts, and cars are very easy to search. Then again, maybe we're just paranoid.

The police say they need to continue busting people for weed because most of B.C.'s $2-billion annual crop is distributed by the elements of organized crime, especially bike gangs. It's also because Americans have a particular taste for our pot: so much of it gets smuggled across the border that the U.S. State Department has branded B.C. a drug-export zone that poses as big a threat to Yankee national security as Colombia or Afghanistan. (Gee, who are the paranoid ones around here?)

But those in the know say the local politics of cannabis cultivation are more complicated. Many of the growers are just regular folks tempted by easy money, trying to pay off mortgages and put their kids through school, pot advocates say. In Victoria, this debate hits the ground at the Sacred Herb hemp shop (106-561 Johnson St.,

Pet Stuff

Kennels

No one to watch Fifi when you go out of town? Check out the services provided by Puppy Love and the Cat's Meow Pet Care Centre (2918 Lamont Rd., 652-2301). Dogs will enjoy the animal playschool (including the "paddle and splash swim program") while cats will dig the climate-controlled environment with its soft music and/or TV services. Add in the 24-hour personnel, on-call vet, special care ward for older pets, full-service grooming and nutritionally balanced meals, and you've got a place more luxurious than most hotels. Also, they can pick up and drop off your non-human friends — which may include llamas, alpacas, rabbits, guinea pigs, birds, and horses. Halliford Canine Country Club (4339 Happy Valley Rd., 478-4082) has similar services, and also features heated floors, 4½ acres of park-like grounds, a "beautique," and day boarding services. It's a "delightful country estate for the discriminating canine," says the promotional bumpf. On the other paw, Happy Time Kennels (1742 Hovey Rd., 652-4331) says that "Cuddling is our specialty." If your pet can't bear the thought of leaving home, then try the live-in pet watchers at Custom Home Watch International (472-2050), Pet Pals (727-9758), and The Housesitters (478-5115), who do plants, too.

Walkies?

While strolling along Dallas Road with your favourite Fido, you're bound to happen across a person with six, seven, or even eight different dogs in tow, all happily yapping as their leashes become a veritable cat's cradle of tangled tow-ropes. They're probably working for one of the many dog-walking services in town: Pet Pampering *(381-5889)*, Play Time Pet Care *(592-0599)*, Pet Pals *(727-9758)*, Tender Loving Pet Care *(882-7297)*, or Club Dog Doggy Daycare *(480-0234)*.

Kibbles and Bits

It's Sunday afternoon and you're out of pet food; where do you go? Best choice is any of Bosley's Pet Food Mart's three locations *(3749 Shelbourne St., 1790 Island Hwy., 491 Burnside Rd. East)*, which are open seven days a week and offer everything you ever thought you'd need for your pet. Closer to downtown, you've got Kelly's Pet Mart *(592-3301)* at Fort and Foul Bay or Oak Bay's Theatre Lane Pet Store *(592-9954)*, both of which are limited to conventional, nine-to-five retail hours. For those who either live in the Gordon Head region or have access to a vehicle, Borden Mercantile *(479-2084)* at Quadra and McKenzie is a good choice any day but Sunday, as is the megastore-style Petcetera *(3170 Tillicum Rd., 380-7990)*, which offers more than 25,000 square feet of pet stuff.

Oh, Poo!

Can't bear to pick up after Rover? No worries. That's why we have the brave folks at K-9 Lawn Care *(474-DOGG)* and Scoopy-Doo Residential Pet Waste Removal *(744-5474)*.

384-0659), which was founded by pot activist Ian Hunter. After he got busted for growing cannabis plants in his store window and threatened with revocation of his business licence in 1998, Hunter sold the enterprise to two employees, who have carried on the Sacred Herb's tradition as a centre for paraphenalia (check out the Cultivation board game) and straight talk about the drug war. As co-owners Chris and Sarah say of their colourful, friendly emporium, "It's a little bubble of freedom."

Mom need help with her arthritis? The Vancouver Island Cannibis Buyers' Club *(381-3262)* and the Vancouver Island Compassion Society *(595-1146)* together supply medicinal marijuana to more than 200 clients who've provided written proof that they suffer from such conditions as cancer, AIDS, fibromyalgia, and chronic migraines. And if you want to take the fight to the ballot box, call Chuck Beyer *(389-8888)*, a local realtor who's the Victoria rep for the new national Marijuana Party. Recent polls show that two out of three Canadians favour decriminalization of the weed, so Beyer says the government is abusing its power by continuing to prosecute marijuana offences. His party could do well in Victoria in the next federal election – that is, if his supporters remember to get off the couch and vote.

Photo: Kevin Barefoot

Bidding Around

Victoria's reputation as an antique centre may limit your chances of finding actual deals on antiques, but your name doesn't have to be Lovejoy to find the occasional gem. Good deals can still be had by patiently sifting through the usual non-retail channels: garage sales, estate liquidations, and, of course, the auction houses. As well as being known as "Antiques Row," Fort Street is also the destination of choice for auction hounds. Kilshaw's *(1115 Fort St., 384-6441)* and Lunds *(926 Fort St., 386-3308)* offer weekly sales, and it's not unusual to find the crowds spilling onto the street in the hopes of taking home a discount masterpiece. With 50 years behind them and a seventh-generation auctioneer at the mic, Kilshaw's 7 pm Thursday night household furnishings auction is a local tradition. While they also handle antiques and fine art, you're much more likely to leave with a steal on a sofa than find any deals on a Degas. Lunds, on the other hand, has carved out a niche as Vancouver Island's premiere auctioneer, so don't be surprised to hear prices well into the thousands at its Tuesday auctions (1 pm and 7 pm). Whereas Kilshaw's pitches the practical, Lunds lobbies for the luxurious, offering theme auctions (fine art, collectibles, jewellery) and high-end estate sales several times a year. Evening auctions often run past midnight, so good deals can be found if you're prepared to wait it out. If you're looking for something a bit more unusual, BDF Auction *(6678 Bertram Pl., 652-0064)* features good vehicles at great prices at their 10 am Saturday car auctions, and real deals on just about everything can always be found up the Malahat at Whippletree Auctions *(4715 Trans-Canada Hwy., 746-5858)*. Their 11 am Sunday "bid and buys" are the stuff of local legend, where an amazing selection of stuff often goes for less than what is morally decent. From vehicles to building supplies and household goods to sporting equipment, their stock changes so rapidly that there's never such a thing as a typical week.

Bath Time

Can't get out but still don't want to wash your terrier in the tub? That sounds like a job for the Groomobile, Victoria's only mobile pet care salon, which operates out of Pet Essentials *(1168 Burnside Rd., 744-3943)*. One call and you've got a complete grooming salon sitting in your driveway.

Get the Point

Looking for some alternative pet therapy? There's a trio of pet acupuncturists in town: Dr. L.M. Bixby *(383-6116)*, Dr. Jennifer Chan *(598-4477)*, and Dr. J.M. Harrison *(598-1067)*. How ever do they get the pups to lie still?

Dead Dog Café

Victoria sports a pair of pet cemeteries for your four-legged loved ones: Family Pet Services Ltd. *(479-3343)* offer distinctive hardwood urns and cremation services, while Glory Bound Pet Crematorium *(812-0646)* specializes in private cremations with urn, or common cremation with other animals. And for those who are having trouble getting over the passing of a four-legged friend, Stefan Faye, M.A. *(920-9629)* is a counsellor specializing in pet loss bereavement.

animal crackers

Every good dog deserves a gourmet doggie treat. Here's where to find some.

Dog's Day Bakery

Located in the tourist strip of lower Johnson Street, their business is mostly wholesale, providing pet stores with fresh baked goods and hotels with bones. They also have woofles (a doggie waffle), puppy cinnamon buns, rawhide lollipops, and sit bites for keeping your dog in line in flavours such as chicken parmesan, peanut butter, and beef 'n' garlic. *543 Johnson St., 386-3647*

Woofles: a Doggy Diner

Located at the entrance to Market Square, steps away from Victoria's other canine bakery, they often refuse service to tourists ordering the apple cinnamon waffles. *#102-560 Johnson St., 385-9663*

Hardware Heaven

Don't know your acrylic latexes from your alkaline oils? Of all the trade stores in town, you'll find the best service and best free advice not at a paint retailer, but at Ace Lumberworld *(3955 Quadra St., 479-7151).* Talk to Ol' Bri', who's always more than happy to share hints and tips from a life spent in paint. (If the conversation runs dry while the paint's getting mixed, try TV westerns, his second-favourite topic.) With their long hours (7 am-8 pm), helpful staff and cheap prices, Ace is the place for your hardware needs.

After that, go with the historic Capitol Iron *(1900 Store St., 385-9703),* which is the really the only choice in the downtown area. You get a good selection, a great staff who aren't above cutting you a deal and a downstairs that does double-duty as both museum and surplus store. Also a big selection of plants, outdoors equipment, clothing, housewares, fabrics, shoes – you get the idea.

In Fairfield, it's definitely Ross Bay Home Hardware in Fairfield Plaza *(1584 Fairfield Rd., 598-7224).* Nice people and a strange but interesting selection that's definitely aimed more at renters than serious builders. In James Bay, the only real choice is Harvey's Read 'n' Rite *(#2-455 Simcoe St., next to Thrifty Foods, 386-9555).* While hardware is not their main focus, it's always surprising what they do have: fuses, paintbrushes, hasps, and hinges, screwdrivers, tape, mactac, screws, nails, tacks, maybe even the occasional hammer … everything you need to keep it together until you can get somewhere better equipped. It's the only hardware store in town where you can also buy stamps, pick up a magazine, choose a greeting card, and cash in a lottery ticket.

Playing Dress-Up

All of us need to pretend we're someone else from time to time – and for every need, there is a business. For costume rentals in the city centre, check out the aptly named Funky Town *(2646B Quadra St., 382-2626)*, which has over 200 outfits, from the Energizer bunny to characters from the *Austin Powers* movies; they also rent tapestries, lava lamps, and all sorts of other '70s goodies to turn your party room into a swinging pad. If you're willing to travel a little farther, be sure to visit Disguise the Limit *(3328 Metchosin Rd., 479-1156)*, which has nearly 1,000 costumes, including a full suit of armour, a Louis XIV ensemble with powdered wig, and a latex Batman body suit ($85 a night, and it gets hot inside); they also rent Scottish formal wear. A bigger selection of classic formal wear, at very reasonable rates, is available from Langham Court Theatre *(805 Langham Ct., 384-2025)*, which also has some medieval and masquerade items in its wardrobe.

Good Cleaning Fun

If you have to go out to do your laundry and you're looking for something more interesting than just watching your socks go round and round, try The Laundry *(1769 Fort St., 598-7977)*, which has Internet terminals, a concession stand, and an art gallery that got started after a UVic fine arts grad complained to the owner that he couldn't find a place to hang his oversized paintings. Another unique laundromat can be found at the Victoria Car Wash *(628 Gorge Rd. East, 386-7021)*, where you can give the Impala a hot wax treatment at the same time your undies are in the spin cycle.

ALTERNATIVE THERAPIES

Crack open Victoria's telephone book, flip to "Health Services" and you'll find listings for more than 100 clinics and consultants, a figure that doesn't even come close to encompassing the true scope of the local alternative healing network. From aromatherapists to practitioners of Traditional Chinese Medicine (TCM), from pranic healers to somatoenergetic consultants, in Victoria it's the M.D.s and G.P.s who often get relegated to the place of second opinions.

Beyond the phone book, good places to find a cure for what ails you include the local healer network Wholenet *(380-7873)*, East-West Health Centre's free weekly acupuncture clinic *(384-4350)*, the annual autumnal Victoria Health Show, or the Bulletin Board on the back page of *Monday Magazine*. You'll also find more than a few TCM practitioners in Chinatown who will be more than happy to check your pulses, look at your tongue, examine your eyeballs and prescribe some rather pungent (but powerful) herbs to get you back on your feet.

Looking for more a path than a cure? You're in luck – Victoria's clinical cup runneth over with schools and training centres for your every healing need. Check out the local alternative healing magazine *Alive*, another great source for information and listings.

DENTAL CASES

Without a doubt, one of the most unique and enterprising dentists around is Donald Bays *(115 Eaton Centre, 381-6433)*, who makes house calls – occasionally, while wearing a white spangled Elvis jumpsuit. Many people in Victoria who need dental care are bedridden or in nursing homes, and Bays helps them out with his mobile air compressor and power drills. Unfortunately, he hasn't quite figured out how to do portable X-rays yet. If you prefer the chair-side manner of women dentists, there are a few in town, including Vicky Ikonomou *(#8-911 Gordon St., 361-4266)* and Olga Dudek *(#206-1595 McKenzie Ave., 721-2221)*. Gillian Bridge *(205 Cook St., 384-4260)* also runs an all-female dental clinic, but don't get your hopes up about getting an appointment; at the time of this writing, they were so busy that they weren't taking on new patients. Finally, if you're looking for preventative dental care on the cheap, check out the dental assistants' program at Camosun College, which can do X-rays, cleanings, polishings, and flouride treatments for little or no cost. Call 370-3191 for an appointment during the school year, September to June.

The Wailing Wall

If you ever end up in the emergency ward of the Royal Jubilee Hospital, at least you can console yourself – and maybe get a good chuckle – by checking out the "Area B" waiting room, and its strange gallery of mishaps. When the wait is particularly long, patients are given paper and crayons to retell the cautionary tale of how they ended up there. The illustrations have accumulated over the years, and now the waiting room is home to an unusal collection of folk art revealing the hazards of youth, and the medical costs of the demon rum. One sketch, for instance, shows a giddy partygoer flinging himself down a staircase and, in the next panel, doing a Travolta imitation in a disco; "Count the number of stairs before jumping in the dark," it warns, "and don't ignore injuries while dancing!" The gallery's open 24 hours, but you may have to break your ankle to see it.

Calling All Newcomers

For those new to living in the Garden City, there's a Welcome Wagon franchise in town. Call *477-2220* if you need to know where to buy your toothpaste.

index

index

index

index

index

index

index

index

index

index

index

index

index

KEVIN BAREFOOT is a graduate of the writing program at the University of Victoria, a contributing editor at *Geist* magazine, and author of *Higher Grounds: the Little Book of Coffee Culture*. He lives in Victoria, if only in his mind.

ROSS CROCKFORD was a Vancouver trial lawyer until 1990, when he moved to Czechoslovakia and spent the next four years writing for *The Prague Post* and drinking the finest beer in the world. Since returning to Canada, he's published work in *Adbusters, Shift,* and *Outdoor Canada*; he's also won a Western Magazine Award and been nominated for a National Magazine Award for "one-of-a-kind" writing. He's been the editor of Victoria's *Monday Magazine* since 1998.

DAVID LEACH is a graduate of and a journalism instructor at the University of Victoria, and the arts and entertainment editor of *Monday Magazine*. He tried to leave Victoria several times before he realized that resistance is futile.

After a decade working backstage, JOHN THRELFALL decided to go to university, where, between a pair of history degrees, he began working as a freelance writer. A one-time TV segment host for *Canadian Biker Television*, three-time columnist ("Full Moon Fever," *Hecate's Loom*; "Paperback Rider," *Canadian Biker*; "The Threl-File," *Monday Magazine*) and full-time practicing witch, John is currently *Monday's* Calendar editor. He has yet to write his thesis.

ALSO AVAILABLE:

Calgary: Secrets of the City
by James Martin
ISBN 1-55152-076-1

Vancouver: Secrets of the City
2nd Edition
by Shawn Blore
ISBN 1-55152-091-5

Available at your bookstore or from
Arsenal Pulp Press
www.arsenalpulp.com
1-888-600-PULP